GEORGE II
Puppet of the Politicians?

Why is George II the forgotten monarch? Despite his lengthy rule (1727–1760), most of us know little or nothing of him.

One answer is the lack of easily accessible source material—George left no diary and he was not a letter writer. But George has also been dismissed for being merely a puppet in the hands of the towering politicians of his time: in particular Walpole, Pitt and Newcastle.

In this new biography—the first for over 30 years—Jeremy Black reassesses this charge, and demonstrates convincingly that George II is a worthy subject of enquiry. Exploiting rich archival resources—including contemporary satire and the letters written *about* the King rather than by him—he amasses evidence that reveals much about George himself. In the process he goes beyond biography to provide a window on the King's world and a clear assessment of a difficult period of consolidation in British history.

Jeremy Black MBE is Professor of History at the University of Exeter. He is one of the leading scholars in the field of British history and has published extensively on the 18th century.

GEORGE II

Puppet of the Politicians?

JEREMY BLACK

UNIVERSITY
of
EXETER
PRESS

First published 2007 by
University of Exeter Press
Reed Hall, Streatham Drive
Exeter EX4 4QR
UK
www.exeterpress.co.uk

The right of Jeremy Black to be identified as author
of this work has been asserted by him in accordance
with the Copyright, Designs and Patents Act 1988.

British Library Cataloguing in Publication Data
A catalogue record for this book is available from the British Library.

ISBN 978 0 85989 807 2

Typeset in 11½/13½pt Garamond
by Kestrel Data, Exeter, Devon

Printed in Great Britain by
Athenaeum Press Ltd, Gateshead, Tyne & Wear

For
Gideon Hollis

Contents

Preface

For a king who ruled for so long (1727–60), longer than any of the Stuart kings of Britain, the relative neglect of George II is surprising. He appears in quiz shows to be categorized as the last British king to lead an army into battle—victoriously, but controversially, at Dettingen in 1743—and, otherwise, is largely ignored. And that despite the drama of these years which included, at Culloden in 1746, the last major battle on British soil and the culmination of the war over the British succession. George was also king when the British empire became the strongest European power in North America and South Asia. Anson sailed round the world in the King's service. James Wolfe died outside Québec fighting for George II and preferring to have written Gray's *Elegy*. In turn, the critics of the political establishment, some of whom had sharp comments to make about George, included prominent writers such as Jonathan Swift, Alexander Pope and Samuel Johnson. The King, however, was seen as a monarch 'in toils', a blustering fool manipulated by others and constrained by the limitations of the royal position.

This biography, which focuses on George's years as king, seeks to redress the neglect. It also offers an opportunity to consider the role of monarchy in early eighteenth-century Britain, as part of a consideration of its political system and culture, and thus to discuss similarities and contrasts with the position on the Continent. The place of the monarch in the long-term development of British politics is also assessed. Part of the achievement of George and his ministers was in bedding-in, accommodating and, perhaps unwittingly, nurturing and developing, the character and methods of a fledgling political system, a system that at times dwarfed the King. Reappraisals of monarchy, the Court, the dynasty, political culture, and the link with Hanover have been advanced by recent scholarship, and throughout the book I will be pausing to discuss how the narrative illuminates George as king in the light of these developments and my own trawl through the archives.

My doctoral thesis, on which I began work in 1978, was on foreign policy and politics in 1727–31, and, for me, in writing about George, there is a sense of at once deep familiarity and coming home. Over the years, I have benefited greatly from the assistance of many archivists and I would also like to acknowledge the support of the universities of both Durham and Exeter. Nigel Aston, Mijndert Bertram, Grayson Ditchfield, David Flaten, Bill Gibson, Anna Henderson, Matthew Kilburn, Clarissa Campbell Orr and Andrew Thompson helped greatly by commenting on an earlier draft. Jane Olorenshaw copy-edited the book sensitively. It is a great pleasure to dedicate this book to Gideon Hollis, a fun fellow and a supportive relative.

Abbreviations

Add.	Additional Manuscripts
AE.	Paris, Ministère des Relations Extérieures
Ang.	Angleterre
AST. LM. Ing.	Turin, Archivio di Stato, Lettere Ministri, Inghilterra
Beinecke	New Haven, Beinecke Library
BL.	London, British Library
Bod.	Oxford, Bodleian Library, Department of Western Manuscripts
CP.	Correspondance Politique
CRO.	County Record Office
Darmstadt	Darmstadt, Staatsarchiv, Gräflich Görtzisches Archiv
Dresden	Dresden, Haupstaatsarchiv, Geheimes Kabinett, Gesandschaften
Eg.	Egerton manuscripts
Egmont	Historical Manuscripts Commission, *Diary of the First Earl of Egmont* (London, 1920–3)
Farmington	Farmington, Connecticut, Lewis Walpole Library, Hanbury Williams papers
GK	Grosse Korrespondenz
Hanover	Hanover, Niedersächsisches Hauptstaatsarchiv
Hervey, *Memoirs*	R. Sedgwick (ed.), *Some Materials towards Memoirs of the Reign of King George II*, by John, Lord Hervey (London, 1931)
HL	San Marino, California, Huntington Library
HHStA	Vienna, Haus-, Hof-, und Staatsarchiv, Staatskanzlei
HMC	Historical Manuscripts Commission
HP	History of Parliament, Transcripts
HW	J. Brooke (ed.), *Memoirs of King George II by Horace Walpole* (New Haven, 1985).
Marburg	Marburg, Staatsarchiv, Politische Akten nach Philipp d. Gr.
MD	Mémoires et Documents

Mo	Montagu papers
Munich	Munich, Bayerisches Hauptstaatsarchiv
NA.	London, National Archives, formerly known as Public Record Office
NAS	Edinburgh, National Archives of Scotland
Newport	Newport, South Wales, Public Library
Polit. Corresp.	R. Koser (ed.), *Politische Correspondenz Friedrichs des Grossen* (Berlin, 46 vols, 1879–1939)
RA	Windsor Castle, Royal Archives
SP	State Papers

Unless otherwise stated, all dates are New Style. Old Style dates are marked (os). Dates after monarchs are their regnal dates, rather than their dates of birth and death. Unless otherwise stated, all books are published in London.

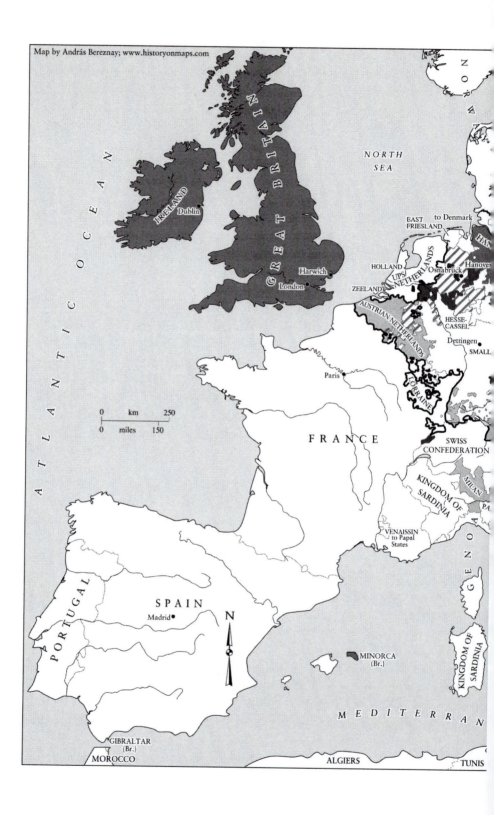

Map by András Bereznay; www.historyonmaps.com

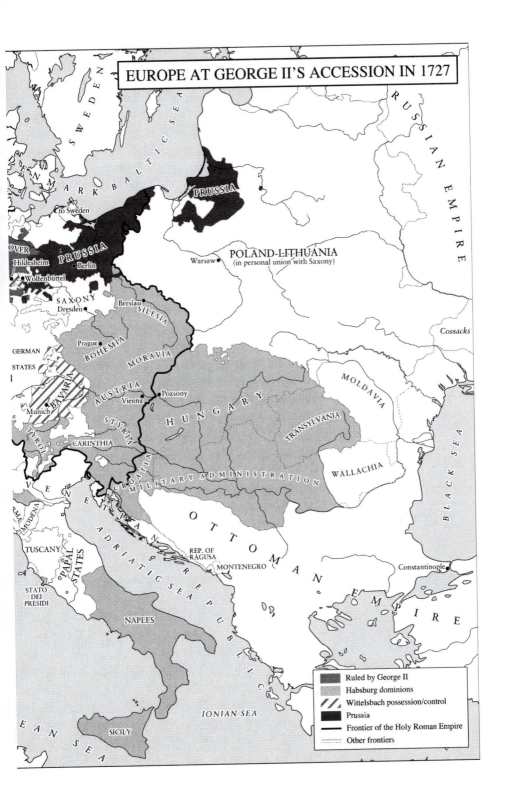

EUROPE AT GEORGE II'S ACCESSION IN 1727

RUSSIAN EMPIRE

SWEDEN

BALTIC SEA

DENMARK

to Sweden

PRUSSIA

PRUSSIA

OVER

Hildesheim

Wolfenbüttel

Berlin

POLAND-LITHUANIA
(in personal union with Saxony)

Warsaw

Cossacks

SAXONY

Dresden

Breslau

SILESIA

GERMAN

STATES

Prague

BOHEMIA

MORAVIA

MOLDAVIA

BAVARIA

AUSTRIA

Vienna

Pozsony

HUNGARY

TRANSYLVANIA

Munich

STYRIA

TYROL

CARINTHIA

CROATIA

MILITARY ADMINISTRATION

WALLACHIA

BLACK SEA

VENICE

MODENA

OTTOMAN

REP. OF
RAGUSA

MONTENEGRO

Constantinople

TUSCANY

PAPAL
STATES

ADRIATIC SEA

REPUBLIC

EMPIRE

STATO
DEI
PRESIDI

NAPLES

IONIAN SEA

SICILY

EAN

SEA

	Ruled by George II
	Habsburg dominions
	Wittelsbach possession/control
	Prussia
	Frontier of the Holy Roman Empire
	Other frontiers

1

The Role of Monarchy in Eighteenth-Century Britain

'The Festival of the Golden Rump', a biting and well-informed satirical caricature on the Court of George II, was published in London in March 1737. The image centres on the naked back of a man standing on a pedestal. This was intended to depict George. His wife, Queen Caroline, injects into his anus the magic potion required to calm his spirits, while Sir Robert Walpole, the prime minister, presides, equipped with a magician's staff. George is shown as a beast who has to be tamed. One of his legs is raised to kick, a reference to the peremptory and irritable George's habit of kicking when in anger. This was also a theme in the caricature 'Aeneas in a Storm', published in January 1737 and referring to George's recent return from his native German territory, the Electorate of Hanover. To judge such comments on George as King, indeed to consider the political world that could present and 'consume' (or appreciate) this image, it is best to assess him against the background of the development of the British monarchy. Those who wish to begin with the narrative of his life therefore should move straightaway to the next chapter. This one, instead, seeks to provide a context for the discussion and judgments offered later in the book, particularly in the closing chapter.

The standard presentation of post-1700 British history is not one that finds much of a positive or prominent role for the monarchy, and this helps explain the neglect of George, who ruled, as the second of the Hanoverian dynasty to hold the British throne, from 1727 to 1760. As television history amply illustrates, however, the situation is very different with pre-1700 history. This reflects popular interest based on good stories and strong personalities, and also academic engagement with the role of key individuals. Monarchy has been seen, and accurately so, as crucial to English and Scottish state-building for the first millennium CE. The Old English state was a product first of the success of the house of Wessex under King Alfred in resisting the Danish invaders in the late ninth century, and, subsequently, was the creation of his successors in the tenth, especially Athelstan and Edgar. This role was seen as continuing, indeed, until, and including, the sixteenth century. Moreover, the failure of Henry VI (r. 1422–61, 1470–1) to sustain a state that spanned the English Channel secured a national character to this state-building. This national character provided the context within which subsequent linkages with foreign dynasties were to be assessed, first, in 1603, the Stuarts, then, in 1689, William III of Orange, and, in 1714, the Hanoverians.

The linkage of monarchy and state-foundation was a process that reaches its apogee with the praise granted to the Tudor dynasty (r. 1485–1603), who indeed played a key role in religious as well as political change. Henry VIII (r. 1509–47) appropriately bestrode the attention of his contemporaries and the political imagination of the age. Elizabeth I (r. 1558–1603) was seen as the saviour of English Protestantism, and thus her accession date was celebrated thereafter as a key anniversary for national independence for at least a century and a half. Reference to Elizabeth was frequently made in the press of George II's day, and she served supporters and opponents of government alike as a symbol of laudatory monarchy.

After Elizabeth, however, the monarchs do, and indeed did, not play so positive a role in accounts of English or British history. James I (James VI of Scotland) resonated not as a key player, but as the intended victim of the Gunpowder Plot of 1605. It was also symptomatic of the newly-grounded position of the monarch in the public imagination that he was remembered as a ruler whose majesty centred in Parliament, and that the Plot had been aimed at both the King and Parliament. This took forward the growing role of Parliament under the Tudors. Earlier, in the fifteenth century, Parliament had not been particularly prominent. Key political developments had focused, instead, on factional feuds and, in the Wars of the Roses, on the battlefield: from the 1450s to the defeat of Lambert Simnel, a Yorkist pretender, who claimed to be the rightful Edward VI, at the battle of Stoke of 1487, which, rather than the battle of Bosworth two years earlier, was the true close of the Wars of the

Roses, not that that will help you in quiz shows. The bloody course of the houses of Lancaster and York resonated with themes of violence that were centuries old. Faction, feud, and civil violence remained significant.

Under the Tudors, though this violence continued, it was, instead, a case of unsuccessful insurrections and not of successful coups or protracted civil wars. Coups were attempted, for example on behalf of Lady Jane Grey in 1553, and by Robert, Earl of Essex in 1601, but they failed. Furthermore, such violence was increasingly associated with the geographical margins of England, as in the Pilgrimage of Grace of 1536, the Western Rising of 1549, and the Northern Rising of 1569, and, more clearly, with Scotland and Ireland. In its place, the major setting and means for political change in England became Parliament. This was seen, in particular, with the ecclesiastical and governmental changes of the Henrician Reformation of the 1530s and, subsequently, with the exposition and defence of the Elizabethan Church settlement and political order. Parliament became more prominent, although, politically, it was not yet central, and, indeed, was an occasion rather than an institution. Changing assumptions, however, made the attempts under James I and, even more, Charles I, during his Personal Rule in 1629–40, to rule without Parliament appear at best irregular and at worst illegitimate. Indeed, the classic Whiggish [liberal, progressive] account of modernization and liberalization in Britain presented, and still presents, successive monarchs as obstacles to progress in the seventeenth century.

In this light, the overthrow of the Stuarts, both of Charles I in the 1640s (and earlier in Scotland) and of James II (and VII of Scotland) in 1688–9, was, and is, seen as necessary in order to achieve progress and, thus, to realize the potential of both country and political system. Put crudely, the monarchs were on the wrong side and therefore were not deemed worthy of serious sympathetic study. The Glorious Revolution of 1688–9, the overthrow of James, his replacement by William III of Orange, and the changes this led to in the Revolution Settlement, were central to the Whig myth, and both the ability to change monarchy, and the political and constitutional changes stemming from these changes were regarded as crucial to the progress of the country.

Thereafter, what is variously termed, limited, parliamentary and constitutional monarchy was, and still generally is, presented in a Whig tradition as definitively British. This is seen as a contrast with both

Stuart kingship and the Jacobite aspirations of the exiled Stuarts, as well as with the Continental monarchy of the period. In short, the British *sonderweg* [unique path] is held, at least in part, to rest on a particular and different type of monarchy, with this type, at least in part, as definition, product and protection of national exceptionalism. This distinctive type of monarchy is seen in terms of the willingness of the monarchs to respond to demands for political 'progress', and that as looking toward William IV's acceptance of parliamentary reform in 1832. Moreover, this willingness is contrasted with the apparent absence of such a situation abroad.

Such an approach, however, leaves scant independent role for the monarchs and, instead, presents the dynamic elements in the political system as forces removed from the world of the royal Court. These elements were seen in terms of progressive parliamentarians and, indeed, of opinion 'out of doors' (outside Parliament) as a whole. The former were presented as especially important by nineteenth-century commentators, while the latter have attracted greater attention from the 1970s.[1]

As a warning, in this linear view of history, about the danger of a throwback to Stuart absolutism, George III's inability to respond positively to American aspirations is held to have caused the serious civil war in the empire known as the American Revolution or the American War of Independence (1775–83), and also to have demonstrated that he was no Whig. The standard teleology presents British monarchy, thereafter, as understanding its place, as seen, in particular, with George IV's very grudging acceptance of Catholic Emancipation in 1829, and also, more positively, with the successive extensions of the franchise [right to vote] in the nineteenth century. Particular attention is focused on the willingness of William IV in 1832 to respond to Whig ministerial pressure, from Charles, 2nd Earl Grey, the prime minister, and his colleagues, and to be willing to threaten to create new peers in order to get the First or Great Reform Act through the obstructive and conservative House of Lords.

This is an account that would be recognized by more members of the public interested in history than by academics. The latter, generally self-consciously, have rejected Whig, teleological and linear history (the terms are to a considerable extent interchangeable), but its apparent excision from the academic sphere has had far less impact on the wider public than might be anticipated. Furthermore, the continued impact in academe of Whiggish assumptions about the nature and direction of progress has been more influential than is generally realized. In part, this is because more aspects of the Whig tradition persist than is appreciated or acknowledged; and, in part, because of the opposite: the dethroning of the grand narrative that the reaction against Whiggery represented led to a reluctance to offer other synoptic accounts. This reluctance, for example, was seen in the Namierite approach to high-political history associated with Sir Lewis Namier, author of *The Structure of Politics at the Accession of George III* (1929), with his focus on the political calculations that led to the establishment of individual ministries. An unwillingness to offer synoptic accounts was also seen in the atomistic, post-Whiggish treatment of the monarchy, in which discussion of particular monarchs and topics did not amount to an overall thesis of the nature and impact of monarchy.

Conversely, the Whig tradition about the beneficial nature of British constitutional and political change in the seventeenth and eighteenth centuries persisted in the assertion of a degree of British distinctiveness that amounted to what has been termed exceptionalism. This affected the presentation of the monarchy as part of a discussion of the general political system in Britain. Ironically, scholars working on Continental history debated the accuracy of the epithet absolutist, as a description of royal governance in the seventeenth and eighteenth centuries, drawing valuable attention, instead, to the limited power and pretensions of Continental monarchs and governments, an approach that greatly qualified the notion of a British *sonderweg*, in terms of a uniquely anti-absolutist system. This debate, however, had only a restricted impact on many of those working on British history.[2]

This limitation was compounded by three factors. First, in so far as comparisons were made, they tended to be between Britain and France, and the latter was misleadingly treated as a paradigm for Continental Europe, with the correlate that, if a Anglo-French difference could be defined, this established a difference between Britain and the Continent: George II was not Louis XV of France (r. 1715–74) and, therefore, apparently, there was no real comparison between British and Continental monarchy. This was not helped by the placing of the Court of Versailles as a model for European monarchy, certainly at the end of the seventeenth century. Secondly, the habit of making comparisons between Britain and the Continent was stronger for those working on the seventeenth century than for political historians working on the following centuries, who tended to concentrate on contrasts. Thirdly, there was scant comparative British eighteenth-century history by foreign scholars, and the valuable work that was produced, for example by French and German writers, did not focus on the monarchy, but rather on the popular politics that seemed most interesting to these scholars, and, indeed, to their Anglo-American counterparts.

The lack of a general thesis about the role of monarchy in Britain was unfortunate, because monarchs played a key part in eighteenth-century European political culture. This was the case in both practical and symbolic terms, and Britain was not excluded from this process, most obviously in practical terms, but also in symbolic ones. Most of the Western world at mid-century, indeed, was ruled by hereditary monarchs. There were alternatives in Europe, in the shape of elected monarchs and republics, but they were relatively unimportant, both on the international scene and in terms of the image of monarchy.

Furthermore, with the exception of the Popes, who were also the temporal rulers of the Papal States in central Italy, but, as unmarried men pledged to celibacy, had no (legitimate) children, the hereditary principle played a role in the prominent elective monarchies that did exist in this period. This indicated an important tendency toward the hereditary principle in the practice of monarchy. Such a tendency was certainly true of the most prestigious monarchy. The experience in 1742 of electing a Holy Roman Emperor who was not (as his predecessors since the fifteenth century had been) a Habsburg, namely the Elector of Bavaria, Charles Albert (who became the Emperor Charles VII), proved so divisive that it was not repeated after he died in 1745, and indeed George II, as Elector of Hanover, had had to be coerced by the threat of a French invasion of Hanover in order to vote for Charles Albert. The Electors were the German Princes (nine from 1692) who had the right to vote for the Holy Roman Emperor, the title given to the ruler who presided over the Holy Roman Empire, which was, in modern terms, Germany, Austria and the Czech Republic, with a few additions in neighbouring modern states. The Emperor had a degree of authority within the Empire, but no real power over the, in effect, independent princes who ruled the major territories within it, such as Bavaria, Hanover, Prussia, Saxony and Hesse-Cassel.

Instead of electing another Wittelsbach (the family of the Electors of Bavaria), or similar prince, successive members of the Habsburg family again became Emperors. First was Francis I, the husband of Maria Theresa of Austria and the son-in-law of the most recent Habsburg

Emperor, Charles VI (r. 1711–40). Francis was elected in 1745, a choice made with the active support of George, who had met and liked him when he visited Britain in 1731. Francis was followed by his son, Joseph II, in 1765, an eventual choice that George had negotiated for actively in the early 1750s when he had pushed hard the Imperial Election Scheme designed to ensure that Joseph be elected King of the Romans and thus next Emperor. Joseph was followed by his brother, Leopold II, in 1790, and then by the latter's son, Francis II, in 1792. He was the last to hold the post, which, as a side-blow to Napoleon's military triumphs, was abolished in 1806.

The hereditary principle also played a role in Poland, although it was an elective monarchy. There the King in mid-century, Augustus III of Saxony, was the son of his predecessor, Augustus II (r. 1697–1733). This, however, was the contested choice that led to the War of the Polish Succession in 1733–5 (see pp. 144–52). The choice of Augustus III was backed by George II and, far more significantly, by a Russian invasion. After Augustus III died in 1763, another Saxon election was thwarted by the choice in 1764 of a Russian-backed Pole, the last King of Poland, Stanislaus Poniatowski. This was helped by the fact that the most suitable Saxon was under-age.[3]

In the republics, there was also an important monarchical element. This was seen with the Doge in Venice, and, far more in practical terms and closer to home, with the *stadholders* (in effect governors) of the Dutch provinces, a position held in the eighteenth century only by members of the house of Orange. The latter indeed was linked to Britain. William III of Orange, the nephew and son-in-law of James II and VII, had had no children, ensuring that the dynastic union of Britain and the Orange interest (1689–1702) had not survived his death, but, in what was seen as a significant choice of partner, William IV of Orange married George II's eldest daughter, Anne, in 1734, and they, in turn, had a son, William V. George backed the Orange interest, particularly in 1747 when anti-*stadholder* regimes in the key provinces of Holland and Zealand were displaced, as William IV seized power with British support. After he died in 1751, Anne acted as regent for the infant William V (1748–1806). In 1787, the British backed William V when he also displaced anti-*stadholder* regimes. Driven out of the United Provinces by French Revolutionary forces in 1795, he spent his last years in exile at Kew, a bridge from the world of his grandfather to a very different posterity.

The monarchical principle was also important in the non-Western world, with coups, for example that overthrowing Sultan Ahmed III in Constantinople, in 1730, not leading to republics, but, instead, to new monarchs. Moreover, although non-monarchical, the Swiss Cantons were oligarchic in character.

The importance of the monarchical principle offers a way to re-examine the position in Britain. There, the background was not one of hostility to monarchy, but of two recent violent responses to particular monarchs and the theories and practice they supported or supposedly represented. When George I came to the throne in 1714, British monarchs had been overthrown twice within the previous eighty years. The rejection of Charles I in the early 1640s had been sustained in a bitter way, somewhat mistakenly termed the English Civil War as it was in fact British in its scope, and a republic had been declared in 1649. The disruption and radicalism produced by the Civil War, however, had led to a reaction in favour of order, and monarchy was restored in the person of Charles I's eldest son, Charles II, in 1660. This was a very popular step.

Subsequently, despite widespread anxiety about his alleged pro-Catholic tendencies, Charles II benefited from concern about instability in the crisis of 1678–81 that began over the Popish Plot and that widened to include the proposed exclusion of his Catholic brother, James, Duke of York from the succession: Charles had no legitimate children. When it came to the crisis, most of the opponents of Charles II had not been willing to push their views to the point of violence, not least because of widespread concern that such violence might lead to both a republic and to Presbyterianism.[4] The Exclusion Crisis of 1678–81, nevertheless, laid the basis for longstanding political divisions. The supporters of Exclusion became known as Whigs, and those opposed as Tories.

James II and VII inherited the throne in 1685 but royal policies became unwelcome to the Tories, who backed the position of the Church of England. The Whigs, already alienated, were developing notions of liberty and consent that directly challenged the practice of royal government. James' autocratic and Catholicising policies proved sufficiently unacceptable to lead, in 1688, to conspiracy, and to a willingness on the part of many (although by no means all) to welcome a Dutch invasion on behalf of William III of Orange. The resulting overthrow of James led to limitations on monarchical power, and not to a renewed attempt to create a republic. Furthermore, although republican views were held during the reign of George II, for example, by Philip, 2nd Earl Stanhope, who voted against the Regency Bill in 1751, few supported them. This indeed was an aspect of the growing rift between British and Dutch political culture, as the latter was far more republican. It was, however, possible in Britain to espouse republican values within the structure of a constitutional monarchy. This was a key reason why the actual republicans, those who wanted to abolish monarchy, were so small a minority.

The crisis in 1688 was dynastic as much as political. Fears about James' intentions had become acute in 1688, when his Catholic second wife, Mary of Modena, had a son, the future 'James III and VIII', who therefore took precedence in the succession over Mary and Anne, his Protestant daughters by his dead first wife. The resulting concern and opposition favoured the plans of James' nephew and son-in-law, William III, the husband of Mary. The chief figure in the Protestant United Provinces (modern Netherlands), William was the leader of opposition in Protestant Europe to the expansionism and aggression of Louis XIV of France. Louis had alarmed Protestants throughout Europe in 1685 by revoking the privileges under which Huguenots, French Protestants, had been allowed to maintain their faith, and a large number had fled to England as refugees, becoming the first large-scale group of religious refugees in England.

Most people in England in 1688–9 did not want any breach in the hereditary succession, and William initially pretended that he had no designs on the English Crown. On 28 December (os) 1688, he accepted only the government of the kingdom from an irregular assembly of peers and former MPs summoned by him on the 26th (os). However, as the situation developed favourably, especially when James had been driven into exile (creating the fiction that he had left the throne vacant), William made it clear that he sought the throne, emphasizing his hereditary claim to it. His seizure of power was accepted, by the Convention he called, in the Bill of Rights of 12 February (os) 1689, which declared the throne vacant and invited William and his wife Mary to occupy it as joint monarchs; William was not willing to concede that Mary should rule alone.

It was possible to minimize the element of innovation by claiming that it was only a vacancy that was being filled; rather than endorsing the more radical notion that James had been deposed. Most people did not want a break with a Protestant monarchy and saw William and Mary as legitimate hereditary heirs. However, all Catholics were debarred from the succession, ending the rights of James's infant son by his second marriage unless the boy became an Anglican. The Bill of Rights, furthermore, dealt the divine right theory of monarchy a fatal blow by obliging rulers to adhere to their subjects' religion. Anne's rights in the succession were subordinated to those of William, so that, when Mary died of smallpox in 1694, the joint-monarchy was succeeded by William ruling alone, and Anne did not come to the throne until 1702 when William died childless. The provision, in the Bill of Rights, that Anne and her issue should come before any issue of William from a second marriage was not necessary. Although Parliament, in 1689, rejected pressure from William for explicitly settling the reversion of the Crown, in the event of William, Mary and Anne dying without heirs, upon Sophia, Electress of Hanover, the succession of George I in 1714 was a direct consequence of 1688–9, and George II would not have been King without James II and VII's overthrow.[5] As a result, what became known as the Glorious Revolution and the Revolution Settlement were the true origins of the rule of the Hanoverian dynasty in Britain. Indeed, the Rockingham Club, founded in 1754 to foster the Whig interest in Yorkshire, speedily commissioned portraits of William III and George II.[6]

The house of Hanover's claim to the English and Scottish thrones (which from the Union of 1707 became the British throne) derived from Elizabeth (1596–1662), the daughter of James VI of Scotland who, in 1603, also became James I of England. In 1613, Elizabeth married Frederick V (1596–1632), a Calvinist stalwart of the Protestant cause in Germany, and the short-lived King of Bohemia in the early stages of the Thirty Years' War (1618–48), as a result of which Elizabeth was known as the 'Winter Queen'. Elizabeth's youngest daughter, Sophia (1630–1714), married Ernst August of the North German Protestant princely house of Brunswick-Lüneburg (1629–98) in 1658. The future George I was the eldest of their large family of six boys and one girl.[7]

There were also restrictions on royal power as a consequence of the Glorious Revolution, restrictions that framed George II's options. The financial settlement for the Crown left William with an ordinary revenue that was too small for his peacetime needs, obliging him to turn to Parliament for support. A standing army was prohibited unless permitted by Parliament, a key limitation on royal power that reflected anger with James's policies. This Revolution Settlement was to be seen subsequently as a decisive break with autocratic practices. In a speech of 1710 supporting the impeachment of the Tory High-Churchman Henry Sacheverell, Robert Walpole, one of the most prominent Whig MPs, made a clear contrast between what he saw as the pre-1688 Stuart doctrine of monarchy and the post-Revolution situation, a contrast that helps explain how Whigs responded to what they subsequently perceived as unwelcome royal initiatives:

> The doctrine of unlimited, unconditional passive obedience [to a monarch] was first invented to support arbitrary and despotic power . . . What then can be the designs of preaching this doctrine now, unasked, unsought for, in her Majesty's reign [that of Anne, r. 1702–14], where the law is the only rule and measure of the power of the Crown, and of the obedience of the people.

There was also a major shift in the nature of monarchy in Scotland, where James's position collapsed in December 1688. The Convention of the Estates, which met in Edinburgh the following March, was dominated by supporters of William, and on 4 April (os) 1689 the Crown of Scotland was declared forfeit, William and Mary being proclaimed joint sovereigns a week later. Catholics were excluded from the Scottish throne and from public office. The contractual nature of the Revolution Settlement, the extent to which the Crown had been obtained by William and Mary on conditions, was far more apparent in Scotland than in England. The offer of the Crown to William and Mary was made conditional on their acceptance of the Claim of Right issued by the Scottish Convention, which stated that James VII (James II of England) had forfeited the Crown by his policies and that no Catholic could become ruler of Scotland nor hold public office. The Scottish Parliament also gained greater independence from William than from his predecessors.[8]

The degree of radicalism in the Scottish constitutional settlement reflected fundamentally different political circumstances from those in England. These included the far greater impact of William's wishes in England. He never visited Scotland. Indeed, the next monarch to do so was George IV in 1822, the visit proving a great success.

As a result of the Glorious Revolution, the effective power of the British monarchy had been lessened, although not as much as the overthrow of James might have suggested. Instead, it was the consequences of the Glorious Revolution that also played a major role. Crucially, William III led Britain into war with France, and this war, the War of the League of Augsburg or Nine Years' War (for Britain, 1689–97), and its sequel, the War of the Spanish Succession (for Britain, 1702–13), proved lengthy and expensive. This forced government into measures to ensure parliamentary support, including compromises with the parliamentary opposition, not least, with the Triennial Act of 1694, accepting that Parliament would meet regularly and that elections would be held at least every three years. The 1690s saw increased party organization, in part because of more elections and of parliamentary sessions becoming more frequent, and in part because royal attempts to govern without relying on an individual party were abandoned. William tried to do so, but, from late-1693, he came to rely increasingly on the Whigs, and, by the following summer, a largely Whig government was in power.

By the late 1690s, the leading Whig ministers, the so-called Junto, held frequent meetings in order to maintain party consistency in government. This was a limitation on the King's freedom of manoeuvre. However, the extent to which William was still able to impose his views indicated his political importance as the arbitrator of both Court factionalism and the ministerial struggle for influence. This role was not really compromised by the emergence of political parties, because they lacked the structure and ethos necessary to provide clear leadership and agreed policy.[9] This situation under William largely prefigured that under George II, not least because their room for manoeuvre was greatly limited as accusations of Jacobitism tainted the Tory option.

In his *Essay on the English Constitution* (1770), Henry Lloyd declared 'A King of England is not only an essential part of the legislative power, but likewise the chief magistrate, head of the church, and commander in chief of all the armies both by sea and land'.[10] The role of the monarch in government was nevertheless diminished by contingencies. William, who was very much a warrior king, helping, like other contemporary monarchs, to set a model for George I and George II, spent much of his reign on campaign, as George II would have liked to have done. William devoted his formidable attention to military and foreign policy issues, rather than to the details of domestic government and politics. Between 1691 and 1697, the army and the navy each cost an annual average of £2.5 million.

William's wife Mary died childless in 1694, and he did not remarry.

His successor and sister-in-law, Anne (r. 1702–14), the second daughter of James II and VII, was able, and not as dependent on her favourites as was believed by some contemporaries, and, as such, was subsequently to become an historical orthodoxy. Instead, Anne, in certain respects, was similar to George II, in that the role of both was to be unduly minimized, and later commentators overly influenced, by hostile contemporaries. The continued role of the monarch as arbitrator was demonstrated by Anne's importance in the struggle for primacy at Court and among her ministers, not least in 1704–5 and also within the Tory ministry between Henry St John, Viscount Bolingbroke and Robert Harley, Earl of Oxford in 1714. As Anne had no domestic programme of change, she was a relatively uncontroversial figure, and indeed political criticism in her reign was centred on ministers, not monarch. Poor health greatly reduced Anne's vigour. She was exhausted by frequent childbearing, and lacked the vigour of such eighteenth-century female monarchs as Elizabeth and Catherine II (the Great) of Russia; although her options were also constrained by the nature of British monarchy, and by the degree to which her reign was lived in the shadow of war. Uncertainty and manoeuvring over the succession moreover was a factor in affecting the response to Anne.[11]

The physical re-location of monarchy was also significant in affecting the perception and reality of its power. Whitehall had been the centre of power over the previous two centuries, at once royal palace and the place of government, but, in 1698, fire destroyed the palace; only the Banqueting Hall remained. This led to a major split. Although there were proposals to rebuild the palace intermittently in George II's reign, Whitehall was not rebuilt as a palace. Indeed, there was a lack of enthusiasm by the monarchs themselves for a new palace on the Whitehall site. As a result, no new palace dominated the town, as, in contrast, did that in Stockholm, begun in 1697 to replace the recently burnt-down royal castle, or Berlin, begun in 1701, to mark the new royal status of the house of Brandenburg, a status that challenged that of the house of Hanover.

Instead, William, Anne and Georges I and II focused Court life on St James's, Kensington and Hampton Court. These palaces, however, were not appropriate as centres of the administration, which was growing as government became of greater scale and complexity. This was particularly so as a consequence of Britain's development as what has been termed a fiscal-military state, one with a sophisticated financial system linked to what was, by contemporary standards, a high rate of military capability and activity.[12] Instead of remaining with the Court, government was rehoused in new buildings on the Whitehall site. This linked civil servants to ministers and kept both physically close to Parliament. At times, the Crown could seem tangential to this nexus or, at best, part of a more multi-faceted governmental process. This was indeed the case, but separating government out made the situation more apparent, and affected royal prestige.

The emphasis on the limited nature of British monarchy in the eighteenth century has usually been functional, in other words a focus on the political system, and one in which the active role of the monarchs seems restricted by constitutional precept and political practice. In part also, however, this is a consequence of the direction of historical research. The central question of research on 'high' political history since the late 1920s has been the existence, nature and impact of political parties, and the role of the monarchy has been distinctly marginal to this discussion.[13] Although the attitude of the monarchs was discussed, there was far greater interest in the nature of political organization and, more recently, in the extent to which parties enjoyed popular support and, more generally, in the nature of popular politics and the perspective this offers on society.[14] The Crown did not play a prominent role in this account, and, indeed, seemed singularly marginal to the latter debate, although the popularity of George I and George II has recently been stressed.[15]

Moreover, the positivist tradition of British political history, with its emphasis on archival sources, found much on offer in the high-political sphere as far as ministers and parties were concerned, but far less for the Crown, particularly for the reigns of George I (r. 1714–27) and George II (r. 1727–60). Neither left much correspondence. This is not so much a case of the failure to retain documents, as of an unwillingness to produce many, although this was not invariably the case. George II wrote lengthy letters to Queen Caroline when he went on his trips to Hanover, but the series has not survived. Indeed, the influential bureaucrat Andrew Stone noted that George II 'never loved to keep papers'.[16] He had not done so as a Prince, and the situation did not change when he became a King. Furthermore, the number of surviving documents by senior ministers marked 'Burn this' suggests that much material that may have made it possible to assess relations between George and his ministers has been destroyed. Comments on the King were particularly sensitive and thus less likely to be committed to paper or to survive.

The shortage of papers makes biography difficult for both George I and George II, certainly in frustrating contrast with the productive George III (r. 1760–1820). In addition, there was no formal mechanism for recording the meetings held by the King. In the case of the papers of a few ministers, principally Thomas, Duke of Newcastle, there are references to the royal role, but, while highly instructive, the references are relatively sparse, and certainly do not present a systematic account of royal views. Thus, the nature of scholarship combined with the interests of scholars to ensure that the Crown received relatively little attention, certainly in contrast to that of prolific politicians, especially Newcastle.[17]

Instead, interest in the Crown among scholars was reawakened from a different direction with the rise of Court studies. Not restricted to Britain, whose Court under the Georges was indeed a model for northern European Protestant Courts, this subject also brought a welcome cosmopolitanism and a comparative context.[18] However, there has been a risk of a different sort of insularity, with a tendency to focus on the interior aspects of Courts and their cultural themes, and sometimes (although fortunately not always) less of an interest in the broader social and political significance of monarchy. This is a topic ripe for examination, and it is one that permits a positive re-evaluation of George's position and role.

The dynamic nature of this question is highlighted by the treatment of other reigns. For example, addressing attention, for the close of the eighteenth century, to the important question of the symbolic role of monarchy, there is the work of Linda Colley arguing that George III took on great symbolic importance as a stalwart of the nation when under threat from Revolutionary France, and at a time when his real political significance (as well as bodily strength) was less than in his early controversial years as King. Colley also suggested that George III was more popular and capable of eliciting popularity than his two predecessors. Colley's first argument is then extended to argue that a decline in the real significance of the Crown was a condition of this symbolic importance, an interpretation in which the role of George I and George II is unclear.[19]

While arresting as a thesis, this approach poses a number of problems. First, as a description of the last years of the century, it postulates a *zeitgeist* (spirit of the age) that offers a less than full description of the variety of opinions on offer about both George III and monarchy, some of which were very critical. Secondly, it is far from clear how the relationship between symbolic and actual power is to be assessed, then and in other periods. Thirdly, there is a tendency to downplay the symbolic role of individual monarchs, and the institution and practice of monarch and monarchy, prior to discussion of this theme for George III's later years. In part, this downplaying reflects the extent to which the Hanoverians lacked charisma, although they were no worse than the eighteenth-century Bourbons, and indeed Louis XV was the focus of more contempt, both personal and political, than George II. There are several pertinent comparisons between George II and Louis XV, but the latter's personal life became a target of pornographic criticism[20] that George was largely spared, though for which he could have provided some material.

More generally, there is also an ahistorical dimension in which, because the symbolic role of the monarchy means relatively little to modern commentators, it is assumed to have meant the same in the eighteenth century. This is seriously mistaken, not least because of the importance of the dynastic clash between the Hanoverian rulers and the exiled Stuarts. Indeed, the Jacobite challenge indicated the centrality of the monarchical theme. This threat remained important until 1746, when Charles Edward Stuart, the eldest grandson of James II and VII, was defeated at the battle of Culloden by George II's second son, William, Duke of Cumberland. Even after both that, and the subsequent enforcement of a new order in Highland Scotland, the Jacobite challenge remained significant for most of the remainder of George's reign. Indeed, the unsuccessful French attempt to invade Britain in 1759 was ostensibly on behalf of the Jacobite claimant. Jacobite success in regaining the throne would have offered the French an acceptable exit strategy to war with Britain in the shape of an apparent guarantee that a British *revanche* for poor peace terms would not subsequently be attempted. Jacobitism by then, however, was dependent on foreign support to a degree that had not been the case in 1745 and, still more, 1715. Nevertheless, the continued relevance of Jacobitism owed something to the role of legitimism in a society that was heavily legalistic and prone to place dynastic issues at the centre of political contention, and a society moreover where religious sanction still counted.[21]

The failure of the '59, the French invasion plan, with the French covering fleet destroyed off the Breton coast by Admiral Hawke in the battle of Quiberon Bay, was followed by the accession of George III in 1760 and by his new policies, which represented a deliberate rejection of the practice of power under George II. Instead, under George III, there was initially a conscious endorsement of the self-styled Patriot cause, a rejection of Continental interventionism as the keynote of foreign policy, a downplaying of the Hanoverian connection, and a deliberate reaching out to the Tories. This was a policy that largely destroyed the possibility of residual English support for Jacobitism, and a reaching out that markedly contrasted with the position under George II, a position that reflected royal choice as well as ministerial convenience.

The demise of the Jacobite option, however, scarcely represented a diminution, still more rejection, of the prominence of royalty in public culture and political life. Instead, the politics of the 1760s were redolent of traditional symbolic themes, particularly the hopes built up around a young monarch, and concern about the intentions of an apparently sinister favourite, John, 3rd Earl of Bute, who became first minister in 1762. George II indeed had been wary of Bute, whose influence over the future George III he regarded as excessive. Regeneration through the rebirth represented by a new King had been the central idea of the Patriot King aspirations that focused on Frederick, Prince of Wales, until his unexpected death in 1751, and then on his son, the future George III. These were aspirations that represented a hostile, or at least critical, response to George II, particularly the elderly George, but this response, nevertheless, still showed the centrality of the Crown and the Hanoverian option. Furthermore, the theme of the Patriot King had itself been taken up by George II, when in opposition in 1717–20 and when he became King in 1727; although this theme was far more muted than the later iterations under Frederick, Prince of Wales, and George III, in large part because of the more powerful identification of dynasty and Whiggery in the 1710s and 1720s. Moreover, a criticism of George II as the 'other', against which ideas were framed under George III, reflected but, even more, helped mould his subsequent reputation.

To take a different perspective in looking at the significance of the British monarchy in a European context, although the position of King-in-Parliament was distinctive and, given able management, helped ensure a state that was stronger than its Continental counterparts, it was not simply in Britain that the authority and power of the monarch were affected by the role of intermediate institutions, in the British case Parliament. Indeed, these institutions were also very important in France. For Britain, it is not appropriate to see this issue simply in terms of restrictions on the Crown, and to measure authority and power accordingly, for example discussing how far George was able to maintain ministers in whom he had confidence in office in 1742, 1744 and 1746. It is more appropriate, instead, to note a common tension across states between the regularization of power, through the establishment and following of agreed administrative procedures, and, on the other hand, the continuing importance of managing patronage networks, the personal intervention of the monarch, and his (or her) determination to affect policy.

In Britain, aside from not knowing most of his dominions, there were restrictions on what the monarch could do arising from the nature of the constitution and the political system. Whatever the royal role in ministerial appointments, Parliament was an important constraint, as its management was not directly handled by the monarch, however much the Court provided an opportunity for the King to meet parliamentarians. George also opened and closed the sessions of the Westminster Parliament, although he never visited Dublin, where there was a frequently independent Parliament, nor the seats of the legislative assemblies in the North American and West Indian colonies.

The King and His Ministers

To move back a level, the role of the Crown itself was made more complex by the dynamic relationship between King and King's ministers, a joint entity that was summarized as the Crown. This was seen, for example, in the exposition of the royal prerogative in foreign policy, that of declaring war, negotiating peace and conducting diplomacy, published in the pro-government *London Journal* of 12 June (os) 1736:

> The power of making war is no power at all, it is only the name of power; because the King can raise no money to carry it on without the Parliament. The power of making peace is a real power of the Crown, and ought to be as . . . the secrecy and dispatch which are required in carrying on negotiations between several contending powers . . . a power which ought to be lodged with the executive part of every government.

In practice, the aggregation of governmental authority and power in the shape of the Crown led to a lack of clarity about whose views were at issue, and this emerged in the frequently bad-tempered conversations between George and his ministers, certainly in so far as they were reported by Newcastle. He anxiously captured George's expressions of anger (see pp. 243–4), although it is less clear that he understood the King's moods.

The small size of government (by modern, and by most eighteenth-century European) standards, and the non-executive role of Parliament, which, anyway, only met for a few months each year, still left many opportunities for royal scrutiny, and initiative, and this extended to a direct part, such as the signing of many documents. The King, for example, signed receipts for Duchy of Cornwall revenues provided to him.[22] In the absence of a real prime ministerial system, or, rather, of a real prime ministerial system as understood today in an age for which continued royal power is an anachronism, and in the absence of collective ministerial responsibility, George was obviously the key fulcrum when ministers disagreed, for they were his ministers, appointed by him. Whether the King saw ministers on their own was regarded as an important point as it provided an opportunity for him to develop individual links. In 1755, when Newcastle was keen to point out that Henry Fox would be given responsibility, not power, he saw George's attitude as crucial in this point, not least in ensuring that Fox did nothing in the House of Commons without previously consulting the Duke.[23] Royal anger and the royal receipt of letters were considered worthy of comment when predicting the fall of ministers.[24]

Furthermore, the physical relationship between monarchs and ministers, with the latter kissing hands on their appointment, standing in his presence, including when discussing government business, and bowing when meeting and leaving the King, offered a visual message of deference, one repeated with others who visited the Court. The royal presence was therefore a staged event, as part of a regular sequence of such events, such as levées. These were staged occasions in which everyone played a role, and did so willingly. The interpretation of the staging, certainly, was a matter in part of perception—deference to one man is subservience to another, but there was little doubt of the message. In part, this helped to explain George's anger when his ministers did not then respond as he believed they should: substance did not correspond to the world of show, a feature characteristic of all societies but, more generally, true of this. George was doubtless encouraged in his expectations by the pliancy of his Hanoverian ministers, although he fully understood the difference between them and his British ministers.

Whatever the differences between him and his ministers, George could generally expect support from within the ministry for his views, which enhanced his pivotal role as far as Crown, government and politics were concerned. This support reflected the lack of cohesion within ministries and, more specifically, the extent to which they were not united on a party basis comparable to what would today be understood by such a basis. In particular, eighteenth-century political parties lacked membership, manifestos and leaderships similar to those of today. As a consequence, it was not possible to contain or control disputes between ministers on the modern basis, and this was accentuated by the idea that they were each the King's ministers and thus directly answerable to him. The collective Cabinet responsibility that developed slowly, in particular under Robert, 2nd Earl of Liverpool, prime minister from 1812 to 1827, and, to a lesser extent, earlier under William Pitt the Younger in the 1790s, was far less apparent under Sir Robert Walpole, prime minister from 1720 to 1742. The title prime minister, moreover, should not be capitalized, as it was not an office (Walpole for example being First Lord of the Treasury), and this helps account for the continued political power, rather than simply influence, of the monarch.

Far from responsibility to the monarch being a theory that was imposed on ministers by the monarch, it was one that provided ministers with an opportunity to defend disagreeing with their colleagues and also to jettison blame. Royal opinions thus acted in a dynamic tension with ministerial politics, the latter providing more opportunities for the former. In 1737, Horatio Walpole, the influential brother of Sir Robert and a distinguished diplomat (as well as the uncle of the writer Horace Walpole), complaining about a failure to co-operate with the Dutch in negotiations over the Jülich-Berg succession, a key issue in German and international power politics, noted that others consulted had concurred with this view, with the exception of the relevant Secretary of State, William, Lord Harrington, who was very much the King's protégé. George was against such co-operation, and Horatio suggested that Harrington's stance stemmed from his 'desire to please the King',[25] a characteristic of Harrington's relationship with the King until 1746, and one shared by a number of other politicians, such as Spencer Compton, 1st Earl of Wilmington.

The tension, as far as governmental responsibility and ministerial cohesion were concerned, between administrative method and royal role also owed something to the extent to which, in Britain as elsewhere, the limited authority of government institutions forced monarchs to act, and to be seen to act. They did so in a system where Court favour was crucial, power not necessarily based upon tenure of office, and only the monarch could arbitrate effectively in disputes. Furthermore, by acting, monarchs fulfilled the goal for which they were brought up and educated.

The Court remained important as a venue for actual politics, and not just symbolism. Political manoeuvres involved the monarch, particularly in the formation of ministries. In Britain, as elsewhere, a continued display of royal favour was important moreover for the maintenance of the authority of ministers, institutions and edicts, although it was insufficient in the face of crisis. Royal backing did not enable the Stanhope/Sunderland ministry to survive attack without reconstruction in 1720, nor Walpole to retain office in 1742, nor Carteret in 1744 and 1746. As a result of these and other episodes, the British monarchy appeared the weakest in Western Europe, indeed a Western equivalent to the 'crowned republic', Poland, or to Sweden during the 'Age of Liberty' from 1720 to 1772. This prefigured the situation in the early 1780s, when the Gordon Riots (1780), the fall of the Lord North ministry (1782), the recognition of independence for the Thirteen North American Colonies (1783), and the political crisis following the overthrow of the Fox-North ministry (1783–4), suggested that Britain was the most unstable state in Europe. Indeed, the situation led a desperate George III, on several occasions, to threaten to abdicate as King and to leave for Hanover.

More generally, British politics might appear particularly unstable to foreigners because of the role of Parliament. However, this role was itself attractive to liberal critics of Continental monarchies, for example Montesquieu and Voltaire, each of whom visited England during George II's reign and was opposed to the less liberal politics of France. In John Chamberlayne's guide *Magnae Britanniae Notitia: or, The Present State of Great Britain* (1726), England was described as:

> an hereditary limited monarchy, governed by the Supreme Head, according to the known laws and customs of the England . . . by the necessary concurrence of the Lords and Commons . . . it hath the

main advantages of an aristocracy, and of a democracy, and yet free from the disadvantages and evils of either . . . reserves enough for the majesty and prerogative of any King that will own his People as subjects, not as slaves.[26]

The reality itself was not particularly harmonious, but the parliamentary system did provide an opportunity for the peaceful expression of different views, as well as for the expression of views of authority and policy without these being the person or policy of the King. Furthermore, parliamentary support ensured that government finances were far stronger than in the seventeenth century, in large part because Parliament provided the guarantee for the national debt. Thus the appearance of instability was greatly misleading as far as the workings of government were concerned; although there was also the serious threat to stability posed by the Jacobite claim on the throne.

The comparative context is illuminating in so far as the role of the British Crown was concerned. Commentators also found the politics of many other royal Courts similarly unstable, or even more so, due to the vagaries of royal favour, not least the changing position of ministers. This can be readily seen in diplomatic correspondence, for instance reports from St Petersburg, where dynastic politics and political arrangements were far more changeable in the first fifteen years of George II's reign than they were in Britain itself. Greater stability was then offered by Elizabeth (r. 1741–62), but this was challenged by factionalism at Court and by the reversionary interest. Furthermore, Philip V of Spain (r. 1700–46) was, with reason, regarded as mentally unstable, and this was seen as affecting the policies of his government. As a form of government, monarchy was particularly dependent on the attitude and role of individual monarchs, which indeed were seen as providing them with an opportunity for greatness. Britain was not exempt from this process. The constitution, as far as both Britain and Hanover were concerned, was far less rigid than the term is often taken to imply, and this left a large role for the monarchs. So did the practice of politics. The reiterated references to royal views in diplomatic instructions are instructive. For example, in 1754, the Secretary of State wrote seeking Dutch advice about the Barrier, the Dutch fortresses in the Austrian Netherlands:

The offensive and unjustifiable conduct of the Court of Vienna upon this point, both as to matter and manner, has raised in His Majesty's breast the greatest indignation; but as the King's first thought will ever be, to preserve that system in Europe which His Majesty has hitherto maintained with equal steadiness and success, the King will not suffer resentment, however well grounded, to bias his Royal mind, or be deterred by the difficulty of the undertaking, from seeking the most prudent and effectual method of preventing the fatal consequences which the ill-judged obstinacy of the Court of Vienna might draw upon all their allies.[27]

George indeed was then regarded as being very angry with Austrian policy.[28] This royal interest extended to issues that might not seem of direct concern to George but that reflected, nevertheless, his sense of the interconnectedness of international relations. Thus, in 1748, Newcastle wrote to William, Duke of Cumberland:

the King has been pleased to give such attention to the Prince of Orange's late instances concerning the maritime complaints of the Dutch merchants, that His Majesty has given orders for passing a new Commission for Prizes . . . for the greater and more easy dispatch of that business.[29]

In Britain (and elsewhere) new ministers sought public shows of royal approval, such as the conferring of noble status on political allies, or the appointment of supporters to posts in royal households. The view of the King was important in the awarding of peerages, and George showed far less alacrity to promote to, and within, the peerage than George III was to do, which lessened the patronage resources at the disposal of the government. Whereas George I and George III promoted to dukedoms, George II, who quickly grasped the need to restrict favours in order to promote the image of a stable monarchy, simply arranged a reversion for the dukedom of the childless Newcastle. The influence of the King was also shown because posts at Court and in government could become influential when favourites filled them, royal favour could qualify the autonomy of institutions, as well as the procedures for appointment and promotion, and those close to the ruler could enjoy considerable influence.

Proximity to the King was seen as an important indication of political views, although not invariably so. There was much interest in who was in favour, and considerable care to 'spin' news accordingly. In January 1734, George, 12th Earl of Morton, a Scottish peer, wrote to his son from London, 'I believe you'll see in the prints [newspapers] that the Earl of Stair had waited on his Majesty and the Queen, but I am informed that neither the King nor Queen took notice of him, or spoke one word to him.'[30] This was important as John, 2nd Earl of Stair was a prominent Scottish critic of the ministry, a leading opposition Whig, and, had notice been taken of him, this would have been interpreted as a lessening of support for Sir Robert Walpole. In part, this was a matter of tensions between Scottish politicians being mediated in London and at Court. In 1754, George responded harshly when James, 20th Earl of Kildare, a leading Irish peer, travelled to London to present to him the case of the opposition to the King's administration in Ireland, an administration led by Lionel, 1st Duke of Dorset.[31]

George's support for Walpole was unwelcome to the latter's opponents, both during his ministry and thereafter. This was reflected in caricatures, with particular outrage expressed in 1742 at what was seen as royal determination to thwart the public wish to see the fallen Walpole punished. In the caricature 'Touch me not; or B-B's Defiance', which was dated April 1742, George and Walpole are shown as two faces on one hand, the first facing Britannia and the latter Justice. George declares to Britannia 'We fear not her nor you'. Beyond Britannia is the ship that will take George to Hanover. Under the illustration appears the verses:

> Behold two Patriots of our British Land,
> Join'd Head to Head, instead of Hand to Hand!
> When two such Noddles are laid close together;
> What Tempests in the State can shatter either?
> I and the King [Henry VIII] the haughty Wolsey cried,
> And all the malice of his foes defied;
> But Robin [Walpole], haughtier still, (to evade Disaster)
> Cries, Touch me if you can, and not my Master.

That August 'Magna Farta or the Raree Show at St. James's' depicted the corruption of the Patriot politicians, with George farting out of a window and wiping his behind with the report of the House of Commons' committee established to investigate Walpole's supposed offences.

Conversely, reluctance to support the ministry on the King's part could also be significant. In 1750, the Pelhams, Newcastle and his brother, Henry Pelham, the two key figures in the ministry, had great difficulty in persuading George to be superficially polite to William Pitt the Elder at the levée, the regular occasion in which the King spoke to people at Court. Pitt was then a junior member of the ministry whom the Pelhams wished to keep content, and thus a show of royal support seemed important to them. It also demonstrated to Pitt that the Pelhams could influence the King.

Newcastle's correspondence the following year indicated his sensitivity to royal acknowledgment. In June 1751, he could write to his leading confidant Philip, 1st Earl of Hardwicke, 'Yesterday his Majesty did not honour me with one word at the levée, though he talked very merrily with my right and left hand neighbours, Lord Granville and my brother . . . and even spoke to my Lord Bath'. As Granville [Carteret] and Bath [William Pulteney] were former opponents of the Pelhams, this was not desirable to the latter, although the continued presence at Court of Granville and Bath was indicative of its importance as a sphere in which relationships were asserted and assessed. Concerns were accentuated by the question of influence during George's visits to Hanover. In March 1748, Newcastle was worried when the King told him that he was determined to go to the Electorate, the first visit since 1745:

> I foresee the greatest difficulties and inconveniences, a peace, and such a peace, as we must, I am afraid, take, to be negotiated, and finally concluded, with the King at such a distance, from this kingdom, and his Council, and possibly by one part of the Ministry, suspected, and distrusted by the other. I am really afraid that my brother in the present temper he is, may decline being in the Regency, especially if it should be determined that I should attend the King to Hanover.[32]

Fortunately for the Duke's piece of mind, he could write in September 1751, 'The King is very gracious, civil, and indeed familiar, both at the levée and in the closet'; referring to the King's Closet where he saw ministers on their own. Whether true or not, Newcastle thought it important to convey this impression. In November 1756, Alexander Hume Campbell recorded that the Duke was 'in high spirits and very merry. He told me the Duke of Devonshire [William, 4th Duke] and he stood twice next to each other yesterday, the Birthday, and the King spoke twice kindly to the Duke of Newcastle, but never at all to the Duke of Devonshire.'[33] The King's conversation was also of importance to diplomats. George's not talking to the French envoy at Hanover in 1752 attracted comment from the Sardinian envoy.[34]

This was a direct royal politics that in part focused on traditional issues and signs of favour. The awarding of the Order of the Garter, for example to Devonshire in 1756, and of peerages and Court offices, were very significant signs, in part because they were regarded accordingly. At a different level of contact and approval, those who played cards with George II in the evening generally then supped late with him, and this gave them a valuable entrée, although not necessarily any real policy impact. George was willing to listen, but tended to make his own mind up, as was also true of his brother-in-law, Frederick William I of Prussia, and both of them could then be stubborn. Monarchs indeed often disliked pressure for favour or support, not least the constant cacophony for patronage. In turn, many ministers fell, as Charles, 2nd Viscount Townshend did in 1730, Tanucci did in Naples in 1776, and Pombal in Portugal in 1777, because they failed at Court, losing, or never having, the backing of the monarch or his relatives. This was a failure that became crucial, as in the case of Townshend, when ministers clashed.

As another demonstration of their political importance, the role of monarchs created serious problems when they were ill, as Louis XV was in 1728 and George III in 1788–9, and as George I and George II generally were not. As a consequence, rumours about the ruler's health were important, and, at times, such rumours were a key aspect of the politics that focused on affirming or challenging the continuity of royal views. Thus, in 1737, when Frederick, Prince of Wales pressed for a greater allowance, it was agreed that reports of George II's poor health encouraged support for his claim, as it was thought that Frederick might succeed soon. As a result, George was advised to return to appearing in public and holding levées in order to show that he was healthy.[35] The role of rumours extended to the condition and position of heirs, not least because anxieties about their health or possible death highlighted the problems that could arise from minorities and regencies.

The role of the King as an individual also attracted attack, literally so with assassination attempts. The Jacobite 'Elibank Plot' of 1751–3 included schemes for the murder or capture of George, but there were also assassination attempts on Louis XV in 1757 (the Damiens affair), and on Joseph I of Portugal in 1759. Prior to the 'Elibank Plot', the Jacobites had not plotted the murder or capture of George II while he had been King, but, in 1722, at the time of the unsuccessful Atterbury Plot under his father, they had realized that it would be necessary to dispose of the Prince.

Rather than Britain being unusual, in having a weak monarchy, it was the case that, even when monarchs were in control of their Courts and ministries, the institutions and personnel of central government frequently proved unresponsive to their demands, particularly if these entailed change. In Britain, as on the Continent, there was also a more general tension in government between respect for privilege and precedent, and the direction of reform policies, a tension that could involve the royal position on either side of this divide.

The rise of the 'public sphere'[36] also focused new attention on monarchs, as they were discussed in the expanding world of print. Newspapers commented extensively on Court activity, and not only in England. A report from Hanover in the *Whitehall Evening Post* of 14 June (os) 1735 during George's visit that year, noted 'the Court is extremely numerous... German noblemen from all parts'. Some comments were not descriptive, but far more critical, indeed hostile. This was also true of caricatures and verses, several of which commented on George's rudeness, specifically his turning his back on critics, as indeed happened; or, instead, presented him as a dupe of Walpole.

Contemporaries also drew specific comparisons between Britain and Continental states. Parallels were asserted in the British press, particularly by opposition writers keen to argue that national distinctiveness and liberties had been overthrown, as a consequence either of corrupting tendencies within British society and/or due to the dangerous, indeed autocratic, inclinations of the government.[37] Looking at British politics through the prism of alleged ministerial corruption made Britain seem similar to Continental states, and this provided a context for domestic criticism of the Crown. The monarch was either blamed for co-operating with this corruption, or criticized for being unaware of it, indeed for being a victim of it, a reminder that, at least in some respects, a strong monarch was sought. In some cases, the process of comparison also made Britain seem like individual Continental states, but dissimilar to others. This was certainly true if attention is shifted to the competence and personality of monarchs.

In the face of similarity, nevertheless, there was also an assertion of differences between Britain and the Continent. If parliamentary government was one expression of the latter, the Hanoverian dynasty was another, because it was presented both as a legal rejection of the Stuarts and as the legacy of the Glorious Revolution of 1688–9. Thus, the Crown was constitutional expression and protection of national distinctiveness, and this gave it support, irrespective of the failings of the individual monarch. At the same time, this argument could serve to justify opposition on the part of those who regarded themselves as loyal, for example both opposition Whigs and ministers disinclined to agree with particular royal views. The expulsion and exclusion of the Stuarts in 1688–9, which had been reaffirmed by Parliament in 1701 with the Act of Settlement, and in conflict against Jacobite rebellions in 1715–16 and 1745–6, had created what was seen, at least implicitly, as a compact, if not a contract, between Crown and people. The *London Chronicle* of 7 May 1757 declared:

> The notions of the Divine Right of Kings to do wrong; of their hereditary indefeasible right to the crown, as an unalienable patrimony; of the unbounded extent of the prerogative above law; these and the like high flying notions have been abdicated with that unfortunate family which acted upon them, and since the Revolution [1688], they are not popular even at court, where these faltering doctrines might expect most favour.

The newspaper was correct. George did not share Stuart views on the royal prerogative, and had no aspirations to act as an autocrat. He also distanced himself from the magical aspect of monarchy: George did not seek to heal sufferers from scrofula, 'the King's Evil', a skin disease, by touching them. This ceremony, last performed, and then frequently, under Queen Anne, with Samuel Johnson a famous beneficiary, instead became a fading memory of a different type and tone of monarchy. William III had not touched for scrofula, and nor had George I. It is significant that George III, although a devoted Anglican, had no aspiration to restore touching. As a further instance of the abandonment of traditional suppositions about monarchy, when, in 1755, the House of Commons debated whether it should sit on 30 January, the anniversary of the execution of Charles I, this was a motion that offended High Church Tories, such as Thomas Prowse, and not the King.[38] A Bill to abolish the commemoration was rejected in 1772.

Instead, George II looked toward a more practical, managerial and philanthropic leadership. This was at once an aspect of his North German Protestant background, and part of a trend toward a civic monarchy. The latter matched a powerful impulse in society seen, for example, in the establishment of the Foundling Hospital, in the work of Sir John Fielding, and in the legislation of the early 1750s on social matters. It is unclear where the emphasis should be placed in assessing George. There is a tendency to focus on the more modern-seeming civic monarchy, but it is probable that greater allowance should be made for the King's background and upbringing. This would lead to an emphasis on the North German Protestant princely culture from which George emerged. Here there is an instructive comparison with his Prussian relatives, with them also sharing his powerful theme of duty, although without the important role of Pietism which was evident in Prussia rather than Hanover where notions of the Lutheran *hausväter* role were more relevant. There may indeed be more differences than similarities between the Lutheran Guelphs of Hanover and the Calvinist Hohenzollerns of Prussia.

The Sources

There are good recent biographies of Anne and George I,[39] but the situation is far less happy for George II (r. 1727–60), a King in deed as well as name, who had a long reign but still lacks a scholarly biography. The neglect of George II is longstanding, although more recent factors in terms of scholarly and popular interest have also played a role. This is an important omission, for, without such a study, the monarch appears as a figure of episodic importance, distinctly secondary to his ministers, and as a restraint on them, rather than as an initiator of issues. To understand the King and his role, it is necessary to consider him not thus from the outside, but rather on the basis of a thorough study that makes use of the surviving sources, very bitty and frustrating as they are in comparison with those for George III. Indeed, having written a biography of George III, it is a major shock to resume earlier work on George II, because the relatively limited amount of material for the latter stands out even more obviously. This is also true in comparison with William Pitt the Elder, whose biography I have also written. Whereas, for example, for Pitt as for George III, there is heartfelt, handwritten material about their relations with their family, including Pitt's fulsome and far from stilted love letters to his wife-to-be, Lady Hester Grenville, there is no comparison for George II.

Without a focus on the King, it is also difficult to understand the Anglo-Hanoverian monarchy, and the problems this created for British ministers. Moreover, the failure to give due weight to George ensures that Britain appears more different from Continental states than it should, and certainly removes a possible way to offer a comparative study with the insights that proposes.

Compared to the wealth of publications on George's leading ministers, especially Walpole, Newcastle and Pitt, there is still very little on the King. This directs attention to the possibility of, and need for, such work. As far as the first is concerned, George left no major series of correspondence. There are indications that, as with his 'I am of your opinion' on a 1736 memorial about the Jülich-Berg crisis, he preferred to annotate letters from ministers, rather than reply to them separately,[40] but relatively few such annotated letters survive. This may reflect the destruction of ministerial correspondence, such as much of that of Walpole in 1742, but, judging from accounts of negotiations with George, for example over ministerial reorganization in 1756 and 1757, it is clear that he preferred to handle matters by conversation rather than correspondence. This was part of the pattern of politics by audience that made the King different, rather than a politics by correspondence in which he would essentially be but one correspondent among many.

The infrequency of royal correspondence is similar to the position with Continental rulers, such as his brother-in-law Frederick William I of Prussia (r. 1713–40), or Frederick I of Sweden (r. 1720–51), but was a marked contrast with the position under his eldest grandson, George III. The contrast reflected a major difference in the style of kingship. Although conscientious and diligent, George II was not a royal bureaucrat. Allowance should also be made for facility with language. George could write English, but it was not his first language and he was less comfortable writing it than his grandson. As a result, for George, there is certainly nothing comparable to the personally written correspondence of George III, which survives in the Royal Archives in Windsor and in the papers of the recipients. This lack makes it difficult to assess George II's views; but, as Ragnhild Hatton valuably showed in the case of George I, the absence of such a correspondence was no reason not to produce a scholarly biography, although, despite her biography, much about that ruler, especially his last years as King, still remained obscure.

The Royal Archives contain relatively little relevant material, and far less for George II than for his second son, William, Duke of Cumberland, and indeed, ironically, for George's Jacobite rival, 'James III and VIII', but sources do exist for the study of George. Alongside a systematic study of the papers of British ministers for relevant material, it is necessary to understand the extent to which diplomatic archives provide a mass of information on the royal Court. Just as British envoys were appointed and paid by George, so foreign diplomats were accredited to the King, not the ministry, they had high-level access to him, and they took particular care to report in detail on the Court. Their frequent conversations with the King, both in the circle at royal levées and, less frequently, in private audiences, ensured that their reports provide a way to study his views.

Thus, in 1727, George told D'Aix, the Sardinian envoy (representative of the King of Sardinia, who was ruler of Savoy-Piedmont), that he had always opposed the Quadruple Alliance of 1718, which had been key to George I's foreign policy, and in 1747, he told D'Aix's experienced and well-connected replacement, Giuseppi Ossorio, with whom he had dealt since 1730, that the success of Allied military operations in Provence would permit the dictation of peace terms to France. In 1750, George told Ossorio's replacement that he was furious with Austria, but, at the same time, he sought to lessen Austro-Sardinian differences.[41] During the Seven Years' War, George pressed the Bavarian envoy on the need for concerted action to preserve German liberty, which was a valuable indication of his views on the international crisis: the argument he employed was a critique of the authority of the Holy Roman Emperor.

Diplomatic reports make it clear how much George took a close interest in European diplomacy.[42] He had, however, few opportunities to meet foreign rulers, although, in October 1731, Duke Francis of Lorraine, later the Holy Roman Emperor Francis I, visited England, and was lavishly entertained. It was presumably as a result of that trip that, in 1736, the Duke told the British envoy in Vienna, 'I rely upon the King singly: not upon treaties, not upon formal promises, but upon what His Majesty has told me over and over again of his goodness for me.' George certainly supported his marriage to Maria Theresa, the Emperor's daughter, and backed him for the Imperial vacancy in 1745.

It is as part of a wider scholarly enterprise that the nature and role of eighteenth-century monarchy, British as well as Continental, can profitably be probed. Such a study provides a way to understand similarities and differences between the two. Moreover, although a stress on the Crown may appear to have little to offer to scholars concerned with other fields, this stress can encourage a re-examination of the role of the monarch in political thought, as well as of concepts and images of authority in lay and religious life. Such a re-examination can be glimpsed from an unusual angle if George's meeting in Kensington Palace on 1 August (os) 1734 with Tomochichi, the Chief of the Lower Creeks, a Native American tribe, is considered. This stemmed from the foundation, in 1733, of the colony of Georgia, named after the King, and the attempt to secure its future in the face of hostile Native American and Spanish interests by alliance with the most powerful local tribe. The chief came to London with James Oglethorpe, the key figure in the foundation of the colony, and he was received by George. The occasion was not recorded on canvas, but it interested contemporaries who saw a meeting between two very different types of monarch. Each, indeed, sought to act in an appropriate manner that was made difficult by a lack of understanding of the priorities of the other. Symbolism thus came to the fore, and George failed to act appropriately as he did not present his visitor with a gift, whereas Tomochichi presented George with 'feathers of the eagle, which is the swiftest of birds, and who flieth all round our nations. These feathers are a sign of peace in our land, and have been carried from town to town there, and we have brought them over to leave with you, O Great King, as a sign of everlasting peace.' There was, unfortunately, no opportunity to perform a war dance for the royal family.

The reciprocal gift-giving of Native American society was important but was not taken so far in Europe, and it is therefore inappropriate to see this failure to present a gift simply as evidence of misplaced avarice on the part of a monarch not noted for his generosity. Nevertheless, despite having the colony named after him, the King had little interest in Georgia, much less the Native Americans. George did, however, lend Tomochichi and his retinue one of his coaches. They toured the Court and were impressed by the size of the palace. The meeting was reported in the press, providing an instance of the scrutiny of kingship that was increasingly seen with changes in British society and public culture.[43]

The meeting also drew attention to the variety offered by monarchy.

This was a variety that was greatly extended in Britain by accounts of past rulers, and by reports of foreign ones, a combination that provided a shifting backdrop against which the current ruler could be judged. Furthermore, this provided a background against which George could consider his own position, for he would have seen dispatches and reports on other monarchs. They frequently emphasized weakness, dereliction of duty, and a reliance on favourites. Thus, in June 1733, Thomas Robinson reported the views of the Austrian government on the new Elector of Saxony, soon to be Augustus III of Poland:

> It is thought that there is not one good head at Dresden to govern the affairs. The Elector is said to be weak, diffident and irresolute . . . His government begins with setting up a declared favourite, whose greatest merit is his knowledge of dogs and horses, but who, it is apprehended, has, without the least tincture of affairs, no small share in them.[44]

In 1748, Cumberland referred to 'the weak behaviour of the Prince of Orange [William IV]'.[45] Such remarks must have encouraged George to activity. He would not have wanted to be seen to fail in his duty.

2

A New Dynasty and a Quarrelsome Prince of Wales

1683–1727

Born in Hanover, on 10 November (30 October os) 1683, George was the eldest child and only son of a marriage designed to help consolidate the North German princely house of Brunswick. His father, another George (1660–1727), was heir to Ernst August, then Duke of Calenberg and Prince-Bishop of Osnabrück. This George was to be better known to history as Elector of Hanover from 1698 and as George I of Britain from 1714 to 1727. The prince's mother was his father's cousin, Sophia Dorothea (1666–1726), the heiress to George William, Duke of Celle (1624–1705), and his parents' marriage was the result of a marital strategy designed to unite the territories of the house of Guelph, a strategy that was a crucial background to the life of the future George II. The new prince was brought up as the heir to his father, who became Elector of Hanover on the death of his father, Ernst August. When the prince was born, the British succession was a very distant prospect, and it was still distant, although far closer, when Ernst August died.

As with most German principalities, Hanover's frontiers were established by feudal, not geographical, considerations, but most of what, in 1692, became the Electorate was between the Elbe and the Weser rivers, the North Sea and the Harz mountains. However, there were also important sections between the Elbe, Mecklenburg, Holstein and the Baltic Sea, and also west of the Weser. Constitutionally, Hanover was the most recent of the nine Electorates in the Holy Roman Empire, the loosely united assemblage of territories that comprised modern

34

Germany and Austria, the Czech Republic, and some bordering areas. The Electors had the right of electing the Emperor after his predecessor died, unless the next Emperor had been elected, as King of the Romans, during his predecessor's reign in order to ensure Habsburg continuity. From 1711 to 1740, the Emperor was Charles VI, the Habsburg ruler of Austria, Bohemia, Hungary, the Austrian Netherlands (Belgium) and much of Italy. Hanover had an essentially agricultural economy, with little industry, and few towns, although there was mining in the Harz mountains in the south of the Electorate. Much of its soil was sandy, which diminished its productivity. Hanover's frontiers lacked strong natural defences and the Electorate was vulnerable to attack. Britain, in contrast, offered the house of Hanover unprecedented wealth, power and prestige, not least as a kingdom.

For the young prince, there was, however, a major difference to the usual pattern of princely upbringing as a result of his parents' divorce in 1694. This arose from the uncovering of his bored mother's affair with Philipp Christoph von Königsmarck, a Swedish Count in Hanoverian military service. Königsmarck was more charismatic, glamorous and sensual than George. Sophia Dorothea and Königsmarck met in 1689 and became lovers in 1692, but the affair did not remain a secret for long, and Sophia Dorothea ignored hints that she should be prudent. Her wish to end her marriage threatened Ernst August's plans to link the Hanover and Celle inheritances and, in July 1694, Königsmarck was intercepted in the Leineschloss palace on a nocturnal visit to Sophia Dorothea, murdered, and probably thrown into the river in a weighted sack, prefiguring the plan made by Rigoletto for the lecherous Duke of Mantua in Verdi's opera, as well as the fate of Rasputin.

Sophia Dorothea was then detained and the marriage dissolved, with Sophia Dorothea regarded as the guilty party and thus denied remarriage, although George I had also taken lovers. George William agreed that his daughter should be confined under his care at the manor house of Ahlden, where she remained until her death in 1726, while George I was given care of their two children, one the future George II. Sophia Dorothea was held under house arrest not so much because of the scandal but to prevent her being a figurehead for the Jacobites or the rival house of Brunswick-Wolfenbüttel, or the Roman Catholic Hanoverians deemed ineligible for the British Succession. The impact of this scandal on the young boy is unclear. It was reported that he had unsuccessfully sought to see his mother after the divorce, and that in 1727 he displayed her portrait which George I had forbidden; but the accuracy of these reports is unclear. So also is the suggestion that his attitude changed when he discovered evidence of the adultery that had resulted in the divorce and his mother's house arrest. Nevertheless, Sophia Dorothea was George II's mother. Sensitivity over her position led, in 1732, to the use of British and Hanoverian diplomats in an attempt to suppress the sale of the *Histoire secrète de la duchesse d'Hanover*, an anonymous and scurrilous work written by Karl Ludwig von Pöllnitz.[1]

The young prince was largely brought up by his paternal grand-parents, Ernst August (1629–98) and Sophia (1630–1714), particularly the latter as Ernst August became increasingly ill from early 1698. George certainly lacked the secure family background his father had enjoyed and, in particular, his experience of maternal love and encouragement. Sophia as a caring grandmother, which she was, was not the same as Sophia Dorothea as a loving mother. It is possible to link George's parents' divorce to his own craving for order and security, but this craving also reflected general suppositions about governance. There is also a need for care in ascribing psychological characteristics to individual histories. Although most élite children were reared by wet-nurses and governesses, the divorce and his mother's effective disappearance may have been traumatic. Indeed, possibly George's later rejection of his son was transferred from his hatred of Sophia Dorothea. This might seem a convenient explanation of George's rejection of the future George II, but the latter's rejection of *his* son, Frederick, Prince of Wales, can hardly be accounted for in such a way.

Instead of his mother, his wife was the dominant woman in the future George II's life. On 2 September 1705, George married the vivacious Princess Caroline of Ansbach, who, like him, was born in 1683: indeed she was older (by eight months), which was unusual and not true of any of the other wives of the Hanoverian kings of Britain. Caroline was the daughter of John Frederick, Margrave of Brandenburg-Ansbach (1654–86), a cadet branch of the Hohenzollern dynasty, and Eleonore (1662–96), daughter of John, Duke of Saxe-Eisenach. Eleonore's second husband, and Caroline's step-father, was Elector John George IV of Saxony; but, as a result of the successive deaths of Caroline's father, step-father and mother, Elector Frederick III of Brandenburg (from 1701 King Frederick I in Prussia) became her guardian. His wife, Sophia Charlotte (1668–1705), was the daughter of Ernst August and thus the aunt of the future George II. The young Caroline spent a lot of time with Sophia Charlotte, who had no daughters, and this proved a stimulating intellectual environment for the young woman.

The marriage between George and Caroline suited the political strategies of the respective houses, and was particularly pushed by Sophia Charlotte and her mother (George II's grandmother) Sophia, although Sophia Charlotte died before it took place, a reminder that the high levels of mortality in early-eighteenth century also affected the social élite. The young George fitted in with what was planned, visiting Caroline incognito at Triesdorf, the summer residence of William Frederick, Caroline's younger brother, the Margrave of Brandenburg-Ansbach, in order to choose her as his wife. The following year, as another link in the dynastic network, George's younger sister, Sophia Dorothea, married Sophia Charlotte's son, Crown Prince Frederick William of Prussia, the future Frederick William I, who was, in the event, to be a bane of George's life.[2]

George and Caroline's first child, Frederick, was born on 31 January 1707; the first daughter, Anne, following in 1709; and two other children, Amelia (1711) and Caroline (1713) were born before George came to England. Caroline was to exercise considerable influence on her husband until her death in 1737. Her reputation in Britain was enhanced by her earlier refusal, in 1704, to surrender her faith for prestige by abandoning the Protestant faith in order to marry 'Charles III', the Habsburg claimant to the throne of Spain, who subsequently became the Emperor Charles VI. This choice was applauded in 1727 in the sermon delivered by John Potter, Bishop of Oxford for the joint-coronation of George and Caroline. The contrast between Caroline's bright, sparkling, witty nature and George's more dour, boorish demeanour was to lead contemporaries, such as Countess Cowper, John, Lord Hervey, and Philip, 4th Earl of Chesterfield to underrate the influence of the latter. Their comments, subsequently published, moulded the portrayal of their relationship.

War was another key influence on the young prince, and understandably so given family background and the circumstances of the age. In 1701, the prince had accompanied his surviving grandfather, George William of Celle, when the latter visited William III in the United Provinces at a time when William was attempting to organize a coalition against Louis XIV. The latter's support for his younger grandson, Philip V, for the Spanish Succession threatened British, Dutch and Habsburg interests.

The rulers of Hanover and Celle joined the Grand Alliance, and this helped their goals, particularly recognition of Celle's acquisition of Sachsen-Lauenburg. Suspicion of France was to be a major theme in George's world view. In 1734, it was claimed by a Wittelsbach diplomat that George had a natural aversion to the very name of France 'the old and bitter enemy of this country' as he told the Speaker of the House of Commons in 1745.[3]

From June to October 1708, the young prince took part in the campaign in the strategic cockpit of the Low Countries against France in the War of the Spanish Succession. He served with bravery in the Anglo-Dutch-German forces at the battle of Oudenaarde, and was never to lose the love of military matters this campaign inspired. Oudenaarde, the third of John Churchill, 1st Duke of Marlborough's famous victories, was a hard-fought battle, in which the fighting lasted for nine and a half hours. The Allied cavalry attack on the French right suffered heavy casualties, as a result of pursuing too far, but the battle was a glorious triumph and the cavalry played an important role in taking pressure off the infantry. The Hanoverian cavalry took a particularly prominent role and inflicted heavy losses on the French. George took a conspicuous part. His horse was shot from under him, and there were fatalities among those near him. Just as the future George I took pride in his military conduct, especially at the battle of Conzbrücke against the French in 1675, so, for the future George II, this was a glorious moment that he was to long to repeat. The battle also played a major role in public commemoration, being celebrated by Whig writers as a sign of his personal dedication to the cause of freedom. Such victories remained a key memory for decades.

The battle, however, brought out the risks of military service, risks underlined by the earlier death of three of his paternal uncles in war, two in 1690 and one in 1703, although, as poor, younger sons, they were all surplus to requirement. At the time of Oudenaarde, George had a baby son, the future Frederick, Prince of Wales, but, in the event of his and George's death, the inheritance would have posed serious problems. He had no brother, and, although he had a sister, there were issues about the inheritance of Hanover through the female line: unlike the British throne, this was unacceptable and, anyway, would have linked Hanover to Prussia. Instead, the next in line would have been George I's unmarried brother Maximilian William, who had converted to Catholicism and was therefore undesirable (and ineligible, under the

Act of Settlement, for the British throne), and then another unmarried brother, Ernst August, who may have been a homosexual. In neither case was an heir available to carry on the line. Thus, military service was a serious risk and it is not surprising that George was not at Malplaquet, the major and bloody battle that occurred a year after Oudenaarde, and at which Frederick William of Prussia was present. Nor was he involved in any of the subsequent dangerous campaigning that lasted until the war ended, for Hanover, in 1714: for Britain, it ended a year earlier, which led to Hanoverian anger with the Tory ministry.

There is no evidence on this point, but this absence of subsequent military service was probably a severe disappointment to George, and may well have been one that conditioned his subsequent response to the possibilities for military service. In some respects, this limitation was a reflection of his parents' divorce. They had only two children, whereas his parental grandparents had had seven, including six boys, which left room for casualties. It may also have been pertinent that, although the future George II had had four children by the end of the war, only one was a boy. Because, however, he went on no further campaigns until 1743, George remained literally close to his wife, with whom he had a strong relationship. Indeed, after 1708 they were not to be apart for long until 1729 when he made, from Britain, his first visit to Hanover as Elector. By then, he had two sons, as well as a third who had died as a baby.

George's dynastic position improved greatly as a result of the Act of Settlement of 1701, which was a response to the winnowing out of the succession. Mary had died childless in 1694, and Anne's only surviving child, William, Duke of Gloucester, followed six years later. William III had not remarried and was sickly, while Anne was now unlikely to have any children who might succeed her. As a result, it proved necessary to clarify the succession and the Act strengthened the Hanoverian claim to the British Succession by putting aside Catholic claimants. These were particularly the house of Savoy, whose claim ran through Charles I's daughter Henrietta, and the Wittelsbach and Modenese houses, whose claims ran through Sophia's elder brothers. Instead, the Act recognized, as William wanted, that the right of succession lay with the now elderly Sophia, George I's mother, now Electress Dowager of Hanover, and her descendants, in the event that, as was expected, neither William nor Anne had any surviving children. This was an important anchoring of the Hanoverian Succession and one that provided a crucial claim of legitimacy. It was very much a case of King-in-Parliament thanks to Parliament. The Whigs in the session strongly supported the Act, while the majority of Tories did not oppose it. Moreover, Parliament went on to pass the Act imposing the Abjuration Oath, which declared that the Act of Settlement and the Bill of Rights should 'be for ever inviolably preserved'.

Under the Act of Settlement, the Hanoverian rulers would have to take coronation oaths commiting them to rule 'according to the statutes in Parliament agreed', and to maintain the Protestant religion as established by law. The parliamentary right to the Crown was to be pushed to the fore, although the Hanoverians also came to claim a hereditary right from Henry II via his daughter Matilda.[4] The latter claim, however, had no weight in Britain. Instead, the parliamentary role was key. It was also paradoxical. 1689 and 1701 ensured that, despite the right of female succession by Mary, there was a degree of elective character to British kingship, but it also grounded the kingship in a parliamentary dispensation designed to ensure permanence. Thus British kingship was very different to that in Poland where the political and constitutional system did not work to the benefit of the Saxon kings.

The Act led to George soon playing a more prominent role in British life. A naturalized British subject from 1705, George gained both the prestigious Order of the Garter and the titles Duke of Cambridge, Earl of Milford Haven, Viscount Northallerton and Lord Tewkesbury, the following year. George was also involved in the politics of placement. This was seen as the Hanoverians responded to Whig attempts to anchor their position in the succession to the Crown, a goal pursued at the expense of both Stuarts and Tories. For the Whigs, an emphasis on the succession was a way to discredit the Tories, as they were, correctly, seen as divided on the issue of the succession and (many of them) as willing to consider a Stuart succession if 'James III and VIII' renounced Catholicism.

Attempts to advance the Hanoverian position publicly were rejected, however, by Anne, who saw a Hanoverian presence as a challenge to her royal majesty, and a reminder of her mortality. They were also un-welcome to the Tory ministers who presided in her last years. Thus, in April 1714, Anne responded angrily to Sophia's attempt to have Prince George summoned to take his seat in the House of Lords as Duke of Cambridge. He had also been thwarted in Hanover as his father was unwilling to let him assist in the governance of the Electorate. It was scarcely surprising that he spent much of his time hunting, an important adjunct to military training, regal deportment and princely image, but not a way to gain governmental experience.

During Anne's reign, the inheritance to which the Hanoverians were to succeed had been changing as the new political order created by and after the Glorious Revolution was both bedded down, and also consolidated through further change. This was not a process that the Hanoverians helped to mould, and if they were kept informed by their envoy, their closeness to the Whigs and their concern about the Tories ensured that they were seen by British politicians as partisan. Parliamentary union with Scotland in 1707 was a key aspect of the process of change. It reflected concerns about the succession, specifically anxiety that England and Scotland would go for different options when Anne died, and tensions over the ability of Scotland to follow a different line in foreign policy. Furthermore, the civil war of 1689–91 had underlined the divisions in Scottish society, and made rule from London seem more attractive than government by Scottish opponents. The powerful leadership of the Presbyterian Church, fearful of exiled Stuarts and Scottish Episcopalians, accepted the Union as a political necessity. The passage of Union through the Scottish Parliament ultimately depended on successful political management, corruption and self-interest. Alongside the security and political dimensions, there were serious economic problems in Scotland. Much of its economy was in a parlous state, and influential circles in Scotland wished to benefit from the economic possibilities of the far larger English market, as well as from those presented by the expanding empire. They were indeed to do so and Scots played a disproportionately large role in the military and commercial expansion of empire. Nevertheless, the short-term political consequences were distinctly unhappy: a large number of Scottish Protestants rejected the new order to the extent that they were willing to rebel in favour of the Jacobite claimant in 1715, albeit without success.

There had been speculation during Anne's reign that Tories would support a Jacobite option and try to block the Hanoverian succession. Indeed, the danger of the Hanoverian option to the Tories was underlined in 1713 by the Electorate's complaints about Britain's abandonment of the, by then, unpopular War of the Spanish Succession by the negotiation of the Peace of Utrecht. This was pushed forward by the Tory ministry despite the bitter opposition of the Whigs. In the event, when Anne died in August 1714, all passed peacefully, largely as a result of inadequate Jacobite preparations and a refusal of several possible foreign backers, particularly France, to provide support. Sophia had already died, aged 84, in June, and George I therefore succeeded. Prince George accompanied his father to London, and both were greeted with great ceremony at Greenwich. The young George became Prince of Wales in September 1714, at the age of thirty-one, although Jacobites disagreed with this designation, leading to the pamphlet *To a Thing They Call Prince of Wales* (1716?), which trumpeted the Stuart cause. The French envoy reported that Prince George himself would 'not suffer the sight of any Tories, regarding them all as Jacobites',[5] while the fecundity of his marriage was seen as a guarantee of the new order, the coronation sermon for George I noting the 'hopeful issue' and the likelihood of 'many more pledges of the lasting happiness of these kingdoms'. At the coronation, the first for a long time in which a Prince of Wales had been present, Mary's crown was adapted for the Prince.

The Prince unsurprisingly pronounced himself pleased with Britain, while he was seen as accessible and pleasant, certainly in contrast to his taciturn, reserved and elderly father. Crucially, the Prince spoke English eagerly, having been taught it in Hanover,[6] although his English was heavily accented, leading to his later being referred to as claiming to hate all 'boets and bainters'.[7] The Prince and his wife were given major roles in Court social life, helping the King to cope with his new position. There were frequent Drawing Rooms and the Prince and Princess also played a part in the balls held at Court. This role was conspicuous and, to that end, they also learned English country dances. There were also dinners with prominent Whig aristocrats. The Prince's reputation for courage was accentuated in December 1716 when he responded actively to a London fire in Spring Gardens, supervising the firefighters and also bravely faced an assassination attempt in Drury Lane theatre. There is no basis for the story retold from Paris in April 1715 by 'Liselotte', Elizabeth Charlotte of the Palatinate, who was George I's first cousin:

> I have heard such a strange story from England . . . I heard that the Prince of Wales saw a play where some actress, supposed to be im-personating the late Queen Anne, pretended to get drunk and flung herself into a chair. Then a milord climbed onto the stage and laid about the actors with a sword, and the Prince is supposed to have ordered his Guards to shoot him down. The entire pit shouted that if a single shot was fired, they would do away with the King's whole party, and the captain of the guards is supposed to have said to the

Prince that shooting might be the thing in Hanover, but in England it just wasn't done.[8]

Meanwhile, following his father's example, George's interests were ranging away from the marital bed. He fell for Mary Bellenden, a Bedchamber woman, but she did not reciprocate. Instead, he turned to Henrietta Howard (c. 1688–1767), third daughter of Sir Henry Hobart, and the estranged wife of the brutal Charles Howard, later Earl of Suffolk. Henrietta in 1714 was appointed Woman of the Bedchamber to the Princess of Wales. She had probably became George's mistress as early as 1713 when the Howards were in Hunover, and remained in this role for his years as Prince, but crucially without limiting Caroline's position as George's leading confidante. Furthermore, Caroline's successive pregnancies indicated that George remained uxorious.

The Prince was given a seat in the Cabinet, the meeting of key ministers, and the Privy Council, a more formal and larger body, but relations between father and son were difficult and became more so. This was a classic feature of dynastic politics: the tension between ruler and heir, and between those who looked to one or the other, and was scarcely new in British politics. Anne, for example, had had cool personal and political relations with William. Furthermore, the dispute between George I and his son looked modest in comparison with what happened elsewhere at this time. Peter the Great had his son and heir, Alexis, a prominent opponent of Peter's Westernizing policies, killed in 1718; while Victor Amadeus II of Sardinia was imprisoned until he died in 1732 by his son and heir, Charles Emmanuel III, when he tried to retract his 1730 abdication. George II's nephew, the future Frederick the Great of Prussia, was to be imprisoned by his father, Frederick William I in 1730, and was made to watch the execution of a close friend, Hans Hermann von Katte, who had aided him in his unsuccessful attempt to flee from Prussia.

The Jacobite rising of 1715–16[9] offered the Prince a valuable opportunity to display courage and substantiate his role, but it was not one that he was offered by his father. Evidence is lacking as to why this was the case. It may not have been a reflection of a lack of parental favour, but rather the need to rely on a professional general accustomed to the command of British units, and, if possible, to the intricacies of Scottish politics; but the contrast with the role that William, Duke of Cumberland was to take in 1745–6 is a striking one, not least because William was considerably younger than his father had been in 1715–16. William was the 'spare' not the 'heir' (the second, not the first, son), which may have been a crucial factor, but, as so often, there is no evidence that this motivated the contrast.

The 1715 rising was an unintended product of the close association between George I and the Whigs, one that was to be sustained under George II. The consequences were helpful for the Jacobites, for George I's support for the Whigs (who, thanks to the resources of government, did well in the 1715 general election) alienated the Tories and helped to strengthen Jacobitism. George distrusted the Tories, whom he regarded as sympathetic to Jacobitism, although he also saw the danger of being a prisoner of a Whig ministry and some Tories, such as Daniel, 2nd Earl of Nottingham, held office briefly, while it was also offered to others, such as William Bromley. However, it was difficult to operate a mixed Whig-Tory ministry. George's replacement of Anne's Tory ministers by a Whig ascendancy left the Tories no option in government service, but the defeat of the '15 indeed lent fresh energy to the purge of Tories. They were excluded from senior posts in government, the armed forces, the judiciary and the Church.

Party politics and ministerial instability since 1688 had revealed the grave limitations of the Glorious Revolution. A parliamentary monarchy could not simply be legislated into existence. It required the development of conventions and patterns of political behaviour that would permit a constructive resolution of contrary opinions within a system where there was no single source of dominant power. The slowness of the development of these patterns was particularly serious as Britain was at war for much of the period and Jacobitism was a significant challenge. The Revolution Settlement had created the institutional tools for a modern state, particularly, in 1694, the Bank of England and the guaranteed national debt, and the constitutional basis for an effective parliamentary monarchy, with parliamentary control over the finances of the state—the aim indeed of many of the critics of Charles II. However, the instability of the ministries of the period suggests that the political environment within which such a monarchy could be effective had not been created.

Differences between King and Prince gathered pace in 1716, when George I forced the dismissal of his son's Groom of the Stole, John , 2nd Duke of Argyll, a rival in the army of William, Lord Cadogan, who enjoyed the King's favour. Military politics were thus intertwined with dynastic ones. Argyll was a favourite of the Prince: they shared an interest in military matters and in women, and had both fought at Oudenaarde, but the King was determined to curb his son's patronage. Despite Argyll's dismissal, the Prince continued to show favour both to him and to his brother, Archibald, Earl of Ilay, angering the King by so doing. During his first visit back to Hanover that year, George I also limited the Prince's rights in Britain as Guardian of the Realm. During that absence, the Prince, nevertheless, played a more active role in British society than he had done hitherto. He took up residence in Hampton Court and dined daily in public, underlining his prominence. Both the Prince and his wife made a special effort to be gracious to all-comers, and everyone who wished to was allowed to see them dine. Argyll was treated very favourably. In September 1716, the Prince went to Portsmouth, where he held a troop review and visited the warships. His reception was very favourable. George I who took pains to have frequent reports sent him on the activities of his son was concerned about his cultivating his own political interest.

The existence of a reversionary interest was itself a cause of serious instability. George I, aged 57 in 1717, was fairly fit, although there had been recent fears about his health, and this meant that there was no imminent prospect of the Prince becoming King. Their relations were poor, with each feeling mistreated by the other. In 1737, Hervey wrote, 'He always spoke of his father as a weak man rather than a bad or a dishonest one; and said . . . his father had always hated him and used him ill.'[10] They did not eat together and avoided speaking to one another.

The tension between father and son led in 1717 to a serious and very public rift that was closely linked to the major division within the Whig party that led to the Whig Split. George I had fallen out with Walpole and his brother-in-law, Norfolk neighbour and political ally, Charles, 2nd Viscount Townshend, when these ministers opposed his Baltic policy, which indeed was motivated by Hanoverian considerations, specifically the possibility of Hanover securing gains from the Swedish empire as a result of the Great Northern War.[11] George's policy, in contrast, was supported by Charles, 3rd Earl of Sunderland and James Stanhope, the two Secretaries of State; and opposition by Walpole and Townshend, who became increasingly prominent as opposition Whigs, helped drive George further into the arms of Stanhope and Sunderland. In turn, Townshend and Walpole looked to his son, whose support for them further alienated his father from both the Prince and these politicians.

Efforts to effect a reconciliation between father and son after the 1717 parliamentary session failed. Stanhope thought that Townshend and Walpole might even have intended to make George I abdicate in favour of his son, although, as so often, evidence is lacking.

Difficulties climaxed in November 1717 in a dispute over the christening of the Prince's second son, George William (1717–18), the first of his children born in England. This was a particularly welcome child as the previous three to be born successfully were girls, while there had been a still-born son in November 1716. George I wanted the new baby named George, while the Princess, who was worried by a prediction about the name, favoured William, a name she thought would also be more agreeable to the British nation,[12] as it was not regarded as Germanic. Indeed, the following son, the future Duke of Cumberland, who was born in 1721, was to be a William. Furthermore, the Prince and Princess wanted as a godfather the Prince's uncle, George I's youngest brother, Ernst August, Prince-Bishop of Osnabrück, and, from 1716, Duke of York and Albany and Earl of Ulster. The King, however, insisted on the conventional choice of the Lord Chamberlain, Newcastle (1693–1768), an ambitious and rising politician whom the Prince detested,[13] and who was closely linked to the Stanhope-Sunderland ministry. After the christening on 28 November (os) 1717, the easily flustered Newcastle was convinced that the Prince had threatened him. The Prince's 'You are a rascal, but I will find you' was heard as 'I will fight you' and as a challenge to a duel. Such a clash, over honour and position, was all too common in aristocratic society, but in this case it had serious political consequences.

The King took the matter in hand, in part for political reasons, treating it as a defiance of both his views and the ministry, and ignored two reasonable letters of apology from the Prince. This reflected the King's longstanding anger with his son. The dispute rapidly led to the expulsion of the Prince from St James's, an order only accepted by the Prince when he received it in writing, and the Prince was also deprived of the protection of his guards, a conspicuous sign of his lack of favour. Instead, the Prince established a rival court at Leicester House. George I, however, took charge of the Prince's children, whom, he insisted, must remain at St James's, an insistence for which he sought and received legal support. George did not act like Peter the Great in his dispute with his son. Instead, with royal heirs as wards of the Crown, a decision unsuccessfully challenged at law by Prince George, there was an emphasis on legality. Nevertheless, there was also a harshness that was seen in the fate of the children and their separation from their mother. Caroline was offered the option of staying with her children, but only if she promised not to communicate with Prince George. She refused, to the surprise of the King, and the events of the next few years were to make the couple even closer, which was important for their subsequent relationship.

The dispute earned the King much criticism, especially when the young George William died after four months.[14] According to the Austrian diplomat Johann Freiherr von Pentenriedter the nobility, unused to the sort of treatment Newcastle had received from the Prince, favoured the King,[15] but this probably reflected the view in the Court circles to which Pentenriedter had access, especially the Hanoverian officials in London. George I also insisted that no one could hold offices in both his own and his son's households, or be received in both. Furthermore, army officers were not allowed to continue in the Prince's household staff. This direct order, telling people to choose one side or the other, produced a scramble for advantage, with Archbishop Wake trying to remain neutral in the midst of the chaos. Newcastle himself became a Knight of the Garter in 1718, as a conspicuous sign of the King's favour. George asserted his control and trust in this manner, displaying both confidence and his control of public rewards.

Forcing courtiers to choose between King and heir caused major difficulties as they sought to respond to both present and future prospects. The public show on the part of courtiers and politicians was matched by one from the rivals in the royal family. The two Courts entertained as rivals, and used their entertaining to try and win support, with the King abandoning his reserved habits and taking a much more public stance. This was true both of what he did and of what he chose not to do. Thus, no ball was held at Court on the Prince's birthday, and the Prince was also banned from attending the theatre at Drury Lane, which had a royal privilege. In turn, the Prince tried to attract attention, for example by putting on musical evenings and organizing horse races. In March 1718, it was reported that the Prince and Princess of Wales conspicuously always spoke English, and that the Prince spoke it well and correctly.[16]

This was an aspect of a key contrast between the Prince and his father. The Prince had considerable commitment to Hanover, and sustained this despite his absence from the Electorate from 1714 until 1729. He also retained a German identity in London, writing in German for example to princely connections. Yet the Prince, unlike his father, was also successful in adopting a British identity. This was seen in particular in his socializing and also with his household servants. In the case of the King, in contrast, these were clearly Hanoverian. The Prince, however, did not go as far as his elder son, Frederick, Prince of Wales, was to do in associating himself with patriotic and nationalistic causes.

British public opinion was not good at sharing: the King was also a Elector, and that inconvenient truth caused trouble since the 'wearing two hats' inevitably created odd situations. Under the Act of Settlement of 1701, the Germans who accompanied the King could not hold Court office or posts in government, and thus they seemed a private, secret world of influence removed from scrutiny and accountability. This fed through into the political anxieties and contention of the period, especially sensitivity about secret influences, providing opportunities for criticism of the Crown. As Prince and King, George II was largely to avoid such attacks, certainly in comparison with his father. There were claims that he favoured Hanover, and these were pushed hard in 1742–4, but the Court of George, first as Prince and then as King, was not conspicuously German. Indeed, as Prince he could be seen, at least in contrast to his father, as British. This prefigured the impression that Frederick, Prince of Wales was to seek, and that George III was to make in 1760. Unlike his grandson, however, George II was to be unable to sustain the initial favourable impression, in large part due to his readily apparent favour for Hanover, to the repeated attacks made on him on this head, and to the unpopularity of the British ministers whom he supported.

In 1717–18, political crisis was increasingly intertwined with that within the royal family. John, Lord Perceval noted that the 'Walpolites' were increasingly seen as 'the Prince's party'.[17] Looked at differently, the two disputes within the royal family fitted into a parliamentary framework, with Court and Leicester House parties at Westminster. The Prince purchased Leicester House in 1718. That year, an attempt at a reconciliation between George I and the Prince failed: the Prince's letter contained no assurance of better conduct, and, when the King asked for one, the Prince was angry.[18] There was also dissension over the Prince's Civil List (annual payment from public funds), with the King trying to siphon off part of the £100,000 per annum guaranteed to the Prince, and disagreement over whom the Prince could employ.[19] The King's terms for a reconciliation were reported:

Provided the Prince would dismiss such of his servants as were disagreeable to the King, and that for the future he would take none but such as should be approved of by His Majesty. That he should give up his children and such a sum for their education as His Majesty should appoint. That he should neither see nor keep correspondence with any but such as His Majesty should approve of, and lastly that he should beg the Dukes of Roxburgh and Newcastle's pardon.[20]

The strong interest shown in the rift from the outset by British and foreign commentators is an instructive guide to their belief in its importance. Reports of a possible reconciliation were eagerly recounted or debated[21] and led to speculation about their likely consequences. There were also reports about more extreme solutions, including that George would oblige his son to return to Hanover, or be seized and removed to a remote dominion, becoming the first member of the royal family to visit America. This was allegedly the idea of James, 3rd Earl of Berkeley, First Lord of the Admiralty, and Charles Stanhope, the Secretary to the Treasury. Two letters to this effect were found in George I's papers when he died in 1727.[22] Foreign interest in the consequences of the rift was seen when Frederick William I of Prussia, George's son-in-law, instructed his envoy Bonet to open links with the Prince.[23] As the Prince had no brothers, it was not possible for the King to think of splitting his inheritance, with the Prince restricted to Hanover or Britain.

The dispute was also reported extensively in the press, much to the fury of the King, who was livid that letters between him and his son were printed.[24] This appeal to the public was unacceptable as far as the King was concerned, but it was characteristic of a developing trend in British public life, and one that was pronounced after the lapse of the Licensing Act in 1695 ended pre-publication censorship. Press reports, in turn, led the government to encourage the publication of accounts that were favourable to it, the *Weekly Journal* of 18 January (os) 1718 urging the Prince to follow the eventually contrite example of Prince Hal, later Henry V, as presented by Shakespeare in his *Henry IV*.

The political crisis denied the Prince any opportunity to win glory in the war with Spain waged from 1718 to 1720 in response to Philip V's determination to make gains in Italy, in defiance of the Utrecht settlement. The key British achievement in the conflict, the victory of Cape Passaro off Sicily in 1718, was a naval one, and most of the fighting on land was done by Britain's ally France, whose army invaded the Basque Country. However, the British also launched an amphibious attack on Spain. An expedition under Lieutenant-General Richard, Viscount Cobham, another Marlburian veteran, attacked and captured Vigo in 1719 and, from there, another force, under Major-General George Wade, captured Pontevedra. Prince George was not given any opportunity to accompany the expedition, just as, that year, he was not part of the response to the unsuccessful pro-Jacobite Spanish invasion attempt on Britain. This must have contributed to an angry sense of exclusion.

The Prince also suffered financially from the political crisis, being replaced, in February 1718, as Governor of the South Sea Company by his father. As the Company was a source of free shares given out as bribes for support, this hit in the short term, although it spared the Prince from the ignominy of the South Sea Scandal in September 1720. This was a crash of what had started as an optimistic commercial prospect, but had basically become a fraudulent financial conspiracy. Similarly, the Prince was not involved in the Harburg Company, which was judged fraudulent by the House of Commons in 1722: instead, his young son Frederick had been made Governor.

Foreign policy remained a major cause of disagreement in Parliament, but concern about George I's views also extended to the government's religious policy. From 1717, in concert with James Stanhope and Sunderland, George backed a policy designed to limit the position of the Established Church in favour of the Nonconformists. They supported the repeal of the Occasional Conformity, Schism and Test Acts, and the passage of an Act to limit the independence of the Universities of Oxford and Cambridge, where most of the clergy of the Established Church were trained. This attempt to win the support of the Nonconformists led to widespread alarm about the future of the Established Church under George. The Occasional Conformity and Schism Acts were both repealed in 1719. The first, passed in 1711, had been designed to prevent the circumvention of communion requirements for office-holding by Nonconformists communicating once a year; the second, passed in 1714, had been designed to make separate education for them illegal.

The political crisis also led to the government's unsuccessful attempt in 1719 to pass a Peerage Bill. This proposal for a restriction of the membership of the House of Lords was intended to prevent the future George II from creating fresh peers when he came to the throne in order to buttress a new ministry that he might attempt to create. The measure thus sought to force the Prince to accept the continuation of his father's ministers, but it was thwarted by Walpole who skilfully orchestrated opposition in the House of Commons. The Bill would have enabled the legislature to restrict executive prerogative power, a major breach of such power. The Great (First) Reform Act of 1832 could not have passed without the threat of new peerage creations, and parliamentary approval of the Treaty of Utrecht of 1713 would not have been possible for the Tory government had twelve peers not been created at the close of 1711.

During the Whig Split of 1717–20, Walpole demonstrated a lesson that was to be crucial also to the politics of George II's reign. He made it clear that a government composed of Whig politicians could not necessarily expect, still less command, the support of Whig parliamentarians, a lesson that his own years in office were to show that he had learned well, and one that George also had to heed. In opposition, Walpole had also found that he could not use co-operation with the Tories to force himself back into office. This prefigured the failure from 1725 against him as first minister of the more famous 'Patriot' platform of the Tory Henry St John, Viscount Bolingbroke and the Whig William Pulteney. Nevertheless, in opposition, Walpole had greatly affected the legislative programme. The rift within the royal family was also to have a resonance after the Prince came to the throne, as it was to be used as a standard by which to judge his own actions when George clashed with his own heir, Frederick. Furthermore, the episode was mentioned during the debate on the Regency Bill in 1751.

The intertwining in 1717–20 of politics and disputes within the royal family ensured that the wish to heal the rift between King and heir was an important factor in Walpole's return to office, while the latter's determination to bring his years in opposition to a close helped end the rift. The resolution of the crisis was also related to the state of the Civil List, the parliamentary grant to the Crown: ending the Whig Split would help ensure that the accumulated debt of the Civil List would be paid off, which would create opportunities for fresh expenditure. There was also tension between, on the one hand, George I's German confidants and, on the other, Stanhope and Sunderland, which improved Walpole's relative position.

Walpole played a major part in arranging, through the offices of Caroline, Princess of Wales, the reconciliation between King and Prince, a reconciliation that the Prince was grudging about. On 23 April (os) 1720, he made his submission to his father, and, next day, the opposition Whigs followed. Walpole steered the Bill for tackling the Civil List debt through the Commons, and the King was able to leave England and set off for Hanover, as he wished, with the political situation eased.

Although once he returned to office Walpole was criticized for defending ministerial colleagues implicated in the South Sea Company, he also benefited from their problems. In April 1721, Walpole became First Lord of the Treasury, while Townshend became a Secretary of State. Walpole still faced issues aplenty, not least Sunderland's continued role at Court, but was now as clearly the dominant figure in the ministry as he had been in the Commons since his return to office in 1720. Within government, a struggle between Walpole and Sunderland for dominance that involved ministerial patronage ended when Sunderland suddenly died of pleurisy in April 1722; James Stanhope had unexpectedly died the previous year. Their former adherents were removed from office, strengthening Walpole's position, although the process took several years. These removals demonstrated the role of the Crown, because royal approval was necessary, as in 1724 when Sunderland's protégé John, Lord Carteret was replaced as Secretary of State for the Southern Department, a post that gave him considerable access to the King. Newcastle succeeded him.

Walpole had played a key role in ensuring government success in the election of 1722. Aside from his policies, Walpole was adept in parliamentary management and in his control of government patronage. He helped to provide valuable continuity and experience to the combination of limited monarchy with parliamentary sovereignty. In the first session after the 1722 election, Walpole displayed his mastery of the Commons, and this remained the case in 1723 and 1724. The failure, however, to appoint the ambitious William Pulteney Secretary of State led Pulteney to go into opposition in 1725 and he created an articulate and active, albeit small, opposition Whig group. Walpole, nevertheless, continued to enjoy substantial majorities in Commons' divisions: 262 to 89 against an opposition motion in February 1726, and 251 to 85 in the debate on the Address in January 1727.

Although relations between father and son were ostensibly mended in 1720 as a key aspect of the political reconciliation of that year, they still remained poor and did not compare to the improved relations between George I and Caroline. The Prince, thereafter, played little part in politics. The spectacular disputes with his father of the late 1710s had been replaced by a mutual coldness, although this was not too serious, as affection between grown men was not a normal aspect of public life, and this was even more the case of fathers and heirs in landed society, including the monarchy. Waiting for your father to die is not the best basis for family harmony, a point that the rising price of property may make more apparent to current and future readers. The Prince, having been humbled in every way, had learned that to continue political defiance would earn him more royal wrath, isolate his followers from offices and perks, and not help the Hanoverian royal family. Continued defiance would be folly and, at the very least, unseemly. George and Caroline had served their apprenticeship, knew the weaknesses of the reversionary interest, and learned to be in harmony with the King after 1720.

The ministry sought to smooth matters, with Spencer Compton, the Prince's adviser, and head of his household, being appointed Paymaster General in 1722, a very lucrative post, and the Prince being informed of policy through the Lord Privy Seal, William, 2nd Duke of Devonshire. The latter had close connections with the Princess,[25] and was to be made Lord President of the Council in 1727. Nevertheless, despite the King's setting off for Hanover in 1720, 1723, 1725 and 1727, the Prince was not appointed regent, which anticipated his later treatment of his own son.

The King also turned down his son's request for a military post in any European conflict that might involve Britain. This refusal challenged the latter's wish to do something useful and to gain renown, or at least tackle boredom. The international crisis of 1725–7 indeed created such possibilities, not least with the serious military threat to Hanover in 1726–7 from Austria, Prussia and Russia, but the King did not wish to risk letting his son have an independent position. Instead, there was talk of George I commanding an army in northern Germany in person. This exclusion was seen as a source of his son's discontent.[26]

Despite this, the Prince did not, as his son Frederick was to do, cultivate his own electoral interest and prepare, in those constituencies he could influence, to oppose the government in the general election due (under the Septennial Act of 1716) at the latest in 1729. Nor did he take the opportunity of a revived opposition in George I's last years in order to push forward his views or goals. In this, he contrasted with the position Frederick was to take in the late 1740s, and this may have sharpened his dislike of his heir. Prince George retained links with the Tories through Sir Thomas Hanmer, a Hanoverian (ie. non-Jacobite) Tory and former Speaker of the House of Commons, but he did not try to develop the relationship to any active end. In 1722, the Jacobite conspirators in the Atterbury Plot planned to have the Prince seized as part of the conspiracy, but the Plot was pre-empted by firm government action and helped strengthen Walpole's position in government.

Meanwhile, the Prince spent much of his time with his family in Richmond Lodge which he had purchased in 1719. These summer stays at his country seat lasted nearly half of the year, and saw the Prince largely avoiding political activity. The prince's family expanded considerably and rapidly. Caroline had suffered a miscarriage in 1718, but healthy children were born in 1721, 1723 and 1724: William, later Duke of Cumberland, in 1721, Mary, later Landgravine of Hesse-Cassel, in 1723, and Louisa, later Queen of Denmark, in 1724. After a further miscarriage in 1725, Caroline had no more children. These three children were in Leicester Square, while Frederick stayed in Hanover throughout the reign, and Anne, Amelia, and Caroline remained under the King's guardianship as had happened as a result of the rift in 1717. There were therefore three different locations for the children. Prior to the 1720 reconciliation, Caroline had been allowed to visit her daughters in St James's frequently, and this remained the pattern thereafter.

George I died in his beloved Germany, early on 22 June 1727, at Osnabrück, en route to Hanover. He had had a stroke on the journey on the 20th. George was buried in Hanover, close to his mother, although it was reported that, in the shape of a large bird, perhaps a raven, a bird renowned for its constancy, he returned to visit his lover, Melusine, Duchess of Kendal, who from 1728 lived in Twickenham, dying in 1743.

On Wednesday 14 June (os) 1727, towards 3 pm, the news reached Whitehall by means of a courier sent by Townshend, who, as Secretary of State for the Northern Department, had been following George to Hanover. Walpole gave order to double the guard throughout London, an unnecessary precaution, but one that reflected the sense of danger-ous transition at the outset of a new reign, and then left for Richmond to inform the Prince that his father had died. Walpole was told to go to Chiswick and take his directions from Spencer Compton.

That evening, George came to London and, the following morning, at 11am, he 'was proclaimed King of these realms at Leicester House Gate and from thence at Charing Cross, Temple Bar and the Royal Exchange. The procession was accompanied by all the officers of the Crown and several other coaches, and all the nobility of both sexes now in town attended at Leicester House and had the honour to kiss their Majesties hands.'[27] Thus, not only George but also Caroline, the first Hanoverian Queen, was acknowledged.

Despite their poor relations, George I provided a model for his son's kingship, more so indeed than the latter ever acknowledged. Both men were diligent in government, interested in the army and committed to the expansion and, even more, security of Hanover. Each, also, continued the pattern, set by George I's father, Ernst August, of a commitment to being an active ruler concerned to govern well and to enhance the interests of his dynasty. These attitudes, moreover, also reflected a more general culture of government in seventeenth-century northern Europe, one that has been described in terms of a well-ordered police state,[28] in other words a carefully regulated government. In his fussy and sometimes bland way, George II sought to fulfil this goal, and he was to do so more effectively than was often appreciated, then or later.

3

The King's Realm

The end of George I's reign provides an appropriate moment to pause and consider the nature of the kingdom that George II inherited. At the global level, Britain was increasingly significant as one of the leading European maritime and colonial powers, indeed the foremost naval power. The *Atlas Historique* of 1705 dedicated to John, 1st Duke of Marlborough, and generally attributed to Henri Abraham Châtelain, described Britain as 'like a well-steered big boat'. This nautical comparison was appropriate, although it also helped suggest why George II, who lacked naval associations, was somewhat marginal to a key concern of the state, unlike Charles I, Charles II and James II, all three of whom, especially the last through military service, had been associated with the navy.

London was not only the capital, the centre of government and legal system, and the seat of both Parliament and the royal Court, but also the focus of a growing global trade system, which benefited from, but was not limited to, the expansion of the Empire. Britain became the leading trans-oceanic trader over George's lifetime, dominating commerce with North America, India and China. Indeed, average annual exports rose from £4.1 million in the 1660s to £12.7 million in 1750, and that in a period of low inflation.[1]

Trade brought money into the country and encouraged industry. Trade brought in goods that were used by George and his family and that can still be viewed today in stately homes. These included the china in Attingham Park, Beningbrough Hall, Dryham, Ham and Saltram, and the lacquer furniture and embroidered silk bed hangings that can be seen in the state bedroom at Erddig. The diet was changed by the import of sugar from the West Indies, the production of which helped drive the slave trade,[2] while tea, coffee and chocolate also all had an impact, and led to the production, purchase and use of new goods, such as teapots.

George's Britain, indeed, was a world power, but it is first necessary to consider the facts of life, facts that spanned from royal family to pauper household. Considering them reminds us that it is as necessary to be wary of finding signs of modernity in the social and domestic life of the period as in its politics. Visiting palaces and stately homes from the period, such as Kensington Palace, it is all too easy to assume that life was in many respects similar to ours. There are few signs for the superficial viewer of more profound contrasts, contrasts that assure us that the very experience of life was totally different. This different experience, in turn, encouraged psychological attitudes that were not those which dominate in modern Britain.

It is best to start with the facts of life, or rather the fact of death. Individual and collective responses to the natural and built environments are affected by the age of the individual observer. Due to lower life-expectancy, the average experience of life for people in the past necessarily came at a younger age than for the average twenty-first century person, and was shaped within a context of the ever-present threat of death, disease, injury and pain. There was still joy and pleasure, exultation and exhilaration, but the demographics were chilling. Alongside longlasting individuals, such as George, and focusing attention on them, in part, as unusual, there were the many lives that were quickly cut short. This was particularly true of infants, but was also the case with adults: in the case of women especially in childbirth.

Members of the social élite were not excluded from this process. For example, like George, Sir Hugh Acland (1637–1713), the owner of Killerton, survived his son, in Acland's case John, and was succeeded by his grandson, another Hugh, who, however, lived only from 1696 until 1728. Other [sic], 3rd Earl of Plymouth, married Elisabeth Lewis in 1730, only to die aged twenty-five, his wife to follow one year later, and the estates to be inherited by the 4th Earl, at the age of eighteen months, under the guardianship of his grandfather. George, like many men, as the result of the death of their first wife, had more than one partner, although he had the second, his longstanding mistress, Madame von Wallmoden, before he was widowed. Of the Parkers of Saltram, four of the five who headed the family between 1649 and 1840 had two wives. Sir Barrington Bouchier of Beningbrough Hall had three wives,

John Hobart, 2nd Earl of Buckinghamshire of Blickling Hall two, and Sir Brownlow Cust of Belton also two.

The aggregate results of such life expectancy were as blunt. After the growth of 1500–1650, Britain's population did not rise greatly for a century. During George's reign, indeed, there were rises in the death rate in both 1727–30 and 1741–2, although the latter rise was the last of the reign. As there was no official census until 1801, population figures are approximate, but a rise in population did not gather pace until the second half of the eighteenth century. Prior to that, the population of England and Wales had not grown greatly during George's life: from 5.18 million in 1695 to only 5.51 in 1711, 5.59 in 1731, and 6.20 in 1751, by when the population of London was about 750,000.

In part, this modest increase was a consequence of the constant presence of disease. Thirty-eight per cent of the children born in the town of Penrith between 1650 and 1700 died before reaching the age of six. Like many parents, George lived longer than several of his children, in his case three, and the consequences of that in terms of fatalism and religious attitudes are worthy of consideration. He also survived one of his grandchildren in the British royal line, Frederick, Prince of Wales's second daughter, Elizabeth Caroline (1741–57). The autopsy on George's second son, George William, who died when only several months old in 1718, revealed that he had been born with the polyp (growth) in the heart that caused his death. Very high child mortality figures continued to be recorded across Britain throughout the eighteenth century, although if childhood was survived, it was possible to live to a considerable age, as George demonstrated.

Defences against disease remained flimsy, not least because of the limited nature of medical knowledge, a problem that affected even the very highest. There was no comparison to modern suppositions that there should be a medical cure for everything, and many, instead, relied on folk remedies and prayer. Medical treatments, such as blistering and mercury, were often painful, dangerous or enervating. They were also no respecter of class. Surgery was primitive and performed without anaesthetics. In 1737, Queen Caroline had an operation for a rupture while fully conscious. She died from the condition in terrible pain. There were also few palliatives for less serious conditions, such as the 'violent cold . . . piles . . . violent pain in one side of his head, and a little fever' from which George suffered earlier in 1737.[3]

Smallpox was one of the most serious diseases. Among those it claimed was Queen Mary in 1694. Immunity was low, not least because a more virulent strain began to have an impact in the second half of the seventeenth century. Both the virulence and the fatality rate of smallpox continued to rise thereafter. It was far more contagious than plague had been, although the fatality rate was lower. In major urban areas, the disease became endemic as well as epidemic, and this proved particularly deadly to infants and children. It was also socially selective, not least because the poor lived at a higher population density than the wealthy. Poor nutrition lowered resistance to disease and to the psychological impact of adversity. Fruit and vegetables were both seasonal and expensive.

Ironically, the crowded nature of palaces helped make them dangerous, and provided a medical basis for the preference for rural retreats on the part of many monarchs. Opportunities for hunting, however, were more important in this preference, and attracted George, like Walpole, west from London.

Initially, inoculation (ingrafting) as a bar to a serious attack of smallpox, introduced from Turkey by Lady Mary Wortley Montagu, wife of the envoy there, was of only limited value, not least because those treated, when not isolated, were a source of infection. Lady Mary had her daughter inoculated in London in 1721. Queen Caroline, who saw herself as progressive in these and other matters, had herself, George and their children inoculated, and actively supported Lady Mary's campaign. Inoculation, however, only became relatively safe after the Suttonian method of inserting solely the smallest possible amount of infectious matter was widely adopted from about 1768.

No comparable progress was made in fighting other serious problems. These included diseases that would not now be fatal to healthy Westerners with access to good medical care, such as intestinal diseases. Furthermore, typhus, typhoid, influenza, chicken-pox, measles, scarlet fever and syphilis were all serious problems. Humans were very much at war with the animal world, although animals capable of inflicting death—bears and wolves—had long been wiped out. However, foxes attacked farm animals, rabies was a problem among the dog population, rats were a serious issue, and bed bugs, lice, fleas and tapeworms were real horrors. It was difficult to protect food supplies from animal attack. People were also vulnerable to fire. Wood and thatch burned readily, and fire-fighting faced many limitations, not least those of water supply and application. In Devon, the town of Tiverton was hit hard in 1726, 1730 and, especially, 1731, the last fire leading to an Act of Parliament that all roofs thereafter should be of lead, slate or tile; while Crediton lost 460 houses to a savage fire in 1743, and much of Honiton was rebuilt after fires in 1747 and 1765.

Many industrial processes were dangerous to others besides the workers, while a large number suffered physical distortion or disease as a result of working methods, for example the impact of milling on breathing. Dressing and tanning leather polluted water supplies, while brick kilns and tile works produced smoke and fumes. There were restrictions on individual noxious practices, for example the pollution of water supplies by some industrial processes, but there was no systematic scrutiny or drive for improvements. Urine was widely used for washing cloth well into the eighteenth century.

Sanitary practices were also a problem, although one that was greatly lessened for the royal family by servants and by the opportunity to move between palaces. Privies were largely an innovation of later in the century: those developed by Alexander Cummings and Joseph Bramah were patented in 1775 and 1778. The royal family, however, did not need to urinate and defecate, like much of the population, in corridors and alleyways. Status provided them with privacy in the midst of the busy Court. For most of the population, there were few baths, washing in clean water was limited, and louse infestation was serious. Those who could afford to wore linen and cotton shifts next to their skins, and these shifts could be regularly laundered. Like other wealthy individuals, the royal family was in a far more fortunate position. Whereas, for most of the population, breath, teeth and skin must have been repellent, they had the opportunity for palliatives. Wealth, however, was insufficient. In 1735, George criticized Bishop Hoadly for 'his nasty stinking breath' and 'nasty rotten teeth'.[4]

Consideration of the position of the bulk of the population highlights the relative quality of the life of the royal family. It is difficult to recreate an impression of the smell and dirt of the life of most. Ventilation was limited and drains blocked. Manure stored near buildings was hazardous and could contaminate the water supply. Effluent from undrained privies and animal pens flowed across streets and also into houses through generally porous walls. Privies with open soil pits lay directly alongside dwellings and under bedrooms. In comparison, royal palaces were astonishing.

The royal position rested on, and was indeed at the apex of, a society in which aristocratic interests and values were powerful. This contrasts with the modern situation in which the royal family is exposed, and obliged to resort to populism, as a result of the decline of this aristocratic world. Instead, far more so than today, the eighteenth century was a propertied society in which inheritance to land was crucial to wealth. Most wealth was still tied up in land. The relationship between capital and income greatly favoured the former—as, in general, was true of British history until the economic growth of the nineteenth century—and the ability to create income without capital was limited.

Imperial expansion and industrialization were both to increase greatly the possibilities for self-advancement. This shift largely followed George's reign, but in some cases the reign had already led to massive wealth. Admiral, Lord Anson, for example, who sailed round the world in the service of George, was a childless self-made man who left his fortune to his elder brother Thomas, who used the money to extend the house and develop the park at Shugborough. In 1746, Henry Talbot, an East India merchant, bought and remodelled Vintage House, near Dorking, one of the many stately homes now demolished. These figures, however, were still uncommon in the period, sufficiently so for there to be grave suspicion about the wealth produced by 'nabobs' who had made their money in India. This hostility to new money, and the newly ascendant, had a parallel in the critical response to the Hanoverians as a new dynasty on the British throne, a response that mirrored that to the Stuarts after they came to the English throne in 1603. At the same time, like many of his subjects, George was uneasy about social mobility, at least in the form of promotion to the peerage.

Although industrial expansion was important, with a major growth in per capita output, agriculture was the principal source of employment and wealth, the most significant sector of the economy, and the basis of the taxation, governmental, ecclesiastical (tithes) and proprietorial (rents), that funded many other activities. Land and its products provided the structure of the social system and the bulk of the wealth that kept it in being. Peasant ownership of the land was limited, and land ownership in Britain was relatively concentrated by European standards. The Agricultural Revolution, introducing crop rotation, nitrogenous plants, and the enclosure of open fields, ensured that more food was available, and also acted as a restraint on its cost.

There was an active land market, and status could be readily acquired, but in most of Britain, especially in areas of established agriculture, the distribution of wealth did not change greatly in the eighteenth century, other than through marriage and inheritance. The pattern of estates also did not alter. The stability of the landed order was one of the striking features of George's reign. Tories might complain that Whig policies discriminated against the landed interest which they claimed to represent, but Walpole brought the land tax down from three shillings in the pound in 1717–21, to two shillings in the pound (10 new pence, 10 per cent) in 1722–6, 1730–1 and 1734–9, and to one shilling in the pound in 1732–3. His protégé, Henry Pelham, First Lord of the Treasury from 1743 to 1754, was similarly committed to peace and low taxation. This was a commitment however that was challenged by George's support for an ambitious foreign policy of Continental interventionism, particularly in 1733–5, and from 1740 on, because that entailed heavy costs, such as subsidies to allies and greater military expenditure.

This serves as a reminder of the social dimension arising from the high politics of the period which can otherwise seem rather remote from the bulk of the population. As social welfare was not a cause of national taxation, the support of foreign policy played a much greater role in public finances than is the case today.

George's ministers came from the landed interest, although talent played a major role in their position. Walpole came from the Norfolk gentry, built a lavish seat at Houghton, and was made Earl of Orford by George, a clear sign of the King's support that was designed to shelter the former minister in the face of demands for punishment. Pelham was Newcastle's younger brother, and Pitt a younger brother of a less prominent landowner. On the other side of the Commons, whatever the political proscription they suffered under George, the Tories were not driven from the land.

Landed continuity had important political, social and cultural consequences for the political world within which George operated. This was a hierarchical society, and there were few challenges to the assumptions that reflected and sustained this situation. The distribution of governmental power and authority fundamentally accorded with the structure of the social system, and not with democratic representation. There were shifts, not least an ecclesiastical pluralism that challenged religious authority following the Act of Toleration of 1689. Nevertheless, the ethos and practice of politics were more conservative than in the seventeenth century (which helped George), and it was possible to encompass political and religious divisions, bar Jacobitism, within the system. Although much commentary naturally related to political tension and disagreements, in some of which the King figured prominently, the extent and impact of this tension were far less disruptive for much of the time than the commentary might suggest. Furthermore, the structure of politics and government, far from precluding debate and discussion, now expected them. Government relied on co-operation, and lacked both a substantial bureaucracy and a well-developed bureaucratic ethos that might provide a substitute for this bureaucracy. Loyalties were largely personal, rather than to the state as such, and this helped focus attention on the person and personality of the King. Politicians, such as William, 4th Duke of Devonshire in 1755, could want George informed that they opposed proposed legislation 'from opinion not desire of opposition'.[5]

More generally in politics, aside from the institutional framework of contention—elections and Parliament—the Court and ministerial context of élite politics was not one of uniform opinions and an absence of debate. It would be wrong to suggest that the British *ancien régime* was stable if that label is intended to imply an absence of debate and of new ideas and initiatives. Yet, with the exception of Jacobitism, there was no permanent struggle with the world of extra-parliamentary politics. There was no such struggle, nor any rigid divide, nor any coherent challenge to the political structure. Indeed, the measure of the conservatism of the period was that stability was a case not of radicalism overcome or resisted, as in the early 1660s, but of a society with few radical options until the crisis created by the French Revolution and the accompanying development of British radicalism in the early 1790s.

The significance of the monarch as the head of the aristocracy, and the mediator of their system of prestige, was underlined by the extent to which the politics of the great houses were crucial in the electoral system. This was true of the more numerous borough (town) seats in Parliament as well as of the county constituencies. Irrespective of whether they actually had any urban property, local aristocrats and gentry could be of considerable consequence in influencing borough representation: the Dukes of Bolton and Chandos in Winchester, the Robartes of Lanhydrock in Bodmin, the Luttrells of Dunster Castle at Minehead, the Dukes of Grafton and the Earls of Bristol at Bury St Edmunds, the Earls Gower at Newcastle under Lyme, and so on. Small towns, however, were not necessarily deferential and this influence was not always uncontentious. In 1747, Derby successfully resisted the usually dominant interests of the Duke of Devonshire and the Earl of Chesterfield, while the Ansons and Gowers were only just successful at Lichfield. This provides a context within which to judge the issues of control for George in the parliamentary representation of Windsor and, far more, Westminster.

In general, particularly in smaller boroughs, the influence of the social élite was strong, but the bustling cities presented a political world that was far more dynamic. This dynamism was one that populist politicians, most prominently William Pitt the Elder, were best placed to marshal, while George felt, at best, uncomfortable and, more commonly, alienated from it. These seats were those that tended to define national issues, and, despite efforts to bring the King closer by propagating loyalty, George tended to be a distant figure in these spheres.

His marginality can be seen by considering the response of the major Midlands manufacturing town of Coventry to the Excise Crisis, the political storm that arose in 1733 over Walpole's proposal to extend the Excise (taxation on goods, equivalent to modern VAT: Value Added Tax). Coventry was dominated politically by the council which was controlled by Dissenters. They used their position to ensure that Whigs were elected to Parliament, although this was not always an easy process. Opponents of the Excise Scheme throughout the country sought to stir up agitation against the government's proposals and to exert pressure on MPs. This caused difficulties for Sir Adolphus Oughton, one of Coventry's two MPs, a ministerial supporter with a constituency opposed to the Excise Scheme, and these difficulties led him to abstain from the division on the Bill on 14 March (os) 1733. On 16 March (os) 1733, however, Oughton was upset by his fellow-Coventry MP, John Neale, speaking for the first time in the House of Commons, to which he had been elected in 1722. Neale declared that Coventry's instructions to its MPs against the Excise Bill were unrepresentative, and that 'he had had a letter from his borough approving of the scheme'. This put Oughton, who had been seeking the governorship of the British colony of Minorca in a very difficult position, an issue that pushed George's views to the fore, for such an appointment depended on the King.[6]

Neale's claim led to a political storm in Coventry and a petition from the town to Parliament against the Excise Bill, a development that exacerbated Oughton's difficulties by highlighting the competing pressures of constituency and ministry. Oughton did not present the petition; that was left to Neale, who had rapidly changed his position, and to William Bromley, a Tory MP for the county, but Oughton abstained in a division on 10 April (os) despite being threatened with the loss of all future promotion. Unsurprisingly, Oughton did not receive the governership of Minorca: royal approval was closely linked to parliamentary conduct.

Coventry was a sophisticated political environment, alert to issues both national and local; and George's role was but tangential to it. The same was true for other towns such as Bristol and Taunton. Edward Southwell, opposition Whig MP for Bristol from 1739 to 1754, complained in 1742 about criticisms from its electorate, 'if I am to suffer or to be run down for every single private vote in an affair where none but those who hear the arguments and pleadings can be judges, it is certain that no man can be more a slave than the representative of so populous a city.'[7]

This public sphere was scarcely new, and in many respects the issues it posed were far easier for George than for his Stuart predecessors because the ministers now played a much greater role in government. This ensured that they were the butt of public criticism and anger. George was to be the subject of much abuse, but it was less than that directed at Walpole. This situation in 1733 set the pattern for the remainder of the reign. No single politician acted as a focus of criticism comparable to Walpole, but Carteret, Newcastle and Fox each played a similar role in obloquy.

George, indeed, was often presented as a victim of his ministers, as in 1749 when the *Remembrancer* of 18 November (os) accused Newcastle and Henry Pelham of corruption and of manipulating the King, as well as the Duke of Cumberland of brutality in his administration of the army. The printer and publisher were arrested, although the impact of such action was limited by the quarrel within the royal family: Frederick, Prince of Wales was willing to indemnify them for any fines. The theme of the King as led astray by sinister ministers was a staple of opposition criticism during the reign as much of it, particularly if not of Jacobite sympathy, did not wish to engage directly with the idea that the King bore a key responsibility for political arrangements that were disliked, or, instead, found it more convenient to attack the ministers. The first issue of the *Monitor*, that of 9 August 1755, declared 'By abusing the power and prerogative of the Crown, and by creating a private and corrupt dependence upon ministers, by bribery and other undue influences, the balance of power between the King and subject may soon be destroyed' and, attacking the Newcastle ministry, proclaimed that the newspaper's goal was 'to emancipate the King from the shackles of an arbitrary administration'.

George indeed saw himself as having to suffer the consequences of a political system in which he had too little power and a political culture that did not seek to help the monarch. Hervey remarked after George's return from Hanover in 1735:

> In truth he hated the English, looked upon them all as king-killers and republicans, grudged them their riches as well as their liberty, thought them all overpaid, and said . . . that he was forced to distribute his favours here very differently from the manner in which he bestowed them at Hanover; that there he rewarded people for doing their duty and serving him well, but that here he was obliged to enrich people for being rascals, and buy them not to cut his throat.[8]

Much of this political drama was played out in London, but this was a city that was not dominated by the King. There was no comparison with Stockholm, Copenhagen, St Petersburg, Berlin, Lisbon and Vienna. Paris was far less dominated by the Crown than these cities, but Paris did not equal the independence of London, not that is until it surpassed London in violent excess in launching the French Revolution in 1789.

London dominated and dominates the public gaze and memorialization of George's Britain. It was the setting for fiction, whether in Alexander Pope's poetry or Henry Fielding's novels. The city also presented a bold and triumphant face to the viewer. In mid-century, Antonio Canaletto, with his splendid canvases, used talents developed to depict Venice in order to show the glories of modern London, as Marco Ricci had done earlier in the century. A modern pride in London was expressed in Canaletto's views, with recent or new buildings such as St Paul's Cathedral, Greenwich Observatory, Somerset House, Westminster Bridge and the rebuilt towers of Westminster Abbey playing a prominent role. A less grand view, but one that also captured the city's expansion, was offered by Richard Wilson in his painting *Westminster Bridge under Construction* (1744).

London was central to English life and culture. The energy of London was captured across the arts and provided the context for much of national culture. Under the shadow of St Paul's were published accounts of the diversions of the capital, such as James Ralph's *The Touchstone: or . . . Essays on the Reigning Diversions of the Town* (1728), and Henry Fielding's *A Trip through the Town* (1735). Neither centred on the royal Court. This was even more true of the particular genre of unbuttoned travelogues, for example *A Trip through London: Containing Observations on Men and Things, viz . . . A remarkable reencounter between a bawd and a sodomite . . . Practice of petty-foggers exposed* (1728).

The backdrop to this activity was the vitality of the capital. London's dominant position owed much to its place in trade and industry, but this also reflected the city's role as the centre of government, the law and consumption, and its position in the world of print, which, after the lapsing of the Licensing Act in 1695, became even more important as a shaper of news, opinion and fashion. London newspapers circulated throughout England, and were also crucial sources for the provincial press. The turnpike and postal systems also radiated from London.

London moreover led the way in national movements and societies such as the SPCK (Society for Promoting Christian Knowledge) and in related activity and lobbying. Despite the primate being the Archbishop of Canterbury, London led in religion. The Archbishop spent much of his time in Lambeth Palace, and ordinands often went to London to be ordained.

London also provided both setting and topics for cultural life. As a subject, it was the most striking in the country until the cult of landscape late in the century. London was presented as a site of liberty, trade and progress, a Whiggish rendition. The capital, however, was also presented, particularly by Tory critics, in terms of moral, political and economic disorder and dissolution. Urban living therefore served to delineate, if not define issues, and the Crown was marginal to these.

The city grew significantly during George's reign as the development of the West End estates of landlords such as Sir Richard Grosvenor and Lord Burlington continued to be developed as prime residential property. The nobility moved west from the Covent Garden area and closer to the royal palace at St James's. Devonshire House was built in the 1730s, Chesterfield House in 1747–52 and the new Norfolk House in 1748–56. Mayfair and St James's indeed became the select side of town. This represented an important realignment socially and politically, but it did not mean that London mercantile and urban interests were cast into the shade. Indeed, far from it, and there was also an important reaction against the polite society that lived to the west. This society was a prime topic of satire and criticism. In the 1740s, Fielding in his novels presented London in terms of a corrupt Court and aristocracy at its West End, with their commerce in vice, and the more acceptable commercial metropolis. Some criticism was driven home directly on George. In September 1738, while walking alone in Kensington Gardens, he was harangued by a male transvestite who got away safely. Four years later, a visit to the pleasure gardens at Ranelagh was also embarrassing:

> The last time the King was at Ranelagh Gardens he had this joke cut upon him, *viz.*, two young fellows were walking by the King, one said to the other, 'where shall we sup?' T'other made answer, 'At the King's Arms.' 'Oh,' says t'other, 'that's too full' (for the Countess of Yarmouth was with him). 'At the King's Head, then.' 'Oh, no,' says he, 'that's very empty.' On which the King made out of the Gardens directly, as well as the young fellows, and they say it caused a great disturbance.[9]

The sense of accessibility captured in this account is notable.

Decorative and architectural work focused more on the city institutions than on royal palaces. Sir James Thornhill in 1725–7 provided painted decorations for the ceiling of the new Council Chamber in the Guildhall, offering Baroque themes and images, with the oval medallion in the centre providing a personification of the City of London as a young woman attended by Pallas Athena (symbolizing wisdom), Peace, Plenty and two cherubs. George Dance the Elder, Surveyor to the Corporation of London, designed the impressive Mansion House, which was begun in 1739. The king lacked an apotheosis comparable to the one depicted by Thornhill for the City of London.

London also developed as a centre of consumption and leisure to which the Court was marginal. The amount of fixed, specialized investment in leisure rose greatly with theatres, pleasure gardens, picture galleries, auction houses and the ubiquitous coffee houses. In 1753, the British Museum was established by Act of Parliament, as the first national museum of its kind in the world. The museum acted as though it were an encyclopaedia, with sequences of rooms, their layout and the juxtaposition of objects within them providing a means of understanding relationships within the world of objects and specimens. This was a world of attempted rationality and applied science that was increasingly prominent. George had relatively little to do with this world, but he continued his father's abandonment of what was at once a Christian rite and ritual white magic associated with the royal touching for the 'King's Evil', the skin disease scrofula, which, it had been believed, was cured by this touch. This represented a rejection of divine right monarchy in favour of the idea of a pragmatic, constitutional monarch who was on the throne as a result of political action, not divine sanction.

London's development greatly influenced that of other cities, not least because of the importance of image. The designs of London's new houses were given wider impact through publications such as Richard Neve's *The City and Country Purchaser and Builder's Dictionary*, which first appeared in 1703, with a second edition in 1726. The pleasure gardens, walks, assembly rooms and squares of London were emulated elsewhere. The social basis of London's development—a major expansion in the middling orders, and a growing practice by the rural élite of spending part of the year there, was matched in regional capitals, such as Norwich and Nottingham, county centres, such as Warwick, and developing entertainment centres, especially spa towns, such as Tunbridge Wells and Bath. Thirty-four new spas were founded in England between 1700 and 1750.

The urban environment for George's well-to-do subjects was changing considerably. Brick buildings with large windows were built in a regular 'Classical' style, along and around new streets, squares, crescents and circuses. Brick replaced timber-frame in houses for the well-to-do, for example in Norwich from the late seventeenth century. In Bristol, Queen's Square begun in 1699 set the fashion for brick-built houses and was joined by Prince's Street (named after Prince George of Denmark) and by King's Square, which was laid out from 1737. This was possibly named not after George but after Kingsdown on the southern slope of which it was laid out. In Bath, John Wood the Elder was responsible for Queen's Square (1728–34), the Assembly Rooms (1730) and the King's Circus, which was begun in 1754.

Alongside light, roomy and attractive private houses for the affluent, numerous public and philanthropic buildings were also built. Theatres, assembly rooms, subscription and parish libraries and other leisure facilities were opened in many towns, alongside public outdoor space: parks, walks and racecourses. The first of what were to be many proprietary libraries, whose members owned shares, was the Liverpool Library, established in 1758. In 1732, York, socially the capital of the north of England, gained magnificent Assembly Rooms that showed that the Palladian style could be used for a public building. Assemblies were first held in Newcastle in 1716, and new Assembly Rooms opened there in 1736. Norwich and Bristol followed suit in 1754 and 1755.

The sociability on offer in such Assembly Rooms was different to that at Court. In the Assembly Rooms, gentility and equality were fused. The assurance of the gentility of those present made it possible in theory for the assembled company to set aside status and to act as equals, sidelining the concerns about social fluidity that played such a corrosive role in mixing. Royal and aristocratic concerns about status might therefore appear absurd, but these concerns were reiterated not only in society, but also in fiction, particularly with anxiety about social mixing. The latter anxiety played a large role in real and fictional dramas about seduction and misalliances. The challenges to honour that led to duels represented another problem related to status. Moreover, rules, cost and the organization of space, both within towns and in individual sites such as buildings, excluded the bulk of the population in the cause of an uneasy mix of hierarchy, status and profit.

The social world that fostered the demand for new buildings and spaces was matched by the wealth of a growing economy, and by entrepreneurial activity to provide many opportunities for artistic skill. Although not all towns moved at the same pace towards what has been seen as an urban renaissance, provincial architects were responsible for fine buildings in many. As a result, the urban fabric changed considerably. Stockton gained a new parish church (1712), customs house (1730), and town hall (1735), Exeter, the Devon and Exeter Hospital (1743), and Norwich, a theatre (1756). New buildings often marked a major change in local consciousness, not least as a replacement of past settings of authority, as with the new Guildhall in Worcester designed by Thomas White and constructed between 1721 and 1727. In mid-century, Nottingham replaced its medieval timber-framed Guildhall with a brick one with a colonnaded front. More generally, the image of towns altered. Timber and thatch were seen as dated, unattractive, non-utilitarian and, increasingly, non-urban, as were the jumble of long-established street patterns. Buildings themselves were seen more brightly as the night was better lit with the introduction of street lighting. The main streets of Lancaster were lit from 1738.

Towns were not separate from rural society. Instead, there were important commercial and social links, and these were strengthened by improvements in communications, not least the postal services used for the letters that provided the structure for a large number of novels, such as Samuel Richardson's *Pamela* (1740) and *Clarissa* (1747). Post Office revenues rose from £116,000 in 1698 to £210,000 in 1755 in a period of low inflation. This rise reflected the foundation of new routes, such as Exeter–Bristol–Chester in 1700, and others that became more frequent, as the London to Bristol, and London to Birmingham services did in the 1740s. The post aided the interchange between towns and countryside that rested on a degree of shared values within British society. Although largely based in towns, enlightened clubs, such as the Peterborough Gentleman's Society founded in 1730, the Brazen Nose Society founded in Stamford in 1736 and the Northampton Philosophical Society founded in 1743, included many landed gentry among their members, mixing easily with local clerics and professional men.

A broadly based interest in culture helped provide the basis for important developments, such as the rise of the novel. Henry Fielding's *Joseph Andrews* alone sold 6,500 copies in 1742. Far from conforming to a common tone, form or intention, novels varied greatly in content and approach, a trend that was encouraged by the size and diversity of the reading public. The absence of a royal role in the action, however, was notable. George did not engage the collective imagination in this fashion. A common theme of the novels was psychological accuracy. The successful novels of Samuel Richardson, such as his first, *Pamela* (1740), were 'true histories' in that they depicted the truth of behaviour, an approach especially suited to the ironic voice he adopted as narrator.

While novels sought to be true histories, conversely historical writing was supposed to capture character. This greatly affected the presentation of George because both John, Lord Hervey and Horace Walpole, major chroniclers as far as posterity was concerned, saw themselves as writing in this light. History did not only offer character out of interest. There was also the overwhelming presentation of history as a morally exemplary tale, a presentation which brought history, novels and journalism together. Far from being differentiated, the relationship of history or politics with morality was strongly focused because of the obvious political importance of a small number of individuals and because of the notion of kingship and governance as moral activities and ones in which moral choices affected success and reputation. The anonymous writer of the *Reflections on Ancient and Modern History* complained in 1746 that 'with modern writers everything is either vice or virtue'. As the relationship appeared timeless, it seemed pertinent to apply admonitory tales in a modern context and to present current figures in historical parallels. The belief that history possessed a cyclical quality contributed to this, as time was not held to compromise the moral power of Classical exemplars. Thus, George's relationships with his ministers could be discussed in terms of historical parallels.

Furthermore, the stress on personal drives, rather than on social, economic, institutional or geopolitical forces, ensured that in history, as in literature, the emphasis was on personality and narrative, and again this is relevant to the understanding of George. Elizabeth Montagu claimed in 1762, 'Few people know anything of the English history but what they learn from Shakespeare; for our story is rather a tissue of personal adventures and catastrophes than a series of political events.'[10] In both history and novels there was an emphasis on individual free-will, not determinism, in short a world that was best understood in moral terms and where there was no sense of changing moral standards.

If this helps explain how George was considered and judged, it is also pertinent for the way in which he looked at the world. It would, however, be inappropriate to see this simply in secular terms, because religious notions about conduct and identity remained important. While it is reasonable to discuss novels when assessing the culture of the period, it is also necessary to underline the extent to which devotional literature was extensively purchased and read. For example, William Law's *A Serious Call to a Devout and Holy Life, adapted to the State and Condition of all Orders of Christians* (1728) enjoyed huge sales, and was influential in the development of Methodism. More generally, there is copious evidence both of massive observance of the formal requirements of the churches and of widespread piety. Sunday schools and devotional literature, such as the chapbooks read by relatively humble people, fostered sanctity, piety and an awareness of salvation.

For many, issues of religious faith overlapped with the occult, in the shape of white or black magic, which was believed to have great influence on the fate of individuals. George was apparently affected by such beliefs, Hervey commenting that he was 'very sure he believed many stories of ghosts and witches and apparitions', while Horace Walpole noted the King's belief in vampires.[11]

Religious observance was linked to strong concern about the condition of fellow-Christians, and this concern provides an unexpected perspective in which to see George, for he was committed to helping the position of Protestants on the Continent, especially in Germany. Thus, the King emerges in a number of lights, if the context of his era is considered. This larger context needs to be borne in mind when making judgments from more particular political perspectives.

More generally, reference to religion serves as a reminder that this was a very different society. There were religious enthusiasts, as there are in all periods, but what was different was the central role of formal religious structures and beliefs. Religious affiliation affected political and other rights, and this was a society in which disagreements over how (not whether it was) best to worship God and seek salvation, how to organize the Church, and the relationship between Church and State, were matters of urgent concern. 'Polite' and 'religious' are not mutually incompatible, and the commonplace image of Hanoverian Britain as a 'polite' society is misleading if that is taken to imply the marginal nature of religious zeal. In fact, despite the claims of other Protestant groups, the established churches were not devoid of energy, and their congregations were not sunk in torpor. The Societies for the Reformation of Manners, for example, indicated the strength and social awareness of Anglican piety. The Church also ordered the past. Probably most people 'heard' history from the calendar of peals of bells commemorating events: Elizabeth I's accession, the defeat of the Armada, the Gunpowder Plot, the martyrdom of Charles I, the restoration of Charles II, and the landing of William III.

In George's reign one of the most noteworthy developments was the beginnings of Methodism. This was a development to which George was linked, not directly but as a consequence of his role in the international Protestant cause. Methodism was initially a movement for revival that sought to remain within the Church of England, supplementing the official parish structure by a system of private religious societies that would both regenerate the Church and win it new members. John Wesley, Methodism's institutional founder, began his evangelical campaign in England in 1738, although George Whitefield, Howell Harris and Daniel Rowlands were already preaching a similar message.

As an instance of North German influence during the reign of George, Wesley combined concern for the Church establishment with first-hand contact with Continental Protestants, particularly the revived Moravian Brethren based at Herrnhut, a German religious community developed by the Pietist Count Zinzendorf, that established a permanent presence in England. Methodism, initially intended by Wesley as a means to reawaken Anglicanism, was thus part of the 'Great Awakening', a widespread movement of Protestant revival in Europe and North America, and it employed many of the organizational features of European Protestant revival, including itinerant preaching and love feasts.

From George's point of view, it was crucial that Wesley, although he criticized some aspects of society, was loyal to the dynasty and the political system. The placing of the King in the litany of loyalty, as well as Wesley's concern about personal and social disorder, and belief in divine intervention were reflected in a letter he sent Matthew Ridley, Mayor of Newcastle, during the Jacobite rising of 1745. He felt bound to write, by the fear of God, love of his country and zeal towards George, as he had been pained by 'the senseless wickedness, the ignorant prophaneness of the city's poor' and the 'continual cursing and swearing, and the wanton blasphemy' of the soldiers, and feared this would endanger divine support.[12]

This idea of divine support might seem to date the reign as a far-off age, but events over recent years have served to suggest that such a teleology is misplaced. This unfortunately may become also true about another aspect of the reign, the confessional antagonism that led to bitterness and suspicion. Methodist meetings sometimes met with a violent response, as in Sheffield (1744), Exeter (1745), Leeds (1745), York (1747) and Norwich (1751–2). In a more systematic and insistent fashion, anti-Catholicism was a powerful force at the popular level and, at least until mid-century, at that of the élite. Prior to then, it was widely believed that Catholicism was on the increase in the British Isles, and on the advance in Europe. The latter was certainly true until the Prussian invasion of Silesia in 1740, and this helped underline George's import-ance to his subjects as the Protestant King.

Suspicions of Catholic disloyalty were indeed increased by the Jacobite threat, and here dynastic factors helped underline confessional animosity. There was an enormous amount of anti-Catholic material both in the culture of print—newspapers, pamphlets, prints and books—and in the public culture of anniversary celebrations, for example of the defeat of the Spanish Armada and the discovery of the Gunpowder Plot. The representation of Catholics was generally crude and violent: their intentions were seen as diabolical, their strength and deceit were frightening. The wish of William Wake, Archbishop of Canterbury from

1716 until 1737, for closer Anglican relations with the French Catholic Church (as well as with the Orthodox and with Continental Protestants) was unrealistic.

Religious antagonism had other manifestations. The small Jewish community grew by immigration, but the strength of popular Anglicanism was demonstrated in 1753. Then a vicious press campaign of anti-Semitic hatred, with popular backing, forced the repeal of the Jewish Naturalization Act of that year, which had made it easier to be naturalized by private act of Parliament, dropping the phrase 'on the true faith of a Christian' from the Oaths of Supremacy and Allegiance.

The King presided not only over the authority of the Church but also that of the state. His position resonated because of the wider echoes of paternalism. Within the family, there was the authority of age and the power of patriarchy. In the local community, there was the power of landowners and employers, and the pressure of neighbours and colleagues. In the wider polity, the possibilities of paternalism were lessened because governmental power and authority were not concentrated, but, instead, widely distributed among a large number of individuals and bodies. Aside from his symbolic role, the King played a role in this distribution of power because much of the formal nature of authority was in his name and was exercised by those chosen, albeit indirectly, at his behest, for example Lord Lieutenants, Justices of the Peace, militia colonels and sheriffs. If the process of patronage was one directed by ministers, it was, nevertheless, in the King's name and his intervention and, more commonly, approval was a reality at certain levels.

At the same time, this was a two-way process. For example, there were about 8,000 JPs in 1760. They were the linchpins of local administration, and, as such, the central figures in the law and order of the localities. The JPs were responsible for the implementation of social policy, a field in which the central government played a little role, but, in doing so, they had to respond to local needs and views. JPs were appointed by the government, and could be removed, but their effectiveness was seen to rest on the degree to which the locally prominent were appointed. This emphasis on co-operation and shared responsibilities was more generally true of the political system within which the King operated, one in which social authority was linked to that of Crown and Church. This co-operation was not simply for mutual benefit but also to further the goals of both political system and its culture or ideology. Thus, in 1727, Bristol Common Council urged George 'to maintain those valuable blessings, the religion, laws and liberties of this Nation'.[13] The King was to make a better effort to do so than is sometimes appreciated.

4

The New King
1727–1731

Splendour and uncertainty ushered in the new reign, the splendour of the rituals of majesty, and yet also uncertainty over who would enjoy George's favour. In practice, however, there was less splendour and uncertainty in 1727 than there otherwise might have been. Coronations were usually occasions that did not match up to expectations, and, instead, all too frequently lacked the ceremonial order that was sought as an affirmation of proper procedure and dynastic achievement. George's coronation was no exception,[1] although the following two were to be even more disorderly. Held on 11 October (os) 1727, the coronation, which was a joint one of King and Queen consort, allowed George to indulge the love of splendour he had displayed while entertaining at Hampton Court when Prince of Wales. The coronation saw the soaring drama of George Frederick Handel's four Coronation Anthems, of which 'Zadoc the Priest and Nathan the Prophet crowned Solomon King' is the most famous, but also, at the close, the confusion in Westminster Hall noted by the Swiss visitor César de Saussure:

> the big doors were thrown open and the crowd allowed to enter and take possession of the remains of the feast, of the table linen, of the plates and dishes, and of everything that was on the table. The pillage was most diverting; people threw themselves with extra-ordinary avidity on everything that hall contained; blows were given and returned, and I cannot give you any idea of the noise and confusion that reigned. In less than half an hour everything had disappeared, even the boards of which the table and seats had been made.[2]

There were also celebrations across the country. In Liverpool, there were entertainments in the Guildhall and a ball, all at the expense of the Corporation, while in Lincoln the firework display lasted for several hours.[3] Whatever the chaos in Westminster, by the time of the coronation, it was clear that the King was securely established. Earlier, George I's death had been seen, instead, by 'James III and VIII', the 'warming pan baby' of 1688, as an opportunity for him to reach for the throne, compensating for the failures he had encountered when he had tried to invade Scotland in 1708 and 1716. Setting off from his court in the papal town of Bologna, James hoped that an up-rising would have broken out in Britain by the time he reached the English Channel, a fundamental misreading of the nature of British politics.

Both France and Austria, however, refused him assistance, and James did less well than he had done on the two previous occasions when, respectively, he had come within sight of Scotland (1708), and briefly landed there (1716). Despite reports to the contrary, James in 1727 did not even reach the Austrian Netherlands (modern Belgium), from where he could have tried to sail to Britain. Instead, he ended his journey in the duchy of Lorraine, then an independent state, whence, as a result of French pressure on Duke Leopold, he moved first to the papal enclave of Avignon and then back to Italy. James's half-nephew, James, Duke of Liria (son of James, Duke of Berwick, an illegitimate son of James II and VII), reported from Vienna that Austrian support would not be forthcoming unless James could show himself at the head of a strong movement, and that the Austrians would not let themselves be persuaded that Britain would declare for James.[4] Thus, Jacobitism posed for George II a far less serious challenge than it had done for George I in the opening stage of his reign. This was an important comment both on the fate of the 1715 rebellion and on the politics of George I's reign.

Conversely, had there been a repetition of the '15 in 1727–8, then George would have had an opportunity to display his military commit-ment as he would have been the obvious commander of the govern-ment forces, not least as no other member of the royal family would have been available. Cumberland was still a baby. It is only helpful to push counterfactuals (what-ifs) so far, but as James did plan a return, it is appropriate to consider what might have happened had George been in command. He would have begun his reign as the Protestant Hero, the leader against James, who had no charisma to match his dynastic claim, and this would have provided a powerful basis of prestige for George and, in particular, in subsequent political crises.

The Austrians were to be proved correct, for, in the event, the accession of George passed without disturbance, a marked contrast to the Tory demonstrations that had followed that of George I. George I had to travel from Hanover, while George II was already in London. Most of the Tory peers, who had not been to Court for years, such as Arran, Scarsdale, Somerset and Strafford, paid their respects to George II, although Charles Caesar, a Jacobite MP, informed 'James III and VIII' that some did so 'hoping to so lull the government asleep that they would disband some of their forces'.[5] At any rate, those Tories, such as Lord Bathurst, who had hoped for royal favour were swiftly disabused. Nevertheless, although the proscription of the Tories and the monopolization of royal favour by the Whigs had helped to provoke the '15 rebellion, there was no comparable response to the continuation of the same situation under the new King. The English Jacobites acted as if they accepted proscription, and were unprepared to run the risks of a rising unless assured of considerable foreign assistance; and both Ireland and Scotland were quiet.

George made a few moves in the direction of the Tories. He was most gracious to those who came to court, sufficiently so that there was speculation that some, such as Sir Thomas Hanmer, a Tory MP for Suffolk, who had been reported close to the Prince in 1718, would be raised to the peerage. George also took steps to increase the number of Tory Justices of the Peace, but he did nothing more than make a few concessions. His instructions to Peter, Lord King, the Lord Chancellor, to increase the number of Tories, included the injunction to 'still keep a majority of those who were known to be most firmly in his interest', which George ordered Lord King to keep secret,[6] suggesting that he was really only seeking with the increase to curry popularity. Although Walpole, in opposition, had sought Tory support in 1718, George, as Prince of Wales, had had little to do with the Tories: the aristocratic clique he mixed with being overwhelmingly Whig.

It has been claimed that the Tories were keen to serve the King, and that George, as King, was willing to turn to the Tories (which would have enlarged the Crown's ability to manoeuvre), but there is little evidence for the second contention, and the first probably underrates the role of Jacobite sympathies. George, at any rate, detested the Tories as the party whose ministry had negotiated the Peace of Utrecht in 1713, ensuring Britain's exit from the War of the Spanish Succession and abandoning Britain's allies, including Hanover, which indeed fought on until 1714. George suspected the Tories of Jacobite inclinations. This was a view that was encouraged by Walpole who presented the Tories in that light and was accused by the *Craftsman* of 2 September (os) 1727 of doing so to strengthen his own position. Such a presentation was difficult for the Tories to disprove, and one that was definitely true for some of them.[7]

There was still, however, the possibility that the new King would transform the ministry. Indeed, the political crisis of 1727 is instructive because it demonstrated the continued power of the monarch for all to see, and also showed the extent to which others had to adapt to him. Whereas George I, when he came to the throne, knew little about British politics, George II, in contrast, had already much experience of them, knew many of the politicians, including all the leading figures in the ministry as well as the opposition Whigs, and had his own ideas.

On the day George was proclaimed King, Newcastle wrote to his co-Secretary of State, Townshend, of 'the concern and distraction we are all in here . . . we can make no judgement of affairs here, in all probability the Speaker will be the chief man'.[8] Indeed, the Honorable Spencer Compton, son of the 3rd Earl of Northampton, and MP for Sussex, was held to be a plausible candidate. Throughout George I's reign, he had been Speaker of the House of Commons, Treasurer to the Prince of Wales and the key adviser to the Prince. In 1722, the ministry, seeking to please the Prince, had bestowed on Compton the extremely lucrative office of Paymaster-General, a post in which he was to be succeeded by Newcastle's brother, Henry Pelham. Arthur Onslow, MP for Guildford, who was in London at the time of George's accession, noted:

> that everybody expected, that Mr. Compton the Speaker would be the Minister and Sir Robert Walpole thought so for a few days . . . the new King's first inclination and resolution, which was certainly for Mr. Compton . . . who had long been his Treasurer, and very near to him in all his counsels. It went so far as to be almost a formal appointment, the King for two or three days directing everybody to go to him upon business . . . but by the Queen's management, all this was soon overruled.[9]

This interpretation of the outset of the reign was to be extremely influential, and was to set the tone for consideration of what came after, both by contemporaries and by subsequent commentators. Many of the statements used to support the interpretation of the events of 1727 that places Caroline's role as central are, however, open to question. John, Lord Hervey, for example, did not begin his memoirs until 1733 or 1734, whilst Onslow's account is based upon papers and correspondence that no longer exist but were transcribed by his son in 1769. These papers were certainly drawn up after Walpole's death in 1745, and their accuracy is open to question. The notes made by Peter, Lord King, the Lord Chancellor, are a more useful source, as he was a senior figure, and as they were made at the time of the events recorded or only shortly afterwards. Lord King's account of Compton's failure does not mention Caroline, but suggests that George was persuaded by personal experience to continue Walpole in power:

> by his constant application to the King by himself in the mornings when the Speaker, by reason of the sitting of the House of Commons, was absent, he so worked upon the King, that he not only established himself in favour with him, but prevented the cashiering of many others, who otherwise would have been put out.[10]

The emphasis on the personal relationship with the King is instructive, as it makes it clear that George formed his own views. Lord King was unsympathetic to Walpole, and his account is a helpful reminder of the degree to which there was no ministry united by party affiliation and discipline, but, instead, a group of Whigs whose tensions could have been manipulated by the King had he so chosen, although the problems caused by the Whig Split of 1717–20 served as a warning about the dangers of doing so.

Lord King presented Walpole as working on George, but there were several obvious reasons why it would have been foolish for the King to remove his leading minister at once. The accession of a new monarch meant that Parliament had to be summoned, the Civil List (the King's grant from Parliament) settled, and elections held for a new Parliament. This was the case after the accession of every new monarch and helped enhance their ability to ensure a new political dispensation, while doing so within a tight timetable. Walpole was greatly needed for these purposes as Parliament sat from 27 June (os) to 17 July (os).

George indeed found the royal speech he made at its opening a considerable burden, unsurprisingly so as he had no experience in public speaking. Furthermore, the Prince had been kept from the functions of rulership during his father's reign. Harriet Pitt noted of the speech, 'I saw him make [it] today, I can't say heard, for His Majesty was in so much confusion he could not put out his voice to be heard.'[11] George certainly was never much of a public speaker, and this was not a role he sought. He pressed for his speeches to Parliament to be as short as possible. George certainly delivered them, and he did not need to give the speeches to the Lord Chancellor to read, as his father, with his poor English, had done. However, these speeches did not turn into occasions in which George II gained respect, prestige or affection.

During the first parliamentary session of the reign, Walpole made himself extremely useful to George, securing an enlarged Civil List of £800,000 yearly. Furthermore, Caroline was given £100,000 a year while George was alive, and £50,000 a year if she became a widow. George, moreover, was to be allowed to keep the surpluses, and these rose with the increased wealth and consumption of the country, for the revenues in question derived in part from excise duties. In the last year of his reign, they were to yield £876,988.

The enlarged Civil List was very helpful to the King who, in part thanks to his growing family, had to think carefully about money. The Household accounts in Windsor suggest that he was pretty careful with his money management[12] and that he (and his father) were much more on top of financial matters than Frederick, Prince of Wales was to be. George, indeed, had a reputation for avarice and meanness,[13] one that persisted throughout his reign, but it is likely that criticism would have been far stronger had he run up substantial debts, as Newcastle was to do, or been dependent on benefactors, as the indebted Pitt and his second son, William Pitt the Younger, were to be. George had learned from the dispute over the Civil List during the previous reign, and ensured that there was less financial independence for the reversionary interest, by altering the wording so that Frederick did not have automatic access, but rather took what his father would give.

Aside from the enlarged Civil List, Walpole's command of the Commons, and the ease with which he secured parliamentary consent for the new fiscal arrangements, were very impressive, though it is doubtful whether politicians seeking to win royal favour would have found it helpful to oppose the Civil List in Parliament, especially at the very start of the reign. They were certainly not to do so with the next reign. Compton lacked Walpole's skill as a speaker, which was a major problem as far as Commons' leadership was concerned.

Possibly as significant was Walpole's success in the elections, the importance of which was obvious to George. These were the first set of elections since 1722. Under the Septennial Act, elections only needed to be held after the accession of a new monarch (which is no longer the case), or at least every seven years (now it is at least every five years). The latter provision made the management of the 1727 elections important, as they would establish the political pattern for a large tranche of the new reign. Indeed, the next general election was not to be held until 1734. The well-informed Saxon envoy, Jacques Le Coq, suggested that Walpole was given an opportunity to display his skill to the King, and that George had decided to delay any governmental changes until after the elections, in order to be in a state to gratify those who had helped with the elections, and those whose help would be needed in the subsequent Parliament.[14] This was a safe move by a monarch who was at once both cautious and prone to lose his temper. Across the reign as a whole, George lost his temper on many occasions, but he made few rash moves.

In 1727, Walpole certainly passed his test with flying colours. After the petitions to the House about contested election returns were heard, a standard means by which the majority was strengthened, the new House of Commons consisted of 415 ministerial supporters, fifteen opposition Whigs, and 128 Tories, a government majority of 272. This was the largest majority since George I's accession. In his lengthy and thoughtful dispatch of 22 July 1727, Le Coq reported that other reasons were also advanced as to why it was against the new King's interest to change the government. First, Walpole's influence with Parliament and with the great chartered corporations—the Bank of England, the East India Company and the South Sea Company—was held to be very important for the creditworthiness and stability of the government. Secondly, to change the ministry was held to be inadvisable for British foreign policy, as new ministers would lack the relevant knowledge, while it was felt that such a change would alarm allies at a tricky diplomatic juncture.

The respective importance of these factors in George's mind is difficult to evaluate. However interested he was in the Civil List, or in the general election, George was probably at least as concerned about the European situation, and, during the first few years of his reign, he was to display far more interest in European than in domestic affairs. Britain's allies certainly expressed some concern about the possibility of a change. Cardinal Fleury, the leading minister of Britain's key ally, France, pressed George to maintain Walpole in power,[15] and concern was also expressed in The Hague, the capital of the other major ally, the United Provinces (modern Netherlands). George may well have been greatly influenced by the view of allies. He also may have been affected by seeing Walpole in opposition in 1717–20, which showed that he could create too much trouble to be left outside government. To have excluded Walpole risked increasing the strength of the opposition Whigs. These 'mays' reflect the problem of writing a biography given the nature of the sources, and the danger of being too assertive in explanation.

Whatever the reasons, Walpole's maintenance of power was clear within a fortnight of George's accession. The achievement, however, was subject to two doubts concerning the King's relations with his leading minister. First, would Walpole be forced to accept many changes in the ministry, and, secondly, would George, anyway, follow the advice of the ministers? William III, for example, had been disinclined to do so. It was widely thought that those associated with George as Prince of Wales would take prominent roles either in the ministry or in offering advice. These associates were a distinctly aristocratic group including Compton and the Earls of Chesterfield, Essex, Grantham and Scarborough. Aside from Compton, few members of this group possessed any governmental experience. Chesterfield was a gentleman of the Prince's Bedchamber. None of the group, aside from Compton and Scarborough, had distinguished himself in Parliament. Aside from Compton, the group was relatively young, and younger than George, who acceded in his forty-sixth year: Scarborough had been born in 1688 and Chesterfield in 1694. Most were worthy of prestigious sinecures, but not of power.

Suggestions, however, were made that they would be raised in the peerage, that several would receive dukedoms, and that they would also gain key posts. These rumours proved to be widely exaggerated. Though some sound supporters of Walpole lost their places, they soon gained others. George's aristocratic friends won a few positions. Essex gained the Rangership of St James's Park, one of the more important posts of its type, as it gave access to the monarch. Grantham was raised to the Privy Council and made Lord Chamberlain to the Queen. Scarborough was appointed Master of the Horse, a profitable post that kept him close to the King, and Sir Charles Hotham a Groom of the Bedchamber. He went on to be promoted within the army, to Colonel in 1732, and Colonel in the fashionable First Troop of Horse Grenadier Guards in 1735. With all these men, it is unclear how much personal ambition they possessed and how far they pressed George for promotion. Most seemed to have been content with honourable, fashionable and profitable posts in the household, but to have shown little interest in gaining the more arduous posts of power. The extent to which their choice throws light on George himself is unclear, not least because the range among which he could choose his friends was limited. Those who served in the Household offices of George and Caroline, while they were Prince and Princess of Wales, took those posts because they were very young (or at least too young for the King), not sufficiently politically powerful to serve the King, or largely second-rate figures who were not interested or able to run with the tough crowd of politicians in royal service. Whereas Walpole was shrewd and competent, Compton was not of his calibre, as became readily apparent in 1727.

It is certainly instructive to consider the fate of George's friends when he had been Prince of Wales. Algernon, 3rd Earl of Essex, a flashy womanizer, was to be envoy in Turin from 1732 to 1738, but, during his embassy, his principal concerns were seduction and securing leaves of absence so that he could visit the carnivals of Italy. He was far from diligent. Hotham's ambition was restricted largely to the army, where he sought a regiment, a goal not attained until 1732. In 1730, he had been entrusted by the King with a key diplomatic mission to Berlin. This miscarried, and Hotham certainly failed to display the necessary diplomatic skills, although his embassy was a very difficult one. Richard, 2nd Earl of Scarborough was highly intelligent and profoundly melancholic, a courtier who ended his life in suicide. He was not, however, noted for conspicuous political skills.

Compton and Chesterfield were more serious politicians, who, between them, might have tried to have led a King's party, or been what were to be called, under George III, King's Friends. John Scrope, Secretary to the Treasury, suggested that Compton was disinclined to accept responsibility for the financial management of the crown,[16] but his maladroit conduct in June 1727 does not mean that he was as weak as has been depicted. Compton was outmanoeuvred by Walpole and lacked his ability, but Walpole took him seriously as a politician. He was removed from the Commons by being promoted to a peerage in 1728 and an earldom (Earl of Wilmington) in 1730. Furthermore, Wilmington was not a leading minister in the 1730s, and did not become First Lord of the Treasury until after Walpole fell from power in 1742. In this role, he was of limited consequence and, anyway, died in 1743.

Philip, 4th Earl of Chesterfield was more pushy, seeking Paris, the most important of the British embassies, and it was believed that George planned to appoint Chesterfield as a Secretary of State after this posting. This was a challenge to Newcastle who lacked diplomatic experience. In the event, Chesterfield received a less influential embassy at The Hague, albeit one that enabled him to offer advice and to correspond in a confidential manner with leading ministers. Chesterfield's ambition, and the favour in which George held him, were to be a major problem for Walpole and his diplomat brother Horatio for several years.

George's favourites played a prominent role in what had become a more active Court. The relatively quiet character of George I's Court had resumed after the reconciliation with his son, in 1720, but, from 1727, the situation was different, not least because there was now a Queen Consort, the dynamic Caroline, as well as a large (and young) royal family. This was to be enlarged when Frederick, Prince of Wales, the member of the immediate family outside the country, was, in 1728, called over from Hanover where he had been since 1714. A larger royal family meant more events, as well as more participants, not least more birthday balls. George and Caroline dined in public as George I had not done in his later years, and there was also a willingness to spend money, that reflected in part the Civil List settlement. The Court became more central to public life.

On 24 July (os) 1727, Newcastle reassuredly remarked that George 'has been pleased to make but very few and those immaterial alterations amongst the late King's servants'. Having mentioned the dismissal of James, 3rd Earl of Berkeley, First Lord of the Admiralty since 1717, and no friend of Walpole, he added 'the other changes are not worth troubling you with'.[17] Charles Stanhope, who had been involved with Berkeley in plans to remove George when Prince of Wales to America, was angrily refused a place on the Admiralty Board by the new King. Nor was he continued as Treasurer of the Chamber. Despite his clash with George in 1717, Newcastle did not lose office, and, although he was not close to the new monarch, he had not been close to his predecessor. Far from being promoted to a senior post, Carteret, who had been a protégé of Sunderland, was sent back to Ireland with diminished powers, and the opposition Whigs were not heeded.

Walpole, who had secured not only his own position, but also those of his colleagues and political allies, was, however, still faced with the problem of defining a relationship with his new master. Five days after George's proclamation, Hill Mussenden, later an MP, stated, 'all that can be gathered for the present is that, whatever side be uppermost, they will not have the same authority, that the last ministry had, since the King seems resolved to enter into all manner of affairs himself'.[18] D'Aix, the Sardinian envoy, reported that George wanted to be informed about everything and that he worked without break from 10 am to 3 pm.[19] George indeed came to the throne determined not only to control his own position, but also to be the master of Britain's government. He had no intention of being a *roi fainéant*, and made it clear, from the beginning of his reign, that he wished to control all the activities of government.

Such a wish of course was not new and, particularly since Louis XIV's bombastic remark in 1661, 'L'État, c'est moi', many monarchs, at their accession to power, spoke of their intention to rule themselves. Indeed, it was expected of them, as the contrast appeared to be rule by favourites. This was widely regarded as a factious, and therefore, dangerous option, and also as a sign of the personal kingship that had been replaced by a commitment to more regular governmental processes. Thus, critics of George and Walpole were to draw comparisons with former rulers and favourites—the Emperor Tiberius and Sejanus, Henry VIII and Cardinal Wolsey, Charles I and George, 1st Duke of Buckingham—in order to imply inappropriate behaviour and the dangers to which it could lead.

George certainly asserted himself in an irregular fashion when he took the copy of George I's will that William Wake, the Archbishop of Canterbury, presented to him at the Privy Council, and did not read it. He went on to have the will declared invalid in Hanover and to take steps to recover the copies of the will that George his father had left with the Emperor Charles VI and August William, Duke of Brunswick-Wolfenbüttel. British resources were used to this end: the Treaty of Westminster of 25 November (os) 1727 with August William included not only a mutual guarantee but also a British subsidy. The will was not mentioned in the treaty, but George's ratification was dependent on its delivery. The government proclaimed the treaty as a triumph of foreign policy, but was far less keen on advertising the amount of money promised to Brunswick-Wolfenbüttel.

There was to be criticism of the King for allegedly suppressing unwelcome legacies with the will, but, in fact, the succession was the key. In the will, drawn up in 1716, with a codicil of 1720, George I had stipulated an eventual division of Britain and Hanover after the death of his then sole grandson, Frederick, the Electorate going to Frederick's second son, if he had one, and, failing that, to the Brunswick-Wolfenbüttel branch of the house of Brunswick.[20] Had the will stood, then Hanover could have become a secondogeniture (inheritance for the second son), as the grand duchy of Tuscany was to become for the Habsburgs, with the Electorate passing in 1760 to Frederick's second son, Edward, Duke of York, and, on his death without heir in 1767, to George III's second son, Frederick, Duke of York. In contrast, although he had been interested, in the mid-1720s, in an eventual separation of Hanover from Britain, George II tended to think Hanover's territorial integrity was best served by the maintenance of the British connection. In 1744, he received this advice from the Hanoverian Privy Counsellors when he consulted them, although anger led him to waver in the late-1750s.

Contemporaries noted that the diligent George threw himself into the business of government, wanted to be informed of everything, and worked hard; indeed so hard that fears were expressed about his health. Hill Mussenden claimed that George was determined to sit in person on the Admiralty, Treasury and War Office Boards, which his predecessor had not done. When George came to the throne, he spoke of his intention to supervise the Treasury in person, and of his determination to cut pay, particularly for officials who held more than one post. It was believed that he would reduce the number of pensions (annual payments, nothing to do with old age) paid from the Civil List. Le Coq argued that these changes were due not to George's avarice, but to a coherent fiscal and political strategy, an attempt to reduce the need for governmental borrowing and the dependence upon parliamentary grants. There is no independent evidence for this suggestion, but it is symptomatic of the belief that George was making a serious attempt to intervene in the processes of government and that he had far-reaching ambitions.[21]

This initial determination persisted and George continued to work hard. Carteret's new instructions as Lord Lieutenant of Ireland, drawn up in October 1727, limited his power over the Irish army and increased that of the King.[22] That month, Alexander, 2nd Earl of Marchmont, had an audience in which George's determination to exercise oversight was clearly indicated:

> I told his Majesty that the Duke of Newcastle had told me that his Majesty had been graciously pleased to order the commission of Clerk Register [Lord Register of Scotland] to be renewed and that his Majesty had ordered a clause to be added to it, that I humbly presumed it was not his Majesty's pleasure to take any perquisite from that small office and give it to the Secretarys or any other office. His Majesty answered, no, that he would not diminish the office but desired to be acquainted with the persons to be named as deputies, because he was informed that Jacobites were brought into these offices, these places being sold, and they were willing to give more money than anybody else, though that had not happened in my time, but that he would not have it to come through the Secretary's office. I told his Majesty that I should take care to lay before him the characters of any persons I should have an occasion of naming to any office in my gift.[23]

Two months later, the manuscript newsletter sent regularly from London to George's uncle, Ernst August, Prince-Bishop of Osnabrück, reported that George was intervening in the pay of his household and guards officers, and devoting a lot of attention to administration.[24] In January 1728, Townshend emphasized the degree to which he kept George informed of all diplomatic correspondence.

Johann Daniel Schöpflin, who was in Britain from September 1727 until the end of January 1728, writing a report about its politics for the French government, claimed that Caroline was important to George's popularity and also wrote:

> The King is much more popular than George I. As much as he can, he tries to make himself popular. His father did not know English and hated the people. George II likes the English and knows the language. The Germans do not take a role in the government of England as they did under George I . . . it appears that George II is more firmly on the throne than his father was.[25]

A general impression of activity and success was created. George encountered opposition, however, and his wishes were not always translated into action. In July 1727, George told Lord King that he expected to nominate to all benefices and prebendaries to which the Lord Chancellor usually nominated, which would have proved a major extension to royal patronage in the Church. When Lord King defended his prerogative, George retorted that William, 1st Earl Cowper, a former Lord Chancellor, to whom he had been politically close while Prince of Wales, had told George that such nominations were a royal right. Two months later, the Sardinian envoy, D'Aix, reported ministerial anger at George's supervision of their activities and at his willingness to listen to others. Le Coq pinpointed another area of tension when he suggested that George's attempts at financial reform were weakening the position of his ministers by denying them an undisputed control of government patronage.[26]

Nevertheless, George did not persevere in his dispute with Lord King over the nominations, a key retreat at the outset of the reign. He also allowed Charles, 2nd Duke of Grafton's views about the appointment of Suffolk JPs to overrule his own wishes to appoint Tories:[27] Grafton, a Whig, was not only the Lord Chamberlain, but also the most prominent aristocrat in Suffolk, and thus this was an issue about local patronage, a key aspect of British governance. D'Aix claimed that the King was easily discouraged.[28] Indeed, George's early enthusiasm for intervening in all the departments of government slowly waned, and Walpole's control of financial affairs was reported as unchallenged by the autumn of 1728. George's ambitions in this direction ceased to be a topic of report. Nevertheless, he continued diligent across much of the range of government, reading documents and signing them promptly. His German Chancery in London ensured that he could also fulfil his obligations as Elector fully and promptly.

For the British ministers, George's close personal interest in the army was only an occasional nuisance, although they would have preferred to enjoy some of the military patronage he wielded, and there were clashes between King and ministers over the issue until the close of the reign. In contrast, it was the possible effects of George's martial temperament upon the conduct of foreign policy that most concerned the government, while, from George's accession until the spring of 1730, there was also considerable uncertainty as to which ministers enjoyed George's confidence in foreign policy. Marshal Villars, a member of the Conseil d'État, where the dispatches of French diplomats were read out and considered, noted in his diary that George was believed to desire war ardently and to wish to lead his army into battle. Le Coq reported the fear that George would push foreign policy with more vigour, although he argued that the King's warlike penchant would be restrained by his allies' opposition to war, by considerations of state, and by the fact that the views of a Prince of Wales were naturally different from those of a King of Britain, a sound analysis of the situation.[29]

Concern about royal bellicosity was to make British ministers worry about his journeys to Hanover, as, once there, George's apparent propensity for violent solutions might be harder to tame. From his accession, George, who had his own sources of information and opinions, not least foreign envoys in London,[30] made it clear that he wished to control foreign policy. At least initially, he read diplomatic dispatches with great attention, and made his preferences among the diplomatic corps apparent. James, Lord Waldegrave, who was appointed to Vienna, was informed 'H.M. expresses a very particular regard for your lordship',[31] while William Stanhope was seen as a favourite.[32] The ministers were particularly worried about George's willingness to take advice from the hyper-active Louis, Seigneur de St Saphorin, a former envoy in Vienna, whom they regarded as meddlesome and unreliable, and who certainly tried to give advice, although St Saphorin returned to his Swiss estate in 1728. However, no Hanoverian minister in the late 1720s or 1730s wielded the influence that Bernstorff and Bothmer had enjoyed in their heyday under George I. Though Bothmer survived until 1732, he did not enjoy George's confidence. Fabrice failed to obtain the diplomatic post he sought in late 1727 and returned to Hanover. The principal officials, Jobst von der Reiche, his son Andreas, and Johann Philipp von Hattorf, were credited with little power, and foreign envoys felt that they had scant influence. In October 1730, Augustus II of Saxony instructed his new envoy in London, Count Watsdorf, to attach himself to the British ministers because their influence was paramount even in what concerned Hanoverian influences, while George ignored his Hanoverian ministers.

George's interests as dynast and as ruler of Hanover were understandably displayed most forcefully in German affairs, a process encouraged from August 1727 until the spring of 1728 by the serious ill-health of the relevant Secretary of State, Townshend. Hanoverian grievances against the manner in which the Emperor, Charles VI, exercised imperial jurisdictional rights fortified George's determination to force him to be a good Emperor. In an instructive guide to George's vivid use of language, the combative tone of his remarks, and his personalization of issues, he told the Prussian envoy that 'if the Emperor trod upon his toe, H.M. would let him know whom he had to do with'.[33]

The issue that caused most immediate problems was relations with Frederick William I of Prussia, who sent Baron Wallenrodt to sound out George about the possibility of a new treaty. George's response, both to Wallenrodt and to the British envoy in Berlin, was curt: the King denied that he had any plans for the marital links with the Prussian royal family that had long been considered. Visiting Prussia in 1723, George I had informally agreed that his grandson Frederick, later Prince of Wales, should marry Frederick William's daughter Wilhelmina, who was George I's granddaughter, while her brother, later Frederick the Great, was to marry a daughter of George II. Frederick William was also irritated by George II's refusal to publish his father's will, as he believed that this had deprived his wife, Sophia Dorothea, of her father's legacy to her. George's response to Frederick William was in part encouraged by his wish to please his ally France, which supported Prussia's Wittelsbach rivals in Germany; but his distrust of his brother-in-law was also important, and was to persist until the death of the latter in 1740. In some respects, the two men were too similar in attitudes and interests. Each was particularly proud of his military service in the War of the Spanish Succession. Given their mutual distrust, it was ironic that this service had been on the same side.

George displayed considerable independence in international affairs, to the irritation of Townshend.[34] He showed his personal interest in diplomacy, in his attempts to develop a league of German princes. In August 1727, Horatio Walpole was informed:

> Your Excellency will perhaps think us too full of the scheme for taking care at the Congress of the Liberties of the Germanic Body, as being pretty strong meat for the Cardinal's [Fleury, the leading French minister] digestion: but My Lord Townshend ordered me to tell you that it arises from the King himself, who sees with regret the Emperor gaining such an absolute influence throughout Germany as may make him an overmatch for us and France too.[35]

From the outset of his reign, in response to concern about the possibility of an Austro-Prussian attack on Hanover, which lacked the military means to defend itself against powerful neighbours, George sought to develop a system of German alliances and to persuade France to threaten Prussia and Austria: the Austrian Netherlands and the Prussian territories in the Rhineland were both vulnerable to French attack. Newcastle noted, 'His Majesty thinks that great attention should be had to the affairs of the North.' The Hanoverian envoy at the Imperial Diet in Ratisbon (Regensburg) received direct orders from London to stir up the German princes against the Emperor.[36] George drafted instructions for Horatio Walpole, then envoy in Paris, which demanded that France provide a declaration that it would respect the rights of Protestants in the Empire,[37] a commitment that was symptomatic of George's concern about the issue. George sought an association of 'a considerable number of princes in the Empire to defend and support the rights and immunities of the whole Germanic body against any usurpations or encroachments on the part of His Imperial Majesty'. It could also serve to protect Hanover. Horatio Walpole was instructed to suggest to Fleury that it would be best if George entered the treaty as Elector of Hanover, rather than as King, but to ask for a convention in which France undertook to provide help if trouble arose on account of the new treaty. Whatever the theoretical distinction between King and Elector, George clearly and explicitly expected his British ministers to be active in the cause, writing to Townshend:

> You will have seen by Count Dehn's letter that Saxe-Gotha has actually acceded to the Treaty, that Hesse-Cassel is coming into it very fast, that they have very good hopes of the Elector of Bavaria, and that they'll press the Bishop of Würzburg to come in . . . I believe it to be high time for me to accede as Elector to this treaty, and I wish you would draw some sketch of those articles that should be added, leaving those out which I can not come into.[38]

Such an attitude was easiest when public attention was limited, but it posed problems for George's British ministers. In the winter of 1727–8, royal diplomatic activity included a meeting of over an hour between Le Coq and Queen Caroline, who told him that George wanted an alliance with Saxony which would strengthen his position in Germany. British ministers were left in no doubt about George's intentions, nor about his sensitivity to his position as Elector. He was particularly concerned about the decree on the Mecklenburg dispute issued by the Aulic Council in Vienna on 11 May 1728. This angered him because it threatened the Hanoverian position in the neighbouring duchy of Mecklenburg, by including Prussia among the administering powers, and because it emanated from the senior jurisdictional body under the control of the Emperor, rather than the Imperial Diet where the German princes were represented. George wrote to Townshend about the issue:

> I am extremely pleased with the Pensionary's letter, and since he wishes we should take the lead we must press the conclusion of the treaty with the German Princes, entering their grievances before the Congress, and support them there,[39]

and again, 'I like your letter to Lord Chesterfield very well, and think it very necessary to send these reflexions along with it for his and the Pensionary's information'.[40] The Pensionary, Simon van Slingelandt, was the leading Dutch minister, the Congress the peace conference called for Soissons in order to settle international disputes. George clearly wanted German issues to receive full attention there. George's concern was readily seen in an anxious letter from Townshend to Horatio Walpole:

> His Majesty's thoughts upon the points of Mecklenburg and Sleswig, on which he is very earnest and would not suffer the least delay to be made. I never saw the King more displeased in my life than he was upon reading what was said in this project and your dispatches upon those two articles. For God's sake, Dear Horace, do your best, both your reputation and mine are at stake.[41]

Sleswig was also an issue that concerned Hanover. The nature of the sources, with diplomatic instructions sent by ministers and over their signatures, is such that royal views are generally difficult to evaluate, but the correspondence between George and Townshend throws considerable light on royal activity and alertness. Townshend's letters to George make it clear that the latter was reading the relevant diplomatic correspondence. One letter touched on an area of particular concern, German politics, 'It will be necessary that the letter to Mr. Sutton should be sent back as soon as your Majesty has read it, it being to go by the post which sets out at two o'clock this afternoon.'[42] Richard

Sutton had become envoy to Hesse-Cassel. George clearly liked Sutton, promoting him in the army and appointing him Governor of Guernsey, a valuable sinecure.

However, other topics were also covered. In March 1728, Townshend wrote to George concerning a letter to Slingelandt, 'This paper has been drawn in some haste, but as the matter presses, it may be sent by the post tonight, if your Majesty approves of it.' George's reply 'I have read this paper with great satisfaction and I don't doubt but it will be liked by the Pensionary', was bland, but Townshend's seeking his consent was pertinent, and other replies by the King were more assertive. An undated reply to an undated request by Townshend, asking if he could send instructions, included:

> I have no objection to these letters going, but the Duke of Newcastle has left out a paragraph relating to the twenty thousand men which the Cardinal offered to send for the Dutch garrisons, and which I think they should be acquainted with as well as of the design of sending new ships to the Indies.[43]

These garrisons established Dutch interest in the fate of the Austrian Netherlands. The winter of 1727–8 also provides indications of George's bellicosity and these suggest that it was a more constant factor than the evidence would otherwise support. The deterioration of Anglo-Spanish relations led to an emphasis on his personal determination and on the role of his dignity:

> the King is most nearly touched with the turn this affair has taken, and will risk the coming to the utmost extremities rather than submit to those scandalous conditions Spain would impose upon him . . . if the Spanish court persist in their unreasonable proceedings, His Majesty must, and will, sooner enter into a war with that crown than suffer his own honour and royal dignity, and the interests of his people to be treated in so ignominious a manner.[44]

It was reported that George and his favourites, especially John, 2nd Duke of Argyll, Master-General of the Ordnance (who had reputedly first persuaded him to have extra-marital affairs), had pressed for war, but that Walpole and the Queen were against it. The Lords' Address in 1728 very much put the government's view that peace was preferable, but it also acknowledged George's martial instincts when it referred to the

> noble self-denial of all the success and glory that might attend Your Majesty's arms in the prosecution of a just and necessary war, when put in balance with the ease, quiet, and prosperity of your subjects. It is a disposition of mind truly great in your Majesty . . . to choose rather to procure peace for your subjects, than to lead them to victories.

This was also a result that reflected the multiple compromises of British politics. George was guided to these compromises, a process that was uneasy, but, nevertheless, which he accepted and, indeed, utilized. If the King made suggestions that were not pursued, that did not indicate that he was inconsequential or readily manipulated, but simply that there were many reasons in international and domestic politics leading toward caution. This, for example, affected George's suggestion, in the autumn of 1728, that the ships of the Ostend Company, the Asian trading company based in the Austrian Netherlands, be seized as a way to intimidate Charles VI, a suggestion that was not pursued. George consistently pressed for what he termed the display of 'spirit', writing for example to Townshend about news from abroad:

> You will see I have not been mistaken when I thought notwith-standing all the pains we have taken, that we should not be able to obtain a good and lasting peace. We must now make use of the good temper the Dutch seem to be in, to obtain by showing a spirit, what we have not been able to get by our condescension.[45]

In the summer of 1728, George, who was frequently reviewing his troops,[46] repeatedly strove to add determination to both allies and his own ministers, for he distrusted the recourse to an international conference. The King temperamentally was averse to what he saw as the delays and equivocations of diplomacy.[47] He was not a natural compromiser. He responded in July to the draft of an answer to Slingelandt, 'This is a very good letter. I wish it may convince the Pensionary, and make the Dutch ministers act with more vigour and concert.'[48] D'Aix reported that Townshend had decided to conform to George's wishes.[49] Foreign rulers were left in no doubt of George's views. James, Lord Waldegrave, a royal favourite, who was sent as envoy to Vienna, was instructed that Hanoverian issues were crucial:

> If the Court of Vienna is sincerely desirous to renew the perfect friendship and harmony which so long subsisted between them and us, they will of themselves see the necessity of doing His Majesty as Elector justice upon several points, upon which the King, and his father, have so long, and with so much reason, complained.

George also directed the pace of policy, deciding on occasion that it was not appropriate to send couriers or, alternatively, urging speed, as when he wrote to Townshend, 'I approve extremely of this letter, as well as of the inclosed paper, and as this matter is of very great importance an express should be sent as soon as possible.'[50]

George's role in policy and concern about Hanover was accentuated when he visited the Electorate in 1729 for his first visit as Elector. This was his first time in Hanover since 1714, but it was to be the first in a regular sequence of visits.[51] The importance of form was shown when Austrian plans to use this visit in order to negotiate a reconciliation were thwarted by George's refusal to notify his arrival to the Emperor, in part because George made it clear that he did not wish to see Count Frederick Seckendorf, the Austrian envoy in Prussia, who had asked Charles to carry the compliments which were the traditional response to this notification. George suspected that Seckendorf was trying to keep Britain and Prussia apart. Charles VI chose to regard the refusal as a slight.[52]

That summer, the Electorate was threatened with Prussian attack as a result of a quarrel over recruiting for the Prussian army, which George saw as an infringement of his sovereignty as Elector. Generally, it is difficult to distinguish royal from ministerial views, but, when Townshend, the Secretary of State with George in Hanover, wrote to Newcastle, it was clear what the King thought:

> I am by the King's express command to acquaint your Grace that His Majesty thinks himself in a very particular manner obliged to the Landgrave of Hesse Cassel upon this occasion, who by his great fidelity and readiness in executing engagements, has extremely contributed to the happy turn which this affair seems now to have taken; his Prussian Majesty's present peaceable disposition being, in

the King's opinion in great measure owing to the early motion of the Hessian troops, and to the apprehensions of a strong diversion on that side in favour of His Majesty.[53]

Hesse-Cassel had become a British ally in 1726, and was paid a British subsidy to keep troops ready for service; and the deployment of the Hessians was regarded as playing a key role in deterring Prussia from attack. As the Prussians pointed out, Hanover was indeed vulnerable.[54] It lacked natural frontiers, had Prussian territory to both east and west, was poorly fortified, and had an army that was smaller than that of Prussia. The establishment was increased after 1727 to reach about 19,000 which was maintained for most of the 1730s, although it rose to 21,000 in 1739 and, as a result of wartime expansion, to 26,471 in 1748. Under Frederick William I, the Prussian army had greatly increased in size, and this considerably accentuated Hanover's vulnerability. George used his first visit as Elector to familiarize himself with the Hanoverian army, not least by holding a series of reviews. These also served the purpose of underlining his determination to resist attack, as well as his value as a potential ally to other rulers, particularly the Wittelsbach Electors of Bavaria and Cologne, who were also vulnerable and whose alliance he sought.

The crisis with Prussia was followed by the revival of the prospect of a dynastic alliance with the Hohenzollerns of Prussia, an issue that attracted George's personal behaviour. In December 1729, Robert Trevor, the son of the Lord Privy Seal and a protégé of Horatio Walpole's, reported from London on how this had been pushed to the fore by the actions of Frederick William I:

> his animosity towards our King seems by his present behaviour to be grown more furious and inveterate than ever; he detests his own children for their being related to him, and makes it his chief pleasure to torment them on that account. Within these few days he has forced his wife [George II's sister] to write an insolent letter of his dictating to our Queen, insisting upon her speedy performance of the hopes she has given her of marrying Prince Frederick to her eldest daughter, and this before February next, and unconditionally, or else that she cannot hinder her husband from disposing of her to somebody else. I'll leave you to judge how this manner of treatment is relished at St. James's, especially after our

King has opened himself so ingenuously, and kindly as he has very lately done upon a plan of reconciliation sent hither from Berlin; in his answer to which after having approved of the methods proposed for terminating the differences of the two Courts about Mecklenburg etc, he offers to exchange the two princesses with, or without portions, and even to allow the Prince of Prussia, if he lives at London, wherewithal to support his rank, provided the King of Prussia returns him hither his present allowance. You certainly know, that our King's contempt for his brother in law is as great as one man can have for another, and I dread the probable consequences of a rancour so violent and so reciprocal.[55]

Equally, Frederick William made no secret of his anger with George and his ministers. In contrast, Caroline and Walpole hoped to end the disputes and to secure a marital union between the houses of Hanover and Prussia. The repeated entreaties of Sophia Dorothea, the Queen of Prussia, had finally borne fruit, even if they had more effect upon her sister-in-law Caroline than her brother George. There is no doubt, indeed, of George's lack of enthusiasm for a new approach to Prussia. His correspondence with Townshend about the projected mission of a British diplomat to propose a marital alliance revealed distrust of Prussia and dislike of the mission. George believed, correctly, that the mission would fail, he feared that it would irritate his allies France and Spain, and was worried his honour would be insulted by Frederick William, an anxiety symptomatic of his more general concern for his honour. George also realized that the mission was incompatible with the negotiations with the Wittelsbach Electors of Cologne, Bavaria and the Palatinate, and he made it clear to Townshend that he regarded the latter as 'of much more consequence'.[56] These negotiations were pushed by the French.

Given this attitude, it might be suggested that the eventual dispatch of Sir Charles Hotham to Berlin was as much proof of George's inability to control the situation as the failure of the negotiations with the Wittelsbachs, the fall of Townshend and the defeat of the aspirations of Chesterfield, who had received much praise from both George and Townshend since he began his mission at The Hague in 1728.

If such an interpretation is adopted, then Walpole can be seen to have defeated both Townshend and George in 1730. However, this was not the case. The selection of Hotham for the mission seems an interesting indication of George's power. Hotham was a Gentleman of the Bedchamber and the hostile Prussian minister General Grumbkow referred to him as a 'créature' of George.[57] George wanted his children married, but he had no intention of yielding to Prussian political demands. The element of personal hostility between the rulers of Britain and Prussia remained significant. A plan drawn up by Townshend and approved by George proposed that, if war broke out, Frederick William ought to be made to lose possessions which made it possible for him to threaten the Dutch and also reduced 'to the necessity of living upon better terms with all the princes of Lower Saxony, than he has hitherto done',[58] in other words with George.

Hotham was ordered to insist on the double marriage of Frederick, Prince of Wales and Wilhelmina, the Prussian Crown Princess, and of Crown Prince Frederick of Prussia and Princess Amelia. Anne, as eldest daughter the Princess Royal of Britain, was designed for William IV of Orange, which was a snub to the Prussians but she was several years elder than Frederick. Hotham's orders were drawn up despite the fact that Frederick William was known to be keen on the marriage of Frederick and Wilhelmina, but opposed to that of Frederick and Amelia, as he believed that the latter would serve to increase the ties between the Crown Prince and his Hanoverian uncle, George. Despite Hotham's reports, and the knowledge that Frederick William had already declared the marriage of the Prince of Wales and Wilhelmina, George and Townshend remained firm. In April 1730, Townshend sent Hotham fresh instructions:

> The King continues firm in the resolution of having the double marriage, as most expedient, and most proper and desirable on both sides. And from this he will never depart, or be brought by any means to consent to make the one, either without, or at any distance of time from the other.

In reply to the Prussian suggestion that, if there was to be a marriage between Crown Prince Frederick of Prussia and Amelia, one of them should be created Stadtholder of Hanover, and the Electorate placed under their authority, Townshend noted that George was willing for Amelia to be Stadtholder on condition that she and Frederick should first come to England 'and make such stay there as His Majesty shall judge convenient'. Finally, George expected Frederick William to settle the Mecklenburg issue on George's terms.[59] These instructions were hardly calculated to produce good relations. Frederick William could not be expected to yield on Mecklenburg, nor on the departure of his heir to England for an unspecified term to England.

Great hopes were raised about the Hotham mission, and it was widely anticipated that a new period in Anglo-Prussian relations would be ushered in, with marital links between the ruling houses, a visit by Frederick William to England, and Anglo-Prussian co-operation in European diplomacy. However, arriving in Berlin at the beginning of April, Hotham found Frederick William more interested in the single marriage. The possibility of a compromise involving two marriages and the establishment of Frederick of Prussia in Hanover was investigated, although it is not clear that George envisaged the succession of Frederick and his intended wife Amelia to both Prussia and Hanover, and the eventual union of these two territories. Hotham claimed of Frederick William, 'It is very plain he will sell his son, but not give him.'[60]

In the event, Frederick William moved against the compromise and the mission became intertwined with serious divisions within the Prussian ministry. Furthermore, the British government tried to ensure the recall of the hostile Prussian envoy, Benjamin Reichenbach, who had close links with the parliamentary opposition, and the disgrace of his ministerial patron, Grumbkow, by sending their intercepted correspondence to Hotham. Britain and Hanover ran a particularly successful postal interception and deciphering system. Frederick William regarded the opening of his ministers' letters as a personal insult, and he reacted violently when Hotham pressed him on the matter. Treating the King's violent anger as an affront to George in the person of his envoy, Hotham left Berlin without an audience of leave. In the event, the future Frederick the Great was to marry Elisabeth Christina, daughter of the pro-Austrian Frederick, Duke of Brunswick-Bevern in 1733, and his sister Wilhelmina was to marry the Margrave of Bayreuth in 1731.

The politics of George's early years as King, both domestic and international, culminated with the resignation of Townshend in May 1730, and his replacement, as Secretary of State for the Northern Department, by William Stanhope, who had been created Lord Harrington that January. Generally, the 1729–30 crisis is presented in terms of deteriorating relations between Walpole and Townshend, George's role being discounted. However strong Walpole was, it was widely reported in diplomatic circles in late 1729 that George preferred Townshend's policies, by which diplomats meant his foreign policy. If this is correct, then the crisis of 1729–30 is of major importance, as the fall of Townshend can be seen as a foretaste of 1742 and 1744, when George was forced to part with Walpole and Carteret respectively, both against his better judgment. Indeed, Townshend's resignation can even be seen as a second stage of failure or, at best, being outmanoeuvred, a stage that came after the continuation of Walpole's pre-eminence in 1727 and that preceded George's inability to intervene in 1733–5 in the War of the Polish Succession (see pp. 145–6).

George's views and role in the winter of 1729–30, on both foreign policy and, even more, ministerial politics, are in fact obscure. George was a monarch prone to conversation in the royal Closet and not an industrious correspondent. However, as a sign of his confidence in Townshend, with whom he had had close links during their time together in Hanover in 1729, he had approved the exclusion of other ministers from knowledge of the secret correspondence between Townshend and the French diplomat Anne-Théodore de Chavigny, in which the two men tried to settle difficulties over the projected subsidy treaty between Britain and the Wittelsbach Electors, an objective that was important to George's German policy.[61]

This secret diplomacy was a longstanding pattern. Early in the reign, Townshend wrote to George, 'This is a private letter I intend to write to Mr. [Horatio] Walpole, if Your Majesty approves of it. And as it is a secret correspondence which only your Majesty knows of, I beg no mention may be made of it before the Duke of Newcastle', this earning the reply, 'This letter is very well drawn and you may depend upon the secret.' The correspondence continued, Townshend subsequently writing, 'The inclosed are some rough thoughts which I have thrown together, and if your Majesty approves them, I will send them privately to Mr. Walpole', earning the reply, 'I believe this letter may have a very good effect, I desire you to send it with the first opportunity.'[62]

George was fully receptive to the practice of manipulating Newcastle so that the Secretary of State sent formal instructions to diplomats that matched those of the *secret du roi*, a practice that left the fig leaf of ministerial accountability in place. Townshend wrote to George in July 1728, 'The inclosed is a draught of a letter I propose to send privately today to Mr. Walpole if it has your Majesty's approbation: and in that case, I believe your Majesty will think it proper to give orders to the Duke of Newcastle to write the same in your Majesty's name', this earning the reply, 'I like this letter very well, and will speak to the Duke of Newcastle in the same way.'[63]

Walpole's early biographer, William Coxe, claimed that Townshend fell because the Queen helped Walpole block his attempt to replace Newcastle by Chesterfield, an explanation that left scant independent role for George. Coxe wrote 'He became more obsequious to the King's German prejudices, paid his court with unceasing assiduity, and appeared to have gained so much influence that he thought himself capable of obtaining the appointment of Chesterfield.'[64] Caroline, who had distrusted Townshend for some time, especially in 1716–17, was also believed to have played a direct role in the fall of the minister. The latter's grandson, Thomas, 1st Viscount Sydney (after whom the Australian city was named), wrote a letter many years later that nevertheless possesses an immediacy missing in other sources. It makes abundantly clear the Court context of ministerial politics, the importance of royal favour, and the role of personal honour in court and ministerial relationships. After recounting a violent altercation between Townshend and Walpole, Sydney continued:

> The way in which I have heard this unusual want of temper in Sir Robert accounted for was this: the two ministers had some secret, which they had agreed to keep to themselves, but they had both imparted it in confidence to the Queen. Her Majesty was unfortunately jealous of the too great cordiality, which subsisted between those who were to carry on the public business, and thought that a little jealousy of each other might make both more manageable; she therefore thought proper to let each of them know, that the other had trusted her. Sir Robert was just come from making this discovery. The Queen was much concerned and mortified at the effect of her own manoeuvre, never intending or suspecting that matters would have been carried to any violence. She was very sorry to be reduced to choose between them, but had no hesitation in making choice of Sir Robert when she was forced to decide . . . Townshend attempted to make a separate personal interest with the King while abroad with him [in 1729], independent of the Queen. It is unnecessary to say that her Majesty on the return of the King overthrew the whole fabric.[65]

Townshend was certainly criticized for his pro-Hanoverian stance. In January 1730, Horatio Walpole complained of Townshend's 'endeavours to make all means Electoral preferable to all other considerations, which is entirely agreeable to the King's sentiments'.[66] George's support for whoever backed the interests of the Elector of Hanover was a given among commentators. In turn, Townshend criticized his rivals for failing to support Hanoverian interests. Although the Prussian envoy, Benjamin Reichenbach, a diplomat close to the opposition Whigs, claimed that Townshend was fed up with George's brutal manners, it was widely accepted that he was George's favoured minister. Reichenbach reported that George did not want him to go, but was obliged to maintain good relations with Walpole in order to obtain money.[67] The very fact that the Secretary of State, the minister concerned with foreign policy, should leave office in accordance with the wishes of the First Lord of the Treasury indicated the willingness of the Crown to accept the implications of parliamentary monarchy, but was also a product of the dynamics among these men. These included a growing lack of interest in the political struggle on the part of Townshend.

As in 1733, when Walpole was unable to persuade George to dismiss Harrington and Scarborough, so in 1730 Walpole had to wait for Townshend to resign. He appears to have decided finally to do so not because of George's position, but rather because of his frustration at the constant opposition of Walpole to his plans. Far from this being disastrous for the King, George, however, had his protégé, William Stanhope, succeed Townshend. Stanhope met George's criteria. He was well-connected, had diplomatic experience and had been an army officer. It was claimed that Walpole and the Queen had attempted to gain the post for Horatio Walpole, but had been thwarted by George. True or not, George had gained a pliant Secretary of State from the crisis, and this is as significant as his failure to sustain Townshend, or to replace him with Chesterfield, or Sir Paul Methuen, a former diplomat and Secretary of State whom George was also keen to appoint. Methuen had been a member of the Whig opposition in 1717–20, and had subsequently served in the Household, first as Comptroller (1720–5) and then as Treasurer (1725–30). The King knew him well. Horatio Walpole, in contrast, would not have been a King's man, and his officiousness might well have angered George personally as well.[68]

The relationship between George and Caroline, whom Townshend thought unsympathetic,[69] was clearly important in this crisis. As yet, their eldest son, Frederick, was not an important element. He had angered his father by, in the latter's eyes, meddling in the complex weave of North German princely marital prospects, and this had led in December 1728 to his being abruptly summoned to London. Frederick was never again to visit Hanover, for George did not want his heir to take an independent role, and such a role would have been easier had Frederick stayed in Hanover. In this, George repeated the policy of his own father. Frederick, who relished the social, cultural and sexual opportunities of London, did not object. Instead, he came to present himself politically as a 'Patriot Prince', with this patriotism being British and not German. This underlined the wisdom of George in detaching him from what might have been an independent power base in Hanover, but also ensured political problems in Britain.

Frederick was created Prince of Wales in January 1729, soon after taking his seat in the House of Lords. George, however, was not inclined to be generous to his son, financially, personally or politically. Unlike George, Frederick as Prince of Wales was not given a separate parliamentary grant, although, in fairness to George, Frederick was as yet unmarried and therefore, according to the conventions of the period, had less need of a separate establishment. More seriously, Frederick was not made regent in May 1729 when George went to Hanover. Instead, Caroline took the role. Her position remained strong and if George did not take her to Hanover as Electress, he also did not take his mistress, Henrietta Howard, with him.

The ministerial crisis of 1729–30 did not excite much public interest. It certainly attracted less attention than the furore in press and Parliament created by reports of French repairs to the harbour of Dunkirk against the explicit terms of the Peace of Utrecht of 1713. Dunkirk had been a key French privateering base against British trade in the War of the Spanish Succession (1702–13) and these repairs were presented as a sign of a French lack of good faith that vitiated the Anglo-French alliance, and also of the failure of the government to protect national interests. This was not an issue that focused attention on George, and indeed he did not encounter criticism as a result of the Dunkirk issue. Instead, the unpopularity of the French alliance helped shield him from attack because it diverted attention from the pursuit of Hanoverian interests. The latter were more complex than the issues in Anglo-French relations and had less resonance in terms of British public culture.

This helped underline the honeymoon nature of George's early years, a period that was to come to a close, as far as international relations were concerned, when the Anglo-French alliance collapsed in 1731, which left Britain more vulnerable. This honeymoon character contributed to the response to the ministerial crisis of 1729–30. There was no comparison in public attention between the fall of Townshend and that of Walpole and Carteret in 1742 and 1744. The fact that the Queen played a role in 1729–30, but not in 1742 or 1744, does not appear to be relevant here. It is more significant that Townshend was not forced out as a result of parliamentary action, and made no attempt to seek parliamentary backing. As a result, the crisis was not seen as an example of George yielding to public pressure, and thus played little role in his subsequent reputation.

George's obduracy had also been demonstrated in the continuing poor relations with Frederick William of Prussia. The arrival of a new Prussian envoy, Count Degenfeld in August 1730, provided an opportunity to improve these, but there were problems. Hotham was sent to Degenfeld to ascertain whether he had been instructed to apologize for Frederick William's insult to George, in the person of his minister. Degenfeld replied that he had not come to make excuses, and that it was rather the part of George to apologize for his minister's conduct.[70] Matters were not helped by George's refusal to give Reichenbach an audience of leave. This, and other difficulties created by George, delayed Degenfeld's initial audience. When it finally took place, he was treated badly by the royal family.

However, it was to be developments in Prussia that wrecked existing relations, and, still more, the prospect for their improvement. The unsuccessful attempted escape of the Crown Prince from the harsh control of his father by fleeing abroad, and the disgracing of ministers who had opposed Grumbkow, ended the chances of a reconciliation. George's anger at the treatment of the Crown Prince, and Prussian suspicion that George was responsible for the attempted escape, which he had indeed known of, helped to embitter relations. This collusion looked toward Frederick William's later attempts to win the support of the Prince of Wales for his own policy. In response to the escape attempt, the Prussian government declared that Frederick William would not consider any marriage, single or double. Serious moves towards a rapprochement were not to be made again until 1732, and the legacy of personal bitterness between the two monarchs was to wreck that attempt and the others made in the latter half of the 1730s. There were to be no marriages between the two royal houses. The failure to ensure good relations was to be a major handicap to British foreign policy in the 1730s. George's views greatly affected Anglo-Prussian relations, and this underlined the importance of the King.

5

Character and Concerns

Testy and over-sensitive (though certainly insensitive to others), George was a very open character, more prone to outbursts than to dissimulation. The anger he frequently displayed was generally hot not cold, although that did not prevent him from harbouring grudges. Constantly under pressure for favours, and also, in political terms, as a consequence of his royal office, George, however, suffered not only from a lack of control, but from a sense that he lacked control. In 1756, Newcastle recounted a conversation with George detailing the latter's response to the Duke's view that William Pitt the Elder should be appointed a Secretary of State and made Leader of the House of Commons in order to ease the problems of parliamentary management which were seen as particularly acute in the deteriorating international context:

> 'But,' replied the King *peevishly*, 'Mr. Pitt won't come in'. 'If *that* was done', I said, 'we should have a quiet session'. *'But Mr. Pitt won't do my German business.'* 'If he comes into your service, Sir, he must be told, he must do your Majesty's business . . .' 'But I don't like *Pitt. He won't do my business'*. 'But, unfortunately, Sir, he is the only one who has ability to do the business'.[1]

This bluster was a counterpoint to a degree of reserve, indeed hauteur, that was frequently noted and that made George no friends, being seen in part as needlessly pernickety, as in his concern with rank and etiquette. George certainly lacked the easier manner of his wife, who, while maintaining her rank, and interested in genealogy, knew

108

how to use the Court to win popularity and to help support the dynasty. Caroline was social to a degree that George could never match.

The King's personality was an issue because the existence of a Jacobite claimant directed attention to contrasts in character between George and 'James III and VIII'. Moreover, character was probed as an indicator of goals. In practice, Hanoverian by birth, training, loyalty and inclination, pulled between his roles as King and Elector, George was a pragmatist who did not have a pro-active agenda for Britain, other than helping Hanover. Instead, the emphasis was on preserving his position as King and maintaining royal prerogatives. In part, this was a sensible response to circumstances; in part, it was the consequence of a complacency that arose from diffidence, honesty and a measure of dullness. George, nevertheless, was less reclusive and more outgoing than his father, in part thanks to the prompting of his wife.

In about 1745 an engraving by Simon François Ravenet of David Morier's equestrian portrait of George II was published. Presenting the King as a military hero, it disseminated an image of him with which he would have been very happy. George was presented as in fine control of his mighty horse which was seen as engaged in the *passage*, an exercise calling for sustained precision. This captured the King in his role as an exemplary master of controlled power,[2] a mastery and power most readily grasped in military contexts. As an aspect of both character and public role, George was indeed happiest as a military leader, and most so as a commander on campaign. Described, in the House of Lords' Address of 7 February (os) 1728, as 'formed by nature for the greatest military achievements', George associated the army with his *gloire*. His prowess in battle was important to his reputation, Dettingen (1743) providing a fresh burnish to a reputation based on his presence on the battlefield at Oudenaarde (1708). 'George's Combat', a print of 1745, presented George as a ruler who would complete the struggle against France that William III had begun.[3] War seemed a matter of George's destiny, as was indeed also the case for other monarchs.

This was related to the staging of royal power. Like his brother-in-law, Frederick William I of Prussia, George believed that the military reviews he conducted were the most obvious and impressive display of his power and importance, and Horse Guards in London was in part redesigned to this end. In Sir John Thornhill's depiction of the royal family in the Painted Hall at Greenwich, George, as Prince of Wales, was shown, like his father, as wearing armour. Military interests were a bond between the two men. Once King, George II held a series of regimental reviews which gave him an opportunity to acquire a close knowledge of the army. He had the Guards' regimental reports and returns sent to him personally every week. When he reviewed his troops, he did so with great attention to detail, which tended to mean a stress on appearance. This is recorded, for a review of the Hanoverian troops held at Bemerode in 1735, in a large painting by J.F. Lüders.[4] Reviewing in London was generally conducted in St James's Park or Hyde Park, and was a prominent and public activity that was attended by courtiers and diplomats.

Reviewing was a preparation for war, and George derived great pleasure from his participation in the victory of Dettingen in 1743, a victory in which both British and Hanoverian forces served. This was to be his last command, in large part because his role was subsequently taken by his second son, Cumberland, but, while the War of the Austrian Succession continued, it was not obvious to contemporaries that George would not serve again. Indeed, in 1748, it was briefly suggested that he would go to the Low Countries in order to command the army.[5]

George enjoyed the company of military men, such as John, 2nd Duke of Argyll, Charles Hotham, William Stanhope and Richard Sutton. Indeed, the last three were each given diplomatic posts, with Stanhope also becoming a Secretary of State and Earl of Harrington, the latter a considerable achievement as George was careful about his promotions to the peerage. In addition, Charles Churchill, a protégé of Walpole, was close to the King, whom he served as a Groom of the Bedchamber from 1718 until his death in 1745. Born in about 1679, he was slightly older than the King, who made him a general in 1727 and subsequently promoted him in 1735 and 1739. Churchill was symptomatic of an aspect of military culture in that he claimed never to have read a book. Moreover, George's Hanoverian mistress, Amalie Sophie Marianne von Wallmoden, was the daughter of a Hanoverian general, Johann von Wendt, who held command in the 1740s, and their son became another general.

George certainly knew more than his British or Hanoverian ministers about war, and was determined to control military patronage, although, due to the nature of political exigencies, he had less control over both army and warmaking than Frederick William I or Frederick the Great. Command positions were generally deployed for political purposes in order to reward the ministry's political allies. Opponents, in contrast, lost their posts, a process George accepted, not least because these men opposed *his* ministry, and therefore, in his view, rejected both due deference and his own position.

In Britain, George II sought to end corrupt financial practices in the army, and did his best to further merit as the basis for promotions. Like his father, George promoted the principle of long service as the main way to advancement, a theme that was also to be taken up by his grandson, George III, and did his best to counter the purchases of commissions. Personally signing military commissions, George II used his formidable memory for names to good effect in keeping oversight of the leading members of the officer class. Although his goal, like that of his father, of ending corrupt financial practices and, in particular, officers' pecuniary perquisites, was only partially implemented, the traditional character of proprietary soldiering at troop and company level was fundamentally changed, to the significant detriment of the incidental income of captains. Regimental entrepreneurship, however, largely escaped, and colonels maintained their private financial position until the reign of Victoria. Thus, the interests of the King ran counter to those of the military establishment. When George asked General Churchill what had become of his hautboys [soldiers who played an oboe-type instrument], the General struck his hand on his breeches pocket, so as to make the money rattle, and answered 'Here they are, please Your Majesty, don't you hear them.'[6] This was not the best basis for an effective response to the French army when conflict with France began in 1743.

George's concern about the army, and his association of it with his own prestige, led him to insist that he approve new uniforms, a clear statement of his own role and the subordination of that of colonels. In 1751, moreover, colonels were prohibited from using their own crests in regimental colours or clothing. The new uniforms were depicted in a series of paintings by David Morier that were of interest to George. The Swiss-born Morier, who gained the patronage of Cumberland, was typical of a cosmopolitan nature of Court culture that was most famously exemplified by Handel, but for George most obviously captured by his own origins, his German wife, and the German origins of his most longlasting mistress, the Countess of Yarmouth.

George's concern with the military, of which he was Commander-in-Chief, also ensured that he took a close interest in operations, pressing the ministers on military policy and intervening over command decisions.[7] Individual officers could expect the King to know of their conduct and to have views on it, and, if he did not, this was seen as affecting their chances. In 1731, Colonel John Campbell wrote to Charles, Lord Elphinstone making this clear, and also showing how the royal oversight of patronage worked for Scotland:

> I was at Court . . . when Lord Ilay [later 3rd Duke of Argyll] went into the King's Closet to receive his commands in relation to the Peer [Scottish representative peer] to be chosen in poor Loudoun's place. Just before he went in he showed me a list of eleven or twelve, among which you were. He told me at the same time that he had put your name there that the King might be acquainted with it, and when he came out of the Closet he told me that the King said you were a young lord just come from your travels, upon which he set him right and told him who you were. I said he might have added what would have done you no harm was that you had been a considerable time in the service and had been wounded in it.[8]

In 1740, it was not surprising that Argyll's breach with the government should be attributed to the King's indignant refusal to accept the Duke's demand for the title of Field Marshal.[9] In 1756, when the fall of the Mediterranean base and colony of Minorca to the French in the opening stages of the Seven Years' War reflected a multiple, indeed scandalous, failure in British warmaking, George was frank in his opinions abut military conduct. It was felt that Rear-Admiral Temple West, Admiral Byng's second-in-command, had acted bravely, and he was well-received at the levée on 28 July, a reception that could then be reported in the press. The theme was of George's pleasure that West had done his duty, a concept that was a central theme in the King's life and views. Conversely, he remarked, when receiving Admiral Byng's report, 'This man will not fight', and also harshly treated Lieutenant-General Thomas Fowke, the Governor of Gibraltar, who had refused to obey orders to send a battalion on Byng's fleet to help the besieged garrison of Minorca. Fowke was cashiered, losing his rank and his regiment, and George was reported as saying 'that if he was unfit to serve for one year, he certainly was so for ever',[10] a dismissal of half-measures.

The Byng trial led to controversy over the quality of mercy, not least George's attitudes. The episode provided an opportunity for Henry

Fox, who was trying to embarrass the ministry, to tell the House of Commons on 23 February 1757:

> That during the nine years that himself had been Secretary at War [1746–55], it had been his constant practice on all courts martial to acquaint the King with any favourable circumstances that had appeared. That he had always found His Majesty disposed to lenity, and when he said nothing, the King would ask, 'Have you nothing favourable to tell me?'[11]

In Byng's case, however, George was unsympathetic. He rightly felt that the Admiral had failed to press home the attack, and was also aware that public opinion was hostile to any pardon, telling William Pitt the Elder, then a Secretary of State, '*you* have taught me to look for the sense of my subjects in another place than in the House of Commons',[12] where the ministers could hope to deliver a majority for whatever policy was decided. The execution of the Admiral very much reflected the King's views. Earlier, in 1755, when a socially prominent young naval captain, Lord Harry Powlett, son of the Duke of Bolton, left Hawke's fleet blockading France and took his ship into port to refit without receiving instructions to do so, this led George to become anxious about his bravery. As a result, although Powlett was acquitted, that year, when court martialled, while, in 1756, Newcastle's support helped him to promotion as a Vice-Admiral, he never held another command.[13]

Despite George's interest, and that of his father, these were years in which military quality was put under serious strain, which invites the question of what would have occurred had the Georges and Cumberland not sought to improve the situation, although George's favour for the elder generation of officers may have hindered reform. Army numbers had been heavily cut at the end of the War of Spanish Succession (1702–13), a habitual pattern in British military history. This reflected what would more recently be called the 'peace dividend', as well as the relative weakness of the military interest, and led to a pattern that gives British military history a start-stop character. Hostility on the part of the opposition to a large or, in many cases, any army, combined in its effect with the desire of Walpole to cut government expenditure and therefore taxation, and with his reluctance to become embroiled in European power politics.

As a result, little was spent on the army. Far from training for battle, it was divided into small units. Dedication and morale were not high among officers and soldiers. Instead, absenteeism, cronyism, and the pursuit of the financial benefits of command occupied the time of most officers, a reflection both of the extent to which the army shared in the values of society and of its institutional character. The army was no longer at the cutting edge in tactical practice, let alone debate or innovation. These deficiencies affected the army's effectiveness when George sought, unsuccessfully, to translate his victory at Dettingen in 1743 into strategic effect. They also contributed greatly to the military crisis caused by the Jacobite invasion in 1745.

George, like many other monarchs, also kept a close eye on military developments in other countries. He followed European campaigns with great interest, keeping hold of a map of the Crimea so that he could better appreciate the Russian campaign of 1736.[14] George also showed favour to foreign diplomats with a military background, such as Marquis Seyssel d'Aix, the envoy from Victor Amadeus II of Sardinia at the outset of his reign.

George could also be bellicose. War was an option that did not frighten him, and he preferred it to uncertainty and diplomatic delay.[15] In 1737, George's impatient support for action, especially in the face of insults to the flag, which were seen as affecting the honour of the monarch, encouraged pressure for a firm stance toward Spain over attacks on British commerce in the Caribbean.[16] In 1748, he was seen as the head of a war party determined to keep Britain in the War of the Austrian Succession against France.[17]

In 1755, Sir Thomas Robinson, one of the Secretaries of State, reported that George was not sure whether war with France was not preferable to the limited hostilities then being waged, 'France being so low, we so superior at sea and such the alacrity in the whole nation— England would never have such an opportunity'.[18] Given the problems that were to face Britain at the outset of the conflict, this view was overly optimistic. That spring, Holdernesse noted 'His Majesty's attention to put this country in a state of defence is far from being diminished', while George proposed that Holdernesse go to Hanover via Brussels in order to meet there a Dutch general with whom defensive preparations could be concerted against any French attack on the Low Countries.[19] This was necessary if France attacked there in reprisal for the outbreak of hostilities in North America.

George's bellicosity, however, was tempered by prudence. As a result, reports that he was ready for war, for example against Prussia in 1749,[20] have to be treated cautiously. More generally, George's response to circumstances could be much more ambivalent than his anger might suggest. In September 1729, George had told the French diplomat Chavigny that he would have his revenge on the Austrians for their conduct; the previous year, a leading Austrian minister, Prince Eugene, had written that George was the prime cause of Anglo-Austrian conflict.[21] George's anger was nevertheless compatible, as in early 1728, with attempts to improve relations.

Like his father, George did not show comparable interest in the navy. This reflected his background, but helped ensure that the naval triumphs of the period, particularly the major victories of 1747 and 1759 (the two battles off Cape Finisterre in 1747, Lagos and Quiberon Bay in 1759), did not reflect direct credit on the royal family. George, however, deserves approval for having the good sense to leave naval matters to the professionals, such as Anson. In 1743, he rejected an attempt by the Admiralty to increase the number of admirals to take note of changes in naval organization and tasking since the time of Charles II, but, soon after, he proved willing to accept more than one flag officer of each rank as well as a system that made the retirement of elderly captains much easier.[22]

George's personal interest in the army could be a nuisance to his British ministers, and was so to a degree greater than his interventions in other spheres. They had less room for making concessions in parliamentary manoeuvring over such issues as the size of the armed forces and the policy of subsidies paid to secure the use of Hessian forces, although, in each case, Walpole's desire for economies in order to help cut taxation was unsuccessful. The impact of George's martial temperament upon his conduct of foreign policy also concerned the government.

In Britain, in contrast, George had no particular political agenda, and this was important to the development of political stability. His pragmatism, nevertheless, was accompanied by a certain amount of choleric anger. Presumably passing on information from his brother, Newcastle, Henry Pelham told Sir Dudley Ryder, the Attorney General, in 1753 that, as far as Hanover was concerned, George 'passes his time there much in the same manner as here, and without any more spirit or cheerfulness, but gave rather a freer venture of peevishness when he was among his Hanover ministers than here', which was one response to the differences in his constitutional and political position between

Britain and Hanover. Hanover was a composite state, where the Regency Council managed several Estates, but the independence of the latter was less than that of representative assemblies in the British world.

In 1750, Newcastle provided more direct evidence of royal peevishness: over negotiations for a subsidy to the Elector of Cologne, that was designed to help support the Imperial Election Scheme (see p. 203), 'The King says he will not be so used, and will not give one single shilling; that his German [Hanoverian] ministers are the worst negotiators; that they know no way of succeeding, but *yield*, and *give*.'[23] This was an instructive instance of a contrast between public perception—the King being willing to spend heavily for the sake of Hanoverian and German goals—and a more complex royal response, although in this case George was also showing the degree of care with his own money—as Elector—that he did not display with that of the British government. George's peevishness in the 1750s may have something to do with his advancing age, or there may simply be more evidence for that decade. The medicines and therapies now available for dealing with pain and stress were conspicuously lacking in this period.

Hanover was one of George's major concerns but, like his grandson, George III, this was not a consistent concern. While Prince of Wales, George, as a result of George I's decision, never visited Hanover and he lived a life of British politics in London. The Court had a marked German element, but, for George and Caroline, who never left England after 1714, this no longer personally overlapped with Hanover. Thus, in contrast to George I, there was no significant direct stimulus for the German element in their life and, indeed, the future George II deliberately associated himself with signs of Britishness.

This, however, changed from 1729 when George II first visited Hanover as Elector, and became more marked from 1735, his third visit, when he began a relationship with Amalie Sophie Marianne von Wallmoden, from 1740 Countess of Yarmouth. Hervey sharpened the contrast in his *Memoirs*, but the lengthy passage he wrote in 1735 captured not only George's habit of making stark contrasts—he was not a man for ambiguities nor a king of nuance—but also the range of comments he made:

> No English or even French cook could dress a dinner; no English confectioner set out a dessert; no English player could act; no English coachman could drive, or English jockey ride, nor were any

116

English horses fit to be drove or fit to be ridden; no Englishman knew how to come into a room, nor any Englishwoman how to dress herself, nor were there any diversions in England, public or private, nor any man or woman in England whose conversation was to be borne—the one, as he said, talking of nothing but their dull politics, and the others of nothing but their ugly clothes. Whereas at Hanover all these things were in the utmost perfection. The men were patterns of politeness, bravery, and gallantry; the women of beauty, wit, and entertainment; his troops there were the bravest in the world, his counsellors the wisest, his manufacturers the most ingenious, his subjects the happiest . . . Forced from that magnificent delightful dwelling to return again to this mean dull island, it was no wonder . . . that frowns should take the place of smiles upon his countenance, when regret had taken that of pleasure in his heart.[24]

Giuseppe Ossorio, the perceptive Sardinian envoy, came to a similar conclusion, reporting that year that both George and Caroline were entirely in favour of everything that concerned the name German.[25]

Thanks in large part to his Hanoverian interests, George was very committed to foreign policy, which was a sphere in which the monarch indeed had considerable authority and power, not least the appointment and payment of envoys.[26] This authority was referred to by British ministers, as in 1749, when John, 4th Duke of Bedford, the Secretary of State for the Southern Department, wrote to Joseph Yorke in Paris:

The caution you took in avoiding the receiving any direct proposals from the French Minister by appearing to be entirely uninstructed, is in every respect agreeable to His Majesty, and it is his pleasure that you should in all future conversations of this nature, except in cases with regard to which you shall have received His Majesty's express instructions, avoid entering into particulars as much as possible.[27]

Most of George's few surviving letters relate to foreign policy. Compared to most of his British ministers, George was very knowledge-able in European affairs, well travelled and competent in languages, and this made him better able to give effect to his policies. In contrast,

Walpole never went abroad, Newcastle had not been abroad prior to 1748, and went then only to accompany George, and Pitt, who had spent time, while young, in the United Provinces and France, never travelled abroad once he became an MP.

Furthermore, in foreign policy, British ministers tried to take advantage of George's skill, contacts and commitment. He received information from a number of sources in addition to the British foreign service. The role of the Hanoverian Post Office in providing postal interceptions offered crucial information on international relations, and George also saw the British intercepts. These could give important insights on domestic politics and the views of those near to him. In 1748, Chesterfield claimed that these extended to George's mistress, the Countess of Yarmouth:

> He said that Lady Yarmouth having repeated with some vivacity to a foreign minister what she had said to Lord Chesterfield that she was sorry he went out but could not say it surprised her or that she disapproved of it that this was put into a intercepted letter which the King read.[28]

The King, however, could prove susceptible to manipulation. In 1727, he had shown a determination to control Court appointments when he had dismissed most of his father's Court servants. Given this rift with his father, the new King scarcely knew them. Some, moreover, were Germans. Five years later, however, John, Viscount Perceval recorded a visit from his cousin Mary Dering, Dresser Extraordinary to the King's daughters:

> She gave an instance of how Princes are imposed upon by their ministers. She said that when the King came to the crown his resolution was to continue in his service as chaplains all those who had been so while he was Prince, and to fill up the number belonging to him as King with as many of his father's chaplains as could be admitted, but one of his chaplains he particularly named to be continued on account of some extraordinary services he had done him when Prince. But when the then Lord Chamberlain [Charles, 2nd Duke of Grafton] . . . brought him the lists to sign, he did it without further examination than observing the chaplain's name was there, yet afterwards it proved that the man was removed,

and neither all his old chaplains, nor many of his father's continued, but a good many new persons placed.[29]

It was widely believed that George could be manipulated. Thomas, 3rd Earl of Strafford, a Jacobite and therefore a hostile critic, had claimed in 1727, 'The same violent and corrupt measures taken by the father will be pursued by the son, who is passionate, proud and peevish, and though he talks of ruling himself, he will be just as governed as his father was.'[30] In 1734, Sarah, Duchess of Marlborough, a caustic critic who saw herself as the custodian of the flame of true Whiggery, wrote:

> It is said, His Majesty is much offended at this proceeding with Spain, but I won't answer for the truth of that report. For I can't imagine by what means His Majesty will be rightly informed of it.[31]

Such a comment could be dismissed as gossip in opposition circles, but, shortly afterwards, Walpole's brother, Horatio, a key diplomat, wrote to an Under-Secretary, promising to continue a confidential correspondence 'on condition that my letters shall not be sent with the packet to Kensington',[32] in other words to the King. Newcastle followed the same policy.[33] In 1737, Hervey recorded the verse:

> For nine long years George bullies, sneaks, and treats,
> Pays useless armies and pacific fleets.
> When war's proclaimed he shifts from court to court,
> Loth to engage, yet promising support;
> At length the peace is signed, Sir Robert says it,
> and George, we're told, has read it in the Gazette.

In 1748, Newcastle instructed John, 4th Earl of Sandwich, envoy in The Hague:

> I must beg that whenever there is any thing in your answers, that you would have me keep to myself; and particularly not show the King; you would write it in a letter by itself with nothing but that particular thing in it; for the King very often asks me if I have any private letters from you, and sometimes there are many things that I would willingly show and am prevented by one or two points

flung in, which would be more properly put in a letter by themselves.[34]

The stress on the King's personal activity is notable. Indeed, in 1751,
George was misled about the contents of a letter from George Lyttelton
about opposition links with the late Prince of Wales, as George
Shelvocke, the Secretary of the Post Office whom he questioned, was
persuaded to mislead him about the contents.[35]

George did not countenance being kept in the dark, but he himself
accepted that some issues were best handled by others. In 1735, when
Britain sent a large fleet to the Tagus estuary, to deter Spain from attacking Portugal, a key ally, Harrington wrote from Hanover:

> as Her Majesty [Caroline, in London] will be able to have at all
> times the opinion of those versed in sea affairs, His Majesty orders
> me to acquaint you that he leaves it entirely to the Queen to send
> such orders as Her Majesty shall find necessary, for continuing or
> recalling at the proper session that squadron or any part of it.[36]

Caroline, left in Britain as regent, would of course be guided by the
ministers in London, but there was also a fundamental trust between
the two that enabled George to feel that she could be relied on to make
the appropriate choices when he was abroad. This trust did not extend
to his eldest son, Frederick, once Caroline was dead, and this may have
discouraged George from visiting Hanover in 1738 and 1739, although
the crisis with Spain in the latter years was also a factor.

Aside from deliberate efforts to keep him in the dark, there was
simply not enough time for George, faced with the size of government
business, to supervise all that he wished to control and for him to see
that his orders were carried out. Some of the bold claims he made soon
after his accession about what he would do as King can be attributed
to inexperience and nervous excitement. In the event, in some
spheres, such as the Church and the law, George's interventions were
episodic, although he could be extremely determined in defence of his
prerogatives.

The amount he was expected to do is striking. There is no evidence
of the burden of work comparable to the extensive correspondence
left by George III, which was dated to the minute when he began each
letter, but it is clear that George II was presented with a wide range of

subjects for discussion and decision, and frequently in great detail. Thus, Newcastle's notes for his audiences with George in March and April 1754 included 'to receive the King's pleasure upon' an agreement about the parliamentary representation of Evesham, and, again, 'to lay this affair again before the King and receive His Majesty's orders upon it'.[37]

Although George did not initiate domestic policies, he generally got his way in the choice of ministers, as well as over issues that greatly interested him, such as army patronage and peerage creations. In each case, ministers could have tough fights with the King. The Church was less dear to his interests, but, even so, George could be a determined defender of his views. From the outset, the Walpole ministry was to find it difficult to persuade George to offer preferment to clerics whom he disliked. His influence continued important thereafter and was exercised in particular in favour of those who served as royal chaplain, such as James Johnson, who was also a protégé of Newcastle. Johnson became Bishop of Gloucester in 1752 after he had accompanied George to Hanover for a second time, before being translated to Worcester. Holdernesse wrote to Newcastle in March 1757:

> Judge of my surprise when His Majesty told me today that he had determined to make Gilbert Archbishop of York, and to appoint Thomas to Salisbury . . . the King seems still to intend Younge for Peterborough and Taylor for St Pauls . . . hurt at this unexpected preference given for the Duke of Devonshire.[38]

In the event, John Gilbert, the Bishop of Salisbury, was translated to York, a post to which the post of Lord High Almoner was added. Newcastle had backed York for John Thomas, the Bishop of Peterborough, the Preceptor of George, Prince of Wales, but George II, instead, backed Gilbert. Horace Walpole attributed this to the King's determination to thwart the Princess of Wales and because Gilbert had praised the late Queen. Rather than go to York, Thomas followed Gilbert as Bishop of Salisbury and Clerk of the Closet. Thomas was succeeded at Peterborough by Richard Terrick who was supported by Devonshire. Newcastle saw the King as playing a key role and as being motivated by political considerations. He wrote in March 1757:

> the King told my Lord Holdernesse yesterday that he intended to make Dr. Terrick Bishop of Peterborough. It concerns me the

more, as I am persuaded that this disappointment proceeds from some dissatisfaction with me.[39]

Horace Walpole suggested that George could also be involved in a process of compromise in the Church, as in March 1751, when he recorded:

> The King would not go to chapel, because Secker Bishop of Oxford was to preach before him: the ministers did not insist upon his hearing the sermon, as they had lately upon his making him Dean of St Paul's.[40]

Secker, a favourite of Caroline, had lost George's support when he turned to Frederick, Prince of Wales, but, in 1750, was rewarded with the Deanery in return for declaring his political obedience to the Crown. Walpole commented 'the King was obliged to fling open his asylum to all kinds of deserters; content with not speaking to them at his levée, or listening to them in the pulpit!'[41] Newcastle had reassured George as to Secker's loyalty, but Walpole noted the conditional nature of royal approval. The King's refusal to hear Secker preach was a public act, and the response showed that such acts were noted.

As far as religion was concerned, George was conventionally devout and quietly non-controversial, and he lacked Caroline's interest in heterodox theological speculation. He liked sermons at Court to be no longer than 15 minutes, but this liking was far from exceptional. A strong Lutheran like his father, George also followed his father in conforming to the Church of England, of which he was the head. This was necessary under the Act of Settlement which decreed that the successor to Anne, and any issue she might have, had to join in communion with the Church of England. A Lutheran chapel had been established at St James's Palace for those brought over by Anne's husband, George of Denmark, but both kings used the Chapel Royal, and made their observance of Anglican practice very apparent. As far as Scotland was concerned, George acted as head of the Church of Scotland, the Presbyterian Church, which was necessary as Lutheranism was seen as a challenge to Presbyterianism. In Hanover, George attended Anglican services. George was depicted, in a painting attributed to J. Valentin Haidt, with figures associated with the Moravian Brethren, a German Protestant community that established a presence in England, but most Anglican bishops were not hostile to them, and, in 1749, supported the passage of the Moravian Act which recognized the Moravian Church.

At the international level, George was a keen supporter of the Protestant interest. He was clearly, sometimes ostentatiously, conscious of this dimension of international politics. George, indeed, had a personal heritage as his maternal grandmother, Eléonore Desmier d'Olbreuse, Duchess of Celle, born in Poitou in 1639, had a Huguenot background. Aware of the plight of Protestant communities, George was generous to foreign Protestants, in 1734 giving £1,000 to Swiss Protestant ministers.[42] Two years earlier, he expressed his approval for the work of the SPCK (Society for Promoting Christian Knowledge) on behalf of the persecuted Salzburg Lutherans.

George was also keen to see British diplomacy used to support Continental Protestantism. This support was particularly apparent in Germany, where it was sometimes bound up with the furtherance of Hanoverian interests, but was also seen elsewhere, for example in Poland, and in Savoy-Piedmont (the kingdom of Sardinia), where the British acted as protectors of the Waldensians, on whose behalf George made representation to Sardinian envoys.[43] When in 1728, Townshend proposed showing the French government a draft of instructions for George Woodward, the envoy to Saxony-Poland, this led George to reply 'I believe there are some parts relating to the affairs of religion which will not at all be fit for such a communication.'[44] Woodward was expected to act on behalf of Polish Protestants. The interests of the Protestant city-state of Geneva, which was threatened by pressure from Sardinia, were also of interest to George. He made efforts on its behalf, as in 1754 when he pressed the Sardinian envoy.[45] Hanoverian diplomacy was also used to support Protestant interests within the Holy Roman Empire in the neighbouring Catholic prince-bishopric of Hildesheim, as well as, notably, at the Imperial Reichstag (Parliament) at Regensburg, and in Vienna.

George's preference for friendship with men with military associations, including exiles from the Continent, such as Frederick, Earl of Lifford, with whom he shared in the Malburian legacy, reflected not only his personality and interests but also an understanding of the role of the Hanoverian British monarchy as guarantor of Protestant liberty in a Europe under threat from universal monarchy. This idea of his youth, then focused on opposition to Louis XIV, a cause for which George had fought, was transposed in the 1720s onto the Austria of

Charles VI and in the 1740s focused anew on France, the backer of the Wittelsbachs in Germany and of the Jacobites in Britain. Frederick the Great's willingness to ally with France under such circumstances helped further condemn him in George's eyes.

George was not seen as a threat to the Church of England. There was no controversy under George comparable to that under his father, whose name had appeared on the title-page of the prominent latitudianarian Benjamin Hoadly's controversial 1717 sermon on the text of 'My Kingdom is not of this world', a sermon published with George I's stated and publicly proclaimed approval. In contrast, George II responded to Hoadly as a seeker after preferment rather than as a theological writer. George told Hervey that Hoadly was 'a great rascal' and 'a canting hypocritical knave to be crying "the Kingdom of Christ is not of this world", at the same time that he, as Christ's ambassador, receives £6,000 or £7,000 a year'.[46] This was particularly hard, given that in 1734 Hoadly had used up his credit with Dissenters—at Caroline's behest—to persuade them not to agitate for the repeal of the Test Act during the general election. Hoadly got the plum bishopric of Winchester that year in large part due to his usefulness to Walpole. George's views on religious matters were not much of an issue for concerned Anglicans, and there was no equivalent to the threat believed to arise from the Catholicism of the Jacobite claimant.

George was not noted as a patron of the arts, although he was interested in music. There was no major programme of royal building during the reign, and nothing to compare with George III's extensive works, notably at Windsor, Buckingham House and Kew. George II, instead, followed his father in making little use of Windsor, although they both hunted there. It was, however, distant from the capital. As part of the move from Windsor, celebrations of the Order of the Garter came to be held in London. For his country seat, George in 1719 purchased Richmond Lodge near Kew, which was much closer to London than Windsor, although it was transferred to Caroline's possession in 1727. The plan for a palace at Richmond led to the creation of a model in 1735 that was based on a design by William Kent, but it was not pursued. The same fate befell the plan for a palace for George III at Richmond. The Baroque style of the decorations in the royal apartments at Windsor, produced by Antonio Verrio for Charles II, do not seem to have appealed to George II, whose sensibilities were somewhat different. This was certainly suggested by his response to Verrio's work at Hampton Court. There, the walls of Queen Anne's Drawing Room were covered with silk damask and with Mantegna's magnificent painting the 'Triumphs of Caesar'. Italianate taste was important at Hanover. George's grandparents, his parents, Sophia and Ernst August were keen patrons of the Baroque, and Hanover exemplifies its assimilation among North German princes better than did Berlin. George bought a splendid set of silver furniture early in his reign from the Duke of Brunswick-Wolfenbüttel who was short of money.[47]

In the capital, although Hampton Court, which was a favourite place of Caroline, benefited from building work, there was a shift in favour away from it, a shift that continued that under George I. Instead, Kensington Palace and St James's Palace were more important. Neither was in the busy, built-up heart of the metropolis, the City of London, where there was no royal palace. This was just as well for the health of the royal family. In 1714, the French envoy complained repeatedly about the effect on his breathing of the coal smoke that enveloped London.[48] Although neither Kensington nor St James's was particularly imposing from the outside, in terms of either building or location, both were lavishly decorated, providing richly ornate spaces for royal life, with impressive chandeliers, paintings and tapestries. However, George II did not prefigure George III (or follow Charles I) as a major purchaser of paintings.

George II's views on the visual arts are not easy to distinguish. The drawings in the royal apartments in Kensington are listed, but it is unclear whether George had as much interest as his wife. Those delivered for her use were marked in the list.[49] When he told William Kent that he had renovated Rubens's fresco at the Banqueting House 'exceeding well', the remark does not indicate specific artistic individual sensitivity, although, had George had such, his reserved nature would not have necessarily have allowed him to express it. At Kensington, Kent was a more restrained decorator than Verrio or, indeed, Thornhill. The extent to which this shift reflected royal taste and can be seen as a move away from high Baroque, possibly a move that can be linked to the North-German Baroque of George's background, is unclear. Kent, the Architect to the Board of Works, was also responsible for designing the new Horse Guards, the headquarters of the army's staff.[50] The late-seventeenth century building was demolished in 1749 and a new building begun in 1750. The supervision of the project was in the hands of John Vardy, who had worked with Kent since 1736.

To turn from buildings, George Frederick Handel was prominently linked with the royal Court. At George's request, he produced and conducted the four anthems for the coronation in 1727, and in 1743 celebrated George's victory in battle by writing the *Dettingen Te Deum*, which was performed later that year at St James's Palace, a triumphant moment in the King's life. Handel's *Music for the Royal Fireworks* followed in 1749, to celebrate the Peace of Aix-la-Chapelle of the previous year, although mismanagement of the expensive fireworks combined with poor weather to spoil the occasion. Handel, however, derived his money not from royal sponsorship but from the busy entrepreneurial possibilities of the London market. These, in turn, provided opportunities for George and his Court which, at least in the 1730s, went regularly to the theatre, as well as to attend concerts and to visit the opera. George also enjoyed masquerades, which scarcely suggests that he was a kill-joy.

The cultural activity of the King was part of his public role and led to comment, as in January 1737 when there was surprise that he had not attended the opera on the first Saturday after he returned from Hanover, 'as most people thought he would to show he was safely arrived'.[51] Some of the King's activity was hardly public. George was also an active patron of the German enamellist C.F. Zincke, but this form was scarcely central to British culture. As a related instance of his interest in miniatures, George also had his collection of coins, an activity associated with antiquarianism and Classical learning. Key household appointments relating to cultural activity, however, were held by government connections. Ripley, Comptroller of the Board of Works from 1726 until 1738, worked for Walpole on his new seat at Houghton, while Charles Dartiquenave, who in 1726 became Surveyor-General of the King's Gardens, was a Whig socialite.

George was also the subject of the arts, not only in music, poetry and paintings, but also in statuary. This was seen in Henry Cheere's statue of him in the grounds of Hartwell House, although the Society of Merchants of Bristol in 1731 turned down the proposal to raise a statue for the King. Instead, it was decided that one to William III should be erected. It has, however, been suggested that the proposal for a statue for George was an insidious Tory plot to derail the William III proposal. Other members of the royal family were also the subject of artistic depiction. The silver medalic ticket struck by Henry Jernegan in 1736 to promote his lottery prize depicted Queen Caroline on the reverse watering a group of palm trees, an image of her nurturing the Carolinas in North America. Caroline was involved in promoting Jernegan's auction.

Queen Caroline was far better read than her husband and made a major contribution to building up the royal library,[52] while Frederick, Prince of Wales was a much more important and discerning patron of the arts than his father. George was not particularly interested in books and was nowhere near as well read as his grandson, George III. Hervey readily contrasted King and Queen in this sphere, writing of the former:

> The King used often to brag of the contempt he had for books and letters; to say how much he hated all that stuff from his infancy; and that he remembered when he was a child he did not hate reading and learning merely as other children do upon account of the confinement, but because he despised it and felt as if he was doing something mean and below him.[53]

The reference to social position was instructive, as George was very conscious of issues of rank. Chesterfield referred to 'the sterility of his conversation'.[54] However, George II did make a major contribution when, in 1757, he donated the royal library of 10,500 volumes to the new British Museum.

It is indicative that one of his friends, Charles, 2nd Duke of Grafton, who was born in the same year as George, and was Lord Chamberlain from 1724 until his death in 1757, was blunt, keen on hunting, indeed died as a result, and did not read books. The longevity of Grafton's tenure, which contrasted with the two far shorter tenures of office in 1715–24, reflected George's preference for continuity. Furthermore, he liked men he was comfortable with around him at Court, and Grafton readily met the bill.

George may deliberately have maintained his quality of bluffness. It was not incompatible with a social life which included masquerades and theatres, and helped the King maintain visibility to the social élite. Although George might appear boorish, nevertheless, when he went to Hanover in 1755 the most recent French plays were sent to him. They were performed at the palace of Herrenhausen, which had a good example of a Baroque garden, in the outdoors *Gartentheater*, where the flats (theatrical scenery) consisted of rows of trees and gilded marble busts.

Although John Theophilus Desaguliers, a popular lecturer, made astronomy popular at Court, George showed relatively little interest in science, and the royal role in the Royal Society declined during his reign. Yet, the scheme for a university for the Electorate of Hanover at Göttingen planned under his father was brought to fruition, and this was an achievement of which he was very proud. George indeed visited the university in 1748, and, aside from the celebrations there, the occasion was recorded for British readers in a *Short Account of His Majesty's late journey to Goettingen and of the new university there*.[55] The university, which was designed to raise the profile of George as a German ruler, not least in competition with Prussia, and also to extend Hanoverian influence,[56] was to make a major difference to the Electorate's cultural and intellectual life.

Science and intellectual pursuits, however, held less interest for George than they were to do for George III. Instead, as with much of the social élite, cards proved a major activity for George II, not least in the evenings and in indifferent weather. He was playing cards in 1751 when he was told that Frederick was dead. 'Fritz ist tot' he bluntly remarked to the Countess of Yarmouth.

Hunting was more of a passion than education, and it was a passion he could pursue especially well in his native Electorate,[57] where the wooded slopes of the Harz mountains offered particular possibilities, not least due to its being far less crowded than the Thames Valley. The royal forests in Britain had been neglected under the later Stuarts, and Windsor Forest required afforestation in order to make it suitable of stag hunting.[58] In 1735, George hunted wild boar in the Harz, an activity of which his British subjects were informed through the press, for example the *Daily Post Boy* of 16 August (os). George, who had a stud in Hanover, hunted from horseback and was an accomplished horseman. The Saxon horse was the motif of the Hanoverians. In England, George preferred to hunt around Richmond, and this encouraged his interest in the Thames Valley. The hunting was good, care was taken to ensure that animal stocks were kept up, and George frequently hunted stags. In the 1750s he went to Richmond on Saturdays as well as on either Wednesdays or Thursdays.

Time spent hunting and reviewing troops reflected not simply George's commitment to his *métier* as a ruler, but also his love for activities that combined drama, the open air and a sense of adventure. These activities and resonances can be put together to refer to George as a late-Baroque monarch, a description further illuminated by reference to his favour for the theatrical music of Handel. However, the extent to which such cultural characterization is a matter of possibly misleading subsequent classification has to be accepted. Furthermore, as indicated above in the case of William Kent, it is also possible to point in the case of George to departures from the high Baroque.

With George, an emphasis on ritual and precedence, a characteristic of Baroque monarchy, although not only of that, can frequently be seen. In replying to Townshend, when the latter sent draft instructions to Edward Finch, appointed envoy in Stockholm in 1728, George wrote, 'there has been left out how he is to behave as to his rank in relation to other envoys of crowned heads. For as of late the French minister has affected a precedency, he [Finch] must be instructed to take care to keep every thing upon strict equality.'[59] This was an important theme. In 1735, Horatio Walpole, then envoy in The Hague, was instructed to restrict the claim for precedence by the French envoy, 'You will publicly support the King's indisputable right to an equality with his most Christian Majesty.'[60] Moreover, when allies did not keep him informed, George also felt slighted and was angry. This can be linked to his sense of honour and integrity. Indeed, in 1732, Ossorio described George as piquing himself on his sincerity, honour and probity.[61]

At the same time, George could show a degree of civility and care that contrasted with the general presentation of him as boorish and difficult. In 1731, after Hervey, generally a bitter critic, had a fit in the Queen's Drawing-Room, he reported, 'The King assisted with more goodness than his general good breeding alone could have exacted and has sent here perpetually',[62] the last a reference to George's concern to see how Hervey was. George, however, lacked much of a sense of humour, and certainly did not appreciate irony. He is reported to have refused to allow the print of William Hogarth's *The March to Finchley* (1750) to be dedicated to him, allegedly commenting 'I hate painting and poetry too. Neither the one nor the other ever did any good. Does the fellow mean to laugh at my Guards?' Hogarth had depicted the troops preparing to march from London to Finchley in December 1745, in order to defend the capital from the advancing Jacobites, in an unheroic, but very human, light, not least sharing the scene with prostitutes. Hogarth responded by dedicating the engraved version to Frederick the Great, terming him an 'Encourager of Arts and Sciences', which was an indirect, but nevertheless sharp, criticism of the King.

Irony was not the sole problem. George found relations with his children difficult, not that that was unusual for eighteenth-century monarchs. When the children were young, he could be harsh, as when he imitated William IV of Orange's way of walking to Anne, who was due to marry the Prince: Lady Suffolk reported:

> that the King even walked about the room, mimicking the Prince of Orange and said, Anne, he is even worse than I represent him—if you think you cannot bear him, I can still break the match; but if he comes over, you must marry him. The Princess replied, she would marry him if he was a monkey.[63]

George was also capable of sensitivity and remorse. When his daughter Louisa died in 1751, George, in response to her last letter from Denmark, where she was Queen, broke out into expressions of tenderness, and was reported as saying, 'I know I did not love my children when they were young, I hated to have them running into my room, but now I love them as well as most fathers.'[64] Fourteen years earlier, the complexities of George's personality were captured by Hervey when he discussed George's response to the drawn-out fatal illness of his wife. Amongst Hervey's praise was the claim, 'that he had passed more hours with her than he believed any other two people in the world had ever passed together, and that he never had been tired in her company one minute', but, at the same time, Hervey captured George's angry restlessness and frustrated meddling:

> . . . yet so unaccountable were the sudden sallies of his temper, and so little was he able or willing to command them, that in the midst of all this flow of tenderness he hardly ever went into her room that he did not, even in this moving situation, snub her for something or other she said or did. When her constant uneasiness, from the sickness in her stomach and the soreness of her wound, made her shift her posture every minute, he would say to her, 'How the devil should you sleep, when you will never lie still a moment? You want to rest, and the doctors tell you nothing can do you so much good, and yet you are always moving about. Nobody can sleep in that manner, and that is always your way; you never take the proper method to get what you want, and then you wonder you have it not'[65]

Allowance should be made for the nervous tension of this period, and Hervey clearly liked presenting George as a ridiculous and tiresome foil for his own ability and wit, but the contradictions of the King's character are captured in this account. More generally, discipline was the key theme in his relations with his family, which helped account for the longstanding tension with Frederick, Prince of Wales.

Concern about dynastic options was another key theme. George, like other rulers, was committed to the status of his dynasty. This was very much in accord with the recent history of his family. The house of Hanover was only lately established, under George's grandfather, Ernst August, in 1692, as an Electorate, and even more recently, under his father in 1714, as a kingdom. The latter position was contested by the Stuarts, while Hanover's role in north Germany was challenged by the Hohenzollerns of Prussia, the Wettins of Saxony and, to a lesser extent, the Wolfenbüttel branch of the Guelph family. Furthermore, its authority was overshadowed by the claims of the Holy Roman Empire which were pushed particularly hard under Charles VI (r. 1711–40), especially in the 1720s. This created issues for the Hanoverian dynasty, some of which cannot be readily segregated as royal or Electoral.

Marriage was a focus of several issues, as it reflected, sustained and strengthened prestige, and thus served to affirm power. The need to choose Protestant spouses had been accentuated by the requirements arising from the British Crown, as the Bill of Right and the Act of Settlement made Protestantism a key prerequisite. Protestantism indeed was a theme much vaunted in Hanoverian marriages, especially those of George II to Caroline, and of his elder daughter, Anne, to William IV of Orange. The emphasis on Protestantism, however, ensured that the most prestigious dynastic prizes were outside the range of George or his family. George indeed pointed out in 1737 that 'for Protestant princesses there is not great choice of matches'.[66] The Hanoverians could not marry with the Habsburgs, the Bourbons or the Wittelsbachs, and the conversion of the main Electoral branch of the Wettins and the Duke of Württemberg to Catholicism further reduced their options. As a result, the house of Hanover could not repeat its dynastic success in gaining Britain by advancing claims when the Habsburg dynasty came to an end in the male line in 1740, as both the Wittelsbachs and the Electoral branch of the Wettins did as a result of earlier marriages. Nor was a member of the house of Hanover able to stand for election as King of Poland when the position fell vacant in 1696, 1733 and 1763, for Poland was also a Catholic state. Instead, the Wettins held the crown of Poland from 1697 until 1763, this, alongside Church preferments, being the gain they derived from their conversion.

Religion was not the sole issue in missing out on potential prizes. Frederick the Great was mistaken in 1749 when he expressed concern that George would support his son Cumberland or his son-in-law, Frederick of Hesse-Cassel, for the Swedish throne when Frederick I died without legitimate issue.[67] In the event, Frederick the Great's brother-in-law, Adolf Frederick of Holstein-Gottorp, succeeded in 1751.

Within the parameters of Protestant Europe, the house of Hanover did not do spectacularly well. Neither a princess of Ansbach, a Hohenzollern, for George II, nor one of Saxe-Gotha for his elder son Frederick, was much of a catch, although efforts were made to play up both. George I and George II in the 1720s and early 1730s actively and repeatedly pursued a much better option, a double marriage scheme with Prussia: the heirs of Prussia and Britain were to marry a princess of the other house. This scheme, however, failed totally under George II, with serious political results during the reign of Frederick William I of Prussia (r. 1713–40). Double marriage schemes were much in favour, another being pursued with Denmark in 1743.

Despite his failure with Prussia, George was able to marry three of his five daughters into European ruling houses.[68] His eldest, Anne, the Princess Royal, in 1734 married William IV of Orange, whom George compared to a baboon. The house of Orange was the closest the Dutch came to a royal house, and one that the Stuarts had twice been happy to marry royal daughters into: the daughters of Charles I and James II and VII, to William II and William III respectively. Anne's wedding was postponed to 1734 due to William IV's illness, but was a splendid occasion that was the first royal wedding in Britain since that of Charles II's niece, the future Queen Anne, to Prince George of Denmark in 1683. The choice of William IV as groom reflected much credit on George, as it underlined the Protestantism of the dynasty and associated it with a family distinguished in British history, rather than simply another German princely family. There were many celebratory receptions, and much writing and bellringing.

Amelia, whom George had seen as a possible wife for Frederick the Great, and Caroline never married, prefiguring the situation for several of George III's numerous daughters; although George II's unmarried daughters did not have illegitimate children unlike (probably) at least one of their grand-nieces, the daughters of George III. However, Mary, the fourth daughter of George II, married Frederick of Hesse-Cassel in 1740. Hesse-Cassel was one of the leading German Protestant states, as well as a major military support for its neighbour Hanover. George had worked during his visits to Hanover at strengthening relations with Hesse-Cassel. Frederick's father was William VIII, the administrator of Hesse-Cassel for his elder brother, Frederick I of Sweden, who had no legitimate children; so the marriage was a prestigious one. It proved disastrous, however, and the spouses separated. The willingness of Frederick to become a Catholic, news of which circulated from 1754, compounded difficulties. In 1754, George's advice and his guarantee of any provisions on behalf of Mary were sought. George was determined to protect his daughter's position, and, to strengthen his pressure, he sought to have the Dutch government join him in his measures, which was also a way to use family pressure more effectively, as his daughter Anne, the widow of William IV of Orange, was then regent for the infant William V. George wanted to keep Frederick's children away from his influence and claimed a right to intervene on their behalf.

This was not simply a family issue but also involved power politics in Germany, with, in particular, a concern that Hesse-Cassel would be wooed by Frederick the Great, then an opponent of George in international relations.[69] At the same time, Frederick's willingness to guarantee the Protestant position in Hesse-Cassel also led to approval, and, to an important extent, anticipated the co-operation between Frederick and George in international power politics that developed later in 1755: family politics looked toward foreign policy. That, however, did not end George's anxiety about Hesse-Cassel.[70] In 1756 the 'utmost zeal and assiduity' was called for in ensuring that Mary obtained an independent financial provision and did not have to live with Frederick of Hesse-Cassel.[71] A life annuity was settled on Mary, and in 1760 she became regent of Hanau, part of the Hesse-Cassel inheritance.

Hesse-Cassel brought together British foreign policy, Hanoverian goals, and dynastic drives, and serves as a reminder that in some circumstances they were not really separable. The issue also underlines the extent to which family issues did not only involve sons, but could also involve daughters. Had George II had brothers, as George I had done and George III did, the situation might have been even more complex, but his parents' divorce helped him to avoid this eventuality.

Louisa, the fifth daughter of George II, married in 1743 the heir of the Danish crown, later Frederick V, but died in 1751. This marriage, which was intended to match that discussed for William, Duke of Cumberland with Frederick's sister Luise, looked back to that of the future Queen Anne with Prince George of Denmark, and forward to the disastrous marriage of George II's granddaughter, Caroline Matilda, with Christian VII.

Until the debacle of 1757, George much admired Cumberland, who had inherited his father's love of the army, but he did not try to win him a principality, as Philip V of Spain (r. 1700–46) successfully sought to do in Italy for two of his sons by his second marriage, Don Carlos, who became ruler of Parma and later of Naples (and eventually Charles III of Spain), and Don Philip, who became ruler of Parma. Osnabrück, a Hanoverian secondogeniture by rotation, could have served Cumberland, but it did not fall vacant until the following reign, when Cumberland's great-nephew, George III's second son, Frederick, Duke of York, became, as an infant, the ruler. Ossorio's suggestion in 1748 that George might support an independent Belgium under Cumberland's rule was without foundation. Cumberland, moreover, did not marry. To have done so was unnecessary for dynastic reasons once Frederick, Prince of Wales had his numerous family, and George probably wished to be spared the cost of a larger establishment for his second son.

Nevertheless, Cumberland was a key instance of the wider impact of the royal family in the shape of several adult children who participated in wider society. This was true of Cumberland, by his military career and particularly his journey to and from Scotland in 1745–6, of Amelia by her progresses to Bath, echoing those of Queen Anne earlier in the century, and of Frederick, Prince of Wales. From George's viewpoint, the last emerged most clearly as a nuisance, if not an obstacle to sound politics, but in the perspective of the development of the monarchy, Frederick's careful construction of an attractive image of rulership was important for the future, not least with his concern for the unfortunate, an ideal of an active kinship independent of the dominant political factions, and his visibility to the public. All were rehearsed at various times before his death in 1751. Cumberland was refused permission by George to take part in the 1744 campaign,[72] but, the following year, was made Captain-General and took a brave role at the battle of Fontenoy.

Dynastic concerns helped accentuate George's interest in Hanover and this was very much reflected in his travels. Like his father and grandson, George never visited Ireland, Scotland or Wales. Indeed, the politics and patronage needed to handle Ireland and Scotland were not seen as requiring the royal presence. Instead, they were the task of ministers, in London, Edinburgh and Dublin. George was fit enough to visit both, and had the time to do so, but they were not on his agenda. This was not simply a matter of the counter-claims of Hanover, because most years George did not visit the Electorate, a point that is overlooked due to the focus on his trips there. He could have visited both Ireland and Scotland by sea, as George IV, who was far less fit, was to do.

Furthermore, George II did not visit northern England, despite a rumour in 1731 that he intended to do so, while, further south, what he saw was seriously limited. There was no equivalent to Charles VI's visit to Graz and Trieste nor his journey to Prague, let alone Peter the Great's journeys, as Czar, to Copenhagen and Baku. The job of showing Francis of Lorraine around the country in 1731 was left to ministers and courtiers. For George, England essentially meant the royal palaces near London, nearby hunting areas, and the routes to and from ports from which he could sail to Hanover. This was principally Harwich, but, due to a storm on the way back from the 1735 visit to Hanover, included Rye in 1736. George also visited Cambridge, to receive the degree of D.D. from the university, and Newmarket in 1728. He did not anticipate his grandson, who travelled more widely in England, visiting Cheltenham, Exeter, Plymouth, Southampton and Worcester (none of which were visited by George II), though not yet the North of England.

George was not particularly grand. He liked ceremonial, but he liked it controlled, within his reach, and without excessive effort unless it had a practical function such as a military one. A French memorandum at the close of his reign, when George was somewhat withdrawn, argued that he lacked a proper Court and that there was scant external pomp or theatre of majesty. The writer claimed that George lived in a town where trade alone was valued, and clearly thought the monarchy weakened by this situation,[73] an account that says more concerning French attitudes than about British views. Indeed, this style of kingship appears to have suited George and he seems to have sustained it with few problems. This looked toward the modesty of George III's kingship. Despite the difference in their styles, particularly their attitude towards women, with George III showing the uxoriousness and gentlemanly care that his grandfather lacked, there was much in common between the two men, and neither was as flashy as Frederick, Prince of Wales. The habit of playing cards in the evening with family members and trusted courtiers linked both men, and helped give a subdued, quiet and even intimate, tone to at least part of the royal day. George II also liked backgammon.

George II's lack of grandness was linked to his persistent reputation for economy, which, to critics, meant a meanness that demeaned the Crown, as well as the King personally.[74] This, however, was not so much a personal foible as a frugal response to the problems of running a royal household and supporting a large family. The latter was an issue for George II, like his eldest son Frederick, and also for George III, who, similarly, had a persistent reputation for economy.

Although Hanover, Brunswick and Prussia were all keen to compete with France in cultural infrastructure, the royal style also drew on Protestant North German traditions of princely activity, with their emphasis on duty, frugality and service, themes expressed in the support shown by George II and Caroline for Thomas Coram's Foundling Hospital in London, which opened in 1741 and sought to join philanthropy to the strengthening of a Protestant empire.[75] Nevertheless, the tone of Court life also responded to a lack of social self-confidence on the part of George I, George II and George III. In part this was concealed by the reserve of the first, the bluster of the second, and the industry of the third, but none was a natural conversationist. Ironically, the North German traditions were in keeping with what was to be a general shift in European royalty toward a more intimate style.

Intimacy in George II's case did not mean easy relations either with his family, his ministers or himself. He was often gruff and he frequently snubbed his wife. Ossorio suggested in 1748 that George's frequent bad temper hindered his projects and those of others.[76] However, George was not simply a master of insensitive bluster. For example, Henry Fox, in late 1756, when parting rather unhappily from royal service, described an audience, 'He was calm, serious, full of anger, but determined not to show it.' George had been blunter in responding to Fox's patronage requests 'He now wants to set his dirty shoe on my neck.'[77] Orford, who, as Walpole, had had long experience of dealing with the King, advised Henry Pelham in 1743 on how best to manage George:

> Address and management are the weapons you must fight and defend with: plain truths will not be relished at first, in opposition to

prejudices, conceived and infused in favour of his own partialities; and you must dress up all you offer, with the appearance of no other view or tendency, but to promote his service in his own way, to the utmost of your power. And the more you can make anything appear to be his own and agreeable to his declarations and orders, given to you before he went, the better you will be heard: as, the power to treat with such persons, as should be necessary to carry on his service in your hands; the encouragement and hopes to be given to the Whigs, by you, as arising from himself.[78]

The response to the King in part reflected the uncertainty within Britain as to what royal behaviour should constitute. Court life was far from a fixed pattern. Indeed, George II's accession in 1727 continued the variation over the previous century in the style and content of Court activity, and in its accessibility across the political spectrum. In each of these criteria, the variation had been very considerable. Under George II, there was an attempt to make Court life more attractive and accessible than had been the case under his father, but this depended heavily on Caroline and was weakened, first, when the reversionary interest emerged in the shape of a defiant Frederick, Prince of Wales, and, second, when she died in 1737. Nevertheless, despite the more reserved style that followed Caroline's death, as well as George's lengthy absences in Hanover, there continued to be an established shape to the royal year, with celebrations for example for the King's birthday, although when George returned late from Hanover, as from his 1736 and 1750 trips, these celebrations had to be postponed. There were parallel celebrations in Hanover. In 1755, George, Viscount Nuneham, later 2nd Earl Harcourt, bought new clothes for the celebrations there for the anniversary of George's accession. He did not, however, find the Court at Hanover entertaining.[79]

Royal life had become quieter after the death of Caroline in 1737, not least because the energy of the young Court of the Prince and Princess of Wales could not, due to personal and political difficulties, be grafted onto the royal Court. The Prince's opposition, like that of his father under George I, fractured both royal family and Court. Princess Amelia, who did not marry, took over Caroline's social role, but Caroline's sparkle was gone, and George now very much took the view that Court life was a duty, albeit one he consistently performed not least in order to show that he was well.

This was even more the case in the 1750s, as the growing age of George and his children was not matched, after the death of Frederick in 1751, by the grafting on of the new young Court. Instead, Augusta, the widowed Princess of Wales, and her son, the future George III, kept their distance as the distinct Leicester House interest was built up. The retired nature of the King further lessened the appeal of the Court.

George might appear ridiculous to critics, but that view was misleading. He could indeed be emotional when he encountered trouble and could bluster, but this was not a full account of his personality. Sometimes, indeed, his anger was for effect, and comments on his acerbic or gruff personality could neglect the more accommodating nature of the actions taken by the King. George indeed could fume and still remain reasonable. Ministerial private correspondence paid tribute to his centrality to government, whether with praise or with complaint. In June 1740, Hardwicke noted the problem in managing ministerial differences caused by George's visit to Hanover, 'now especially whilst the King is abroad (who when he was here was a kind of centre of unity, at least his final opinion concluded everybody else) the utmost endeavours should be used to preserve harmony and good agreement'.[80] Newcastle, who rarely looked on the positive side, complained four months later about George, presenting him as stubborn and as unduly influenced by a factious colleague: 'we have reason to fear, that our united credit with the King, may hardly be sufficient to induce His Majesty to do quite right, in this great conjuncture, one will govern all, and fill the King's head with complaints and unreasonable jealousies of part of his servants.'[81] Again, the theme was on how George could be manipulated, and therefore on how other ministers had to act in order to counteract such manipulation.

Manipulation, however, was not the key theme. In a state with a practice of power that reflected a mixed constitution, neither George nor others was absolute, and the resulting areas of compromise were prone to debate. George knew the royal role, saw it in theory and practice in 1714–27, and then lived it. He could not single-handedly run the ship of state, and he placed his focus and energies on what most concerned him: foreign policy and the military, and not, for example, on local government in the shape of JPs. George was dutiful. He did his duty, was not, by any intention, an absolutist, sought to conform to the constitution as he knew it, and practised and worked to uphold the dignity of the throne, rather than diminishing it.

Duty was the key theme to how George operated, as well as his expectations of the royal family and the political servants about him. When George did not see duty (as he saw it done) he could be harsh, as to Byng in 1756–7, Cumberland in 1757, and Frederick, Prince of Wales from the mid-1730s. Duty was linked by George to reputation, and George was determined not to lose his reputation by dishonourable conduct. This was a theme he struck when giving audience to Ossorio in 1748.[82] In this case, George focused this point on not letting his allies down. To him, this was an aspect of his duty, as was fulfilling his role as Elector of Hanover, whatever the complaints of his British subjects.

6

George and Walpole:
Double Act or King in the Shadows?
1731–1741

Whatever their differences over foreign policy and ministerial composition in 1729–30 (see pp. 101–4), George supported Walpole in office until his fall in 1742, a fall that George sought to prevent and, subsequently, bitterly regretted. Indeed, in the second major ministerial crisis of his reign, that in 1733, George crucially and publicly backed Walpole against men who had earlier been the King's favourites. The King's position was central because the crisis of 1730 had not ended serious divisions in the ministry and Court. Opposition to Walpole continued.

This opposition could be linked to the dynastic position of the Hanoverians, as was aptly demonstrated in January 1733, when the government was able to intercept and decipher an instruction, sent from Frederick William I of Prussia to Count Degenfeld, his envoy in London, to thwart the intended marriage of William IV of Orange and Anne, the Princess Royal, Frederick William's niece. This instruction reflected the wide-ranging dynastic competition between George and Frederick William. To that end, Frederick William sought to play on animosities within the government which were clearly no secret:

> the jealousy which Robert Walpole has conceived against Lord Chesterfield may be improved by you, if you dextrously insinuate to the former what an overmatch of credit the effecting of that proposed marriage would give to the said Chesterfield with the King and Queen.[1]

Frederick William argued this because of Chesterfield's Dutch links, not least as recent envoy at The Hague. His letter reflected the close eye the Prussians kept on British politics, and the extent to which they understood these in terms of Court rivalries. A struggle to influence King and Queen was seen as crucial in the latter, as indeed was the case.

The 1733 crisis was unexpected because in 1731 and 1732 Walpole had appeared in secure control of the tempo of politics, and much to the benefit of George. The resignation of Townshend in 1730 had ensured that Walpole's position in the ministry was strengthened. He was now able to dominate policy, and this served to support the government's domestic position. The settlement of differences with Austria in 1731, by the Second Treaty of Vienna, somewhat implausibly presented by Newcastle as George 'singly' giving 'peace to all Europe',[2] led to a marked decline in the sense of international crisis. This helped lead to a fall in taxes. Indeed, the land tax fell to one shilling in the pound in 1732 and 1733. Parliamentary majorities for the government varied in 1731 and 1732, not least with opposition over taxation in 1732, but were generally comfortable. The ministry also survived a number of scandals, particularly in 1732.

Ironically, the situation deteriorated sharply in 1733 over what Walpole had not seen as likely to cause a major political storm, namely a proposal to extend the excise arrangements to cover wine and tobacco. He saw the proposal as a technical financial measure designed to make revenue raising more efficient, not least by cutting smuggling, but the opposition exploited fears that the government was going on to tax other commodities, and that it would deploy an army of excise officers to raid homes and control elections.[3] Both were crucial issues. The threat of excise duties on food (which were not in fact intended) seemed to move Britain closer to the image of a heavily taxed and regulated Continental state. The nature of excise powers indeed challenged suppositions about the constitution and the character of British liberties. All dealers and retailers had to register with the excise officials, who enjoyed powers of inspection and summary justice. Excise officers and commissioners were seen as arbitrary figures unconstrained by jury trials. Contemporaries could not believe that Walpole would not use the right to search by excise officers in elections as he had already employed customs officers to this end, for example in Liverpool. Indeed, the critical Master of the Rolls, Sir Joseph Jekyll, 'said he was sorry a Whig ministry would bring in a Bill, a Tory ministry never durst attempt'.[4]

Anti-excise material appeared in opposition newspapers towards the end of 1732, and it was clear that the legislation would be challenged, but it was not felt that there would be any more trouble than had occurred in previous years over such issues as Hessian subsidies. Initially, it seemed as though the session was going well, but, at the same that the government passed its other measures, public criticism of the Excise Scheme rose. On 6 February (os) 1733, Henry Goodricke wrote from London, 'The rising tempest of an excise makes a furious roar in this town . . . people have taken a general and violent prejudice to Sir Robert's proposal even before they know what it is; and elections being so near at hand many members [MPs] will be cautious how they vote full against the bent of their electors.'[5] This concern challenged assumptions about the efficacy of ministerial patronage of MPs.

On 10 April (os) 1733 the government majority in the House of Commons fell to 17. This was against an opposition motion to hear by counsel a petition from the City of London critical of the Excise Scheme. The petition was a testimony to the Scheme's unpopularity and to the opposition's skill in orchestrating a public campaign of criticism. The political temperature rose markedly. During the Excise alarms in London, George, indeed, is reported to have worn a wide-brimmed hat with lead-lining for protection and to have carried a pistol. He also avidly sought news of the debates in Parliament.

The Excise Crisis was more serious because it also brought to the fore tensions within the Whig elite. Chesterfield, Scarborough and Wilmington (the ennobled Compton) sought to exploit the crisis by pushing for a change in ministerial leadership, and Scarborough threatened to resign as Master of the Horse. Furthermore, Harrington was among others who took an ambiguous position in this crisis, while the opposition saw it as an opportunity to challenge the ministry.

Walpole in the end felt it necessary to abandon the Excise Bill on 11 April (os). London was illuminated by opposition supporters to mark the failure of the Bill, and Walpole was burned in effigy, but, by withdrawing the legislation, Walpole ensured that his majority in the House of Commons rose at once. However, this did not end the sense of crisis. The Duke of Bolton, the Earls of Chesterfield and Stair, Viscount Cobham and others, riding a wave of popular opposition, proved willing to co-operate with the Whig opposition in pressing for the removal of Walpole, creating a serious crisis in the House of Lords. In the event, it was George's backing that was crucial to ending the crisis. A number of prominent Whig peers, the Dukes of Bolton and Montrose, the Earls of Marchmont and Stair, and Viscount Cobham, were dismissed for voting with the opposition in the Lords. George was particularly proud of the army and the dismissal of officers, such as Cobham and Bolton, who opposed his minister was a conspicuous demonstration of royal authority and power. Chesterfield lost office (as Lord Steward of the Household), not Walpole.

The dismissals were a public show of royal support. Walpole was also responsible for the royal speech proroguing Parliament on 11 June (os) 1733, in which, the opposition, characterized as those who sought 'to inflame the minds of the people, and by the most unjust misrepresentations, to raise tumults and disorders', were attacked. George's support for Walpole had helped to divide the Court opposition to the minister, for, unlike Chesterfield, Cobham, Stair and several others, Harrington, Scarborough and Wilmington had proved unwilling to push their opposition in the face of royal disapproval. Had they done so, the crisis would have proved much more serious, but Wilmington was always unwilling to act without royal support. In August 1733, John Drummond MP wrote of 'the destruction of Sir Robert, which is not like to happen, for I never saw him easier at Court'.[6] Wilmington and Harrington were forced into acquiescence. However, the dismissals helped lose Walpole the backing in the Commons of the clients and allies of those who were dismissed.

It has been suggested that the expulsion from the ministry of men of talent weakened it. The ever-critical Sarah, Duchess of Marlborough commented in 1740, 'Sir Robert . . . never likes any but fools, and such as have lost all credit . . . I cannot reckon above two in the administration that have common senses.'[7] However, the expulsion also served to increase the stability of the government, because the presence of figures such as Chesterfield, who had been willing in 1733 to intrigue actively with sections of the opposition, had been a disruptive force. Thanks, moreover, to the close relationship between George and Walpole, the political tensions of the years 1714–17, 1720–1 and 1742–4, were not seen at a comparable scale or longevity in the 1730s. Rather than suggesting that Walpole's determination to dominate the government, and George's willingness to let him do so, should be seen as a source of ministerial instability, it is possible to argue that this instability, instead, resulted when Crown–ministry cohesion could not be secured, which was to be increasingly the case at the end of the 1730s as ministerial unity fractured.

Queen Caroline's support for Walpole was seen as very important in the 1730s, and was discussed as such in what was a considerable snub to the King as it implied that he could be readily manipulated. That, indeed, was part of the point of the criticism, which simultaneously implied that opposition was legitimated by this manipulation and also tried to stir up George against the ministry. In 1731, William Pulteney, the opposition Whig leader in the Commons, in public 'alluded to the report that Sir Robert Walpole is only supported by the Queen'.[8] The *Craftsman*, the leading opposition newspaper, in its issue of 15 September (os) 1733, described politics in terms of chess, with Walpole as the Knight: 'see him jump over the heads of the nobles . . . when he is guarded by the Queen, he makes dreadful havoc, and very often checkmates the King.' George testified to the closeness and support of his relationship with Caroline, revealing, soon after she died in 1737, the 'great reliefs and assistance which he found from her calm and masterly disposition and opinion in governing such a humoursome and inconstant people; that her presence of mind often supported him in trying times, and her sweetness of temper would check and assuage his own hastiness and resentment'.[9] Their more critical son, speaking in hindsight, argued that emotion, rather than reason, was the key element. He said of his father, 'no one could manage him but the Queen, and she with tears and fits.'[10] With his stress on order, George did not like shows of disorder by others.

Diplomats also commented on the Queen's influence, François-Marie, Duke of Broglie, the French envoy, reporting in 1730 that Walpole and Caroline were co-operating to quieten George's concerns as Elector about threatening developments in Mecklenburg.[11] Caroline's influence, however, was less than was usually credited, not least because she did not accompany George on his lengthy visits to Hanover, although they corresponded when he was away. Instead, she remained with the children in Britain and acted as regent. Walpole's support from Caroline also had its limits. During the War of the Polish Succession (1733–5), she was more favourable to British support for Austria than Walpole, although less so than George was. This war was touched off by a contest over the Polish throne. Stanislaus Leszcynski was elected King, but the Russians saw him as an unacceptable candidate because of his French and Swedish connections. The Russians invaded Poland, captured Warsaw, and had the new Elector of Saxony elected King. The Poles proved unable to challenge the Russians successfully in the field and a small French force sent to relieve besieged Danzig in 1734 was easily defeated.

Louis XV of France, Stanislaus's son-in-law, however, saw the Russian action as an attack on his honour, and in October 1733 declared war on the Emperor Charles VI, ruler of Austria, holding him responsible for the Russian invasion of Poland. It was also far easier to attack Austria than its ally Russia, and indeed France was joined in so doing by Philip V of Spain and Charles Emmanuel III of Sardinia. French and Sardinian forces easily overran the Milanese that winter, while the French also overran Lorraine, whose Duke was likely to become the husband of Charles's heir, Maria Theresa.

Despite obligations to Austria under the Second Treaty of Vienna of 1731, Britain was neutral in the conflict.[12] However, in contrast to his position as King, George II, as Elector, was active in rejecting a Prussian approach to maintain peace in the Empire jointly (an attempt at neutrality), and, instead, in voicing support for the Emperor, Charles VI. Furthermore, 5,600 Hanoverian troops served in the Imperial army on the Rhine. George had delayed sending his troops in early 1734 when Austria pressed for assistance against France, but the threat, that spring, that a French army under Marshal Belle-Isle, who captured Trier and Trarbach in the Moselle valley in April, would move on to seize the Rhine crossing at Rheinfels and invade Hanover's ally and neighbour, Hesse-Cassel, led George to decide to dispatch them. He also pressed for the occupation of the fortress of Rheinfels by Hesse-Cassel troops, and instructed Thomas Robinson, the British envoy, to exert influence upon Austria to condone such an occupation.[13] This was a clear use of the British diplomatic system for a Hanoverian goal, and one that ignored the spirit of British neutrality.

It is too easy to see the war, as it is generally presented, as an episode in which George's desire that Britain take part in the conflict was thwarted by Walpole, so that, as pro-governmental spokesmen, such as the anonymous writer of the *London Journal* of 1 May (os) 1736 pointed out, Britain and Hanover did not act together in the war. The evidence offered to this end, however, in Hervey's oft-cited *Memoirs*, which dealt at length with the crisis, is insufficient. George certainly complained about his British ministers and the need to consider Parliament, but Hervey's view of George, as a monarch readily manipulated by Caroline and Walpole, presented George in overly simplistic terms, and, crucially, underplayed the King's ability to further his own views. As much of the evidence throughout the period for clashes between monarch and ministers over foreign policy is fragmentary or elusive, it is not surprising that great weight has been placed on British neutrality during the War of the Polish Succession, but the evidence about that only extends so far.

It is also necessary to move away from the theatrical starkness of Hervey's highly coloured palette. Rather than seeing George as an unthinking supporter of the Austrian cause, it is important to note longstanding and continuing tension in the relationship, tension that was also to emerge in the 1740s and 1750s. In part, this was cultural, more specifically the effect of George's clear commitment to German Protestantism. This appeared under challenge from a last upsurge in the Catholic Counter-Reformation, one that was especially associated with an Austria whose cultural values and ideological thrust can be gauged from Charles VI's palace-monastery at Klosterneuburg: George II had no even pale equivalent.

There was also a range of diplomatic issues in dispute in 1731–3 between George and Charles, issues that remained important thereafter during the years of the War of the Polish Succession. Some may appear technical, but each contributed to poor relations and most centred on the geopolitics of power in northern Germany, the area closest to George's concerns. For example, in 1731, the Austrians suggested that George and the Czarina Anna of Russia should reciprocally guarantee their dominions, and that George should undertake to obtain an equivalent for her relative, Karl Frederick, Duke of Holstein-Gottorp for the lands he had lost to Denmark in the Great Northern War (1700–21), a provision that would have gravely compromised Hanoverian interests, as Hanover had gained the Duchies of Bremen and Verden as part of this settlement. George rejected both suggestions, and insisted that Anglo-Russian relations should be resolved by the two powers in separate negotiations.[14] By rejecting the Austrian proposals, George showed his determination to maintain his alliances with Denmark and Sweden.

George's views, however, contributed to a fatal ambivalence that affected Austrian policy in the Holy Roman Empire and, more generally, in northern Europe. The conflicting diplomatic interests of, on the one hand, Prussia and Russia and, on the other, George, proved very difficult to reconcile. Austria tended to support Prussia and Russia, and George was angered and confused by actual or supposed Austrian support for marriages between the houses of Prussia and Brunswick-Bevern (the latter rivals to Hanover), the Prussian cause in Mecklenburg, the Prusso-Russian marriage project, which threatened to link the two states, and the negotiations for the Treaty of Copenhagen of 1732. Each of these seriously challenged George's views as Elector. Disputes over these issues helped to embitter Anglo-Austrian relations and, in particular, to anger George, so that, by early 1733, the alliance was in parlous state.

Furthermore, the commitment to the integrity of the Habsburg succession entered into by George in 1731 was conditional. This commitment was in the shape of the guarantee of the Pragmatic Sanction, the provision under which the entire inheritance was to go to Charles VI's elder daughter, Maria Theresa (he had no sons). George had wished to include in the Second Treaty of Vienna a stipulation that the guarantee would depend upon the husbands selected for Maria Theresa and her sister, 'His Majesty is willing still that none of the Arch-Duchesses should be married to any Prince that might give any just grounds of jealousy as to the balance of power in Europe.'[15] The Emperor, who had offered in 1729 and 1730 to guarantee that no marriage detrimental to the balance of power should be negotiated, felt it was dishonourable to have his daughters' marital choice restricted in a public treaty, and it was therefore decided that a secret article should be resorted to. This article released George as King from his obligations to the Emperor in the event of a Bourbon or Prussian marriage for Maria Theresa.

This very much reflected George's views. In 1728 he had been reported as insistent on such a stipulation,[16] and the ban on a Prussian marriage reflected the fear that Crown Prince Frederick of Prussia would be forced to convert to Catholicism to enable him to marry Maria Theresa, which would have been a fundamental blow to the Protestant interest in Germany.

The secret article served another important function that represented an important continuity between the policies of George I and those of George II. By linking the guarantee to an exclusion of any Bourbon marriage, it restricted the possibility of the Austrians reviving an Austro-Spanish alliance based on the 1725 First Treaty of Vienna between the two powers. Concern about this alliance had been key to British policy in 1725–9.[17] Due to the detaching of Spain from this alliance in 1729 and its linkage with Britain and France under the Treaty of Seville, this possibility was no longer a strong one in 1731, but it could not be discounted, and such an alliance was indeed to be suggested in 1735 as a solution to the War of the Polish Succession. The issue was not simply a matter of Hanoverian policy. It also looked back to British anxieties, both those based on the 1725 treaty, and also the concerns created in the latter stages of the War of the Spanish Succession by the prospect of a union of the Austrian and Spanish inheritances in the person of Charles VI, who as Charles III, was the Habsburg candidate for the Spanish throne.

In the event, Maria Theresa was married in a way that fully satisfied George, which helped explain his subsequent pro-Austrian role as Elector of Hanover during the War of the Austrian Succession (1740–8). She married Duke Francis III of Lorraine in 1736, and her sister married his brother Charles, later a prominent general. These marriages had been strongly advocated by George, who had been much impressed by Francis on his visit to England in the autumn of 1731,[18] and had urged the Austrians to declare that the marriage of Maria Theresa and Francis would take place. This serves as a reminder of the cross-currents in relations between George and Charles VI.

Alongside the Hanover-Britain-Austria question, issues were raised by George's anxiety about Prussia. Relations between the two had deteriorated in 1733. There were continued differences over the situation in, and succession to, the territory of East Friesland, a territory based on the port of Emden, the future succession to which was sought by both George and Frederick William. East Friesland would expand Hanover's North Sea coastline, but in Prussia's hands would further a sense of Hanover as surrounded. British diplomats, such as William Finch in The Hague, were instructed to stay in touch over the issue with the ministers in Hanover.[19]

Furthermore, George, as both King and Elector, in the spring of 1733, promised assistance to the Dutch in a dispute over Prussian recruiting that threatened to lead to a Prussian attack. The entire episode throws light on the problems of treating every issue as either British or Hanoverian, and thus of assessing George's policy towards Prussia from the perspective of blame, specifically of narrow Hanoverian views. The episode also illustrates the difficulties of following the opposition propaganda line about the Hanoverian interests driving British policy. Frederick William claimed that the dispute was not the business of Britain. However, both Britain and Hanover would have been affected had Prussia succeeded in intimidating the Dutch, because they were a key ally for Britain and also a possible support for Hanover.

In addition, attempts to stabilize the situation in the Duchy of Mecklenburg, a key issue for George, had failed in 1731–33. The resumption of civil war in the duchy in September 1733 led to Hanoverian, Prussian and Wolfenbüttel movements of troops into it. George used British diplomats to press Austria and Russia to persuade Frederick William to remove his forces, which were the major (though not the sole) limitation on Hanoverian action, but Frederick William broke a promise to do so. In response, in order to ensure more Austrian pressure on Prussia, George delayed the march of his troops to join the Imperial army on the Rhine, which scarcely conforms to the pro-Imperial attitude described by Hervey. In the event, Hanoverian troops continued in Mecklenburg until 1735, and Hanover remained in control of eight districts until a loan was redeemed in 1768. This loan was an important financial asset for George. Prussian units continued in the duchy until 1787.[20] George, moreover, was correctly seen as personally disliking Frederick William, Horatio Walpole observing in 1737 of the Jülich-Berg dispute (about the succession to two Rhenish territories held by the childless Elector Palatine), 'I am persuaded the King would scarce have any share in any accommodation that should give anything to the King of Prussia.'[21]

The order to the Hanoverian forces to march at once to the Rhine was not dispatched from London in 1734 until after letters had arrived from Prince William of Hesse-Cassel warning of the risk of a French crossing of the Rhine. Via the Hessian diplomat, General Ernst Diemar, there were private routes of correspondence between William and both George and Walpole. Diemar had a military background and was keen on hunting, both of which recommended him to George. The delay in ordering the march owed something to a dispute with Charles VI over the conditions of service of the Hanoverian troops, while George, in addition, had refused to send his troops until reassured about Prussian troop moves. At the same time, George's decision followed soon after the Reichstag declared war on behalf of the Empire. The Hanoverian troops reached the Imperial army on 2 June, swiftly earning praise from its commander, Prince Eugene, who had fought in the War of the Spanish Succession, including at Oudenaarde. George respected him, and Eugene had a confidential correspondence with Diemar, which served as an important route for links between London and Vienna, a route that was outside the formal diplomatic mechanisms of both countries.[22] Conversely, during the Austro-Turkish war of 1737–9, George refused to send troops because the Empire had not been consulted.[23]

The dispatch of the troops in 1734 indicated how George's Electoral position provided him with important opportunities for action he lacked as King. He had more authority as Elector than as King, which galled him. This was also grasped by foreign governments. When, in October 1733, Thomas Robinson, the envoy in Vienna, told Count Sinzendorf, the Austrian Chancellor, that an Anglo-Russian political alliance was impossible, as Parliament would never accept Russian demands, he was asked 'if H.M. then as Elector could not enter into a more extensive alliance'.[24] The Hanoverian dimension also created difficulties, in the shape of crossed lines, for British diplomacy. In 1734, Horatio Walpole wrote to his brother about orders received from George to correspond directly with Johann Philipp von Hattorf, head of the Hanoverian Chancery in London:

> this cannot go on for long without being perceived in the office, and consequently by Lord Harrington [Secretary of State for the Northern Department] . . . as it will I suppose relate to His Majesty's demands concerning a negotiation about Bergh and Juliers [Jülich-Berg]; and as I am afraid these demands will be unreasonable and break off the negotiation; it may not be proper that the correspondence should appear in the office.[25]

The dispatch of the troops to the Rhine also underlines the theme of security in Hanoverian policy, as this was the crucial factor in prompting George to act in 1734. It is also notable that there was much reviewing of troops by George on his 1735 visit to Hanover. Far from these reviews being simply symbolic in intention and cultural in background, and indeed providing him with something to do, he wished to be assured of the troops' quality and to send a message accordingly about Hanoverian strength and resolve.

In 1734–5, Prussian threats to intervene in the bitter quarrel between Denmark and the Imperial Free City of Hamburg raised George's concern anew about stability near Hanover, as well as the state of the Imperial constitution, and the respective power of nearby rulers. Denmark seemed, like Prussia, to be aggressively expansionist and absolutist, and George saw himself as the supporter of the constitution and of the rights of smaller powers. Again, however, it is unclear how precisely this issue affected his attitude to the War of the Polish Succession, to British neutrality in the conflict, and, therefore, to his position as King and as Elector.

George's ability to influence policy increased during his absences from London on his trips to Hanover. This made access to him a particularly sensitive issue, as the terms of this access varied with his trips there. During George's visits to Hanover, the correspondence of the Secretary of State who accompanied him tended very much to reflect the personal views of the King. Thus, the sense of George as anxious to justify his position, and as at the end of his tether, was captured in Harrington's 'most secret' letter to Newcastle of 12 June 1735. George, who had seen the report of the recent meeting between British and Dutch ministers to discuss the failure of their attempt to mediate in the War of the Polish Succession, was concerned about the 'justification of his own past and future conduct', and was resolved either to join with the Dutch, if they were ready, to take immediate steps 'for the preservation of the Balance of Europe', by acting against France, or, that failing, to advise Charles VI to settle with his opponents. There was little doubt from Harrington's letter of where George saw virtue lying: 'with spirit and vigour'. His concerns were also apparent: an anxiety that Charles

> either be diverted from pursuing such methods of accommodating his disputes with one or other of the Allies, as he may still probably have in his power, and upon which the safety of all Europe may depend, or tempted to exclude the Maritime Powers entirely from any share in such an accommodation, or even to conclude, as in the year 1725 directly to their prejudice . . . this appearing to the King to be the most prudent and honourable way of proceeding in the present unhappy circumstances, His Majesty has commanded me to put it immediately in execution by giving Count Kinsky [the Austrian envoy] a free and confidential account of the King's sentiments upon his master's affairs.[26]

In short, George held up the danger of Austria turning to Spain (as in 1725) which he correctly saw as detrimental to British interests. The focus in the discussion of British policy and the war tends to be on the period up to early 1735, when Horatio Walpole unsuccessfully attempted mediation. This was a period in which George's role could seem limited, even thwarted, as he was ambivalent about these negotiations. Far less attention has been devoted to the summer of 1735, when George took a much greater role in diplomacy. This looked toward the active part he took in 1741 in trying to rally support for Maria Theresa.

How George's role in 1735 would have developed is unclear, as secret Franco-Austrian negotiations brought the conflict to a close that year, with France abandoning her allies. However, George's search for a new solution serves as a reminder of the danger of judging a subject by simply one aspect or period, in this case the earlier part of the war. Hervey knew far less about George's role in Hanover than that in London.

The emphasis in the correspondence, both in 1735, and on other visits to Hanover, was very much on George's views. The press also stressed his role, the *Whitehall Evening Post* of 14 June (os) 1735 noting 'His Majesty is observed particularly to be locked up for several hours every day with Milord Harrington.' Foreign observers also commented on what they thought to be George's views, and presented George's moves, or their absence, as of significance. Thus, the King's failure in 1735 to notify Frederick William of his arrival in Hanover, or to compliment him on his convalescence, was seen as serious, which indeed it was, as there was a prospect of better Anglo-Prussian relations but it depended on a thaw in those between the two rulers.

It was conventional for the King to be accompanied to Hanover by the Secretary of State for the Northern Department, which had been the case with each of George I's trips, and with the first three of George II's (1729, 1732 and 1735), although, in 1723, both Secretaries of State accompanied George I to Hanover. Robert Walpole's concern about Townshend and Harrington was greatly accentuated by the time they spent with George II in Hanover. In 1736, however, Harrington did not go and, instead, Horatio Walpole went as acting Secretary of State. Whoever accompanied the King experienced problems because the minister found that Hanoverian officials played a major role in policy, at least in relations with Austria and Prussia, and in related matters. Thus, in 1736, the Saxon envoy, who had pressed for the renewal of the defensive treaty between Hanover and Saxony, reported that, because it was an Electoral matter, Horatio Walpole was not kept informed of the negotiations.[27]

In 1736, as later with George's visit to Hanover in 1748 after the close of the War of the Austrian Succession, the immediate post-war period provided opportunities for a fresh start in diplomacy. As in 1748, however, the prospect of better Anglo-Prussian relations was, in part, thwarted by particular Hanoverian interests as interpreted by George, although the views of successive Prussian monarchs were also a problem. In 1736, as in 1729, George was offended by Prussian recruiting in Hanover which he saw as detrimental to his honour and his army. His determination to have this recruiting stopped exacerbated a situation already made difficult by the mutual distrust of the two rulers. In 1737, anger with Prussian recruiting helped lead George to refuse to see Baron Börck, the new envoy in London.[28]

Then and later, George's concern about Hanover, and his far-from-secret personal obstinacy toward Frederick William, were faced not by a united British ministry determined to seek the support of Prussia, but by genuine uncertainty over how best to respond to Frederick William. George was certainly worried about Prussia. When, in March 1738, Louis-Dominque, Count of Cambis, the French envoy in London, urged that George, as Elector, prevent Prussian forces from advancing from Brandenburg to their Rhenish base at Cleves, from which they could exert pressure on Jülich and Berg, George responded that he would not let the Prussians through his territories, but that he was concerned about their strength and wanted Frederick William's anger to fall on France and Austria, and not on Hanover.[29]

George does not appear to have liked Horatio Walpole, who seems to have felt that his role was that of a minder and indeed tried to keep George in the dark about options. His nephew, Horace, commented in 1751:

> With the King he had long been in disgrace, on disputing a point of German genealogy with him (in which his Majesty's chief strength lay) whose the succession of some principality would be, if eleven or twelve persons, then living, should die without issue.[30]

Such a remark was typical of Horace, not least in that it reflected his wish to put the pen in, in this case by ridiculing both those he was referring to. The accuracy of the description may be queried; while, anyway, such issues of genealogy were very important to the East Friesland and Jülich-Berg disputes, each of which involved contested successions. The remark indeed illustrated George's advantage over his British ministers and diplomats by virtue of his (far) superior knowledge of German dynastic politics. George's reputation has suffered greatly from comments such as that by Horace Walpole, but in this case they can be qualified by noting a strong policy clash: Horatio Walpole supported reconciliation with Prussia, if necessary at the cost of Hanoverian interests, and it is not surprising that George allegedly blocked Horatio Walpole accompanying him to Hanover in 1740.[31]

The British press focused attention on relations with Prussia, attention that reflected the importance of George. The *Craftsman* of 20 January (os) 1739, carried a report from Hanover:

> The report which had been spread that the King of Great Britain will take a tour hither next summer is confirmed by our last letters from London, which add, that his Britannick Majesty's principal view in taking that journey, is to have an interview with the King of Prussia, in order to conclude a double marriage between the two royal families, and agree upon some measures proper to be put in execution for the support of the Protestant interest. It is likewise reported that their Britannick and Prussian Majesties will conclude a treaty of alliance together, which some other princes and states will be invited to come into; and that the design of this treaty is to prevent anything that may disturb the respose and tranquility of the Empire.

George, however, was not prepared to accept a reconciliation that sacrificed Hanoverian interests. Furthermore, Horatio was not only a fairly pushy individual, lacking in courtly graces, but also a diplomat who was not from a military background. Furthermore, Horatio was closely identified with good relations with the Fleury ministry in France, not a policy to which George was drawn and one to which he had never been emotionally committed, even when the two states were allied. Horatio himself argued that George's views were harmful to the entire direction of British policy. In September 1739, he wrote to his brother:

> I will tell you in confidence; little, low, partial, Electoral [ie. Hanoverian] notions are able to stop or confound the best con-
> ducted project for the public . . . In the mean time nobody has
> credit or courage enough to speak plainly upon these heads in their
> respective departments; and if you venture to do it sometimes, it is

in a cursory manner. You receive a short answer; domestic affairs employ your time and your thoughts; and the foreign mischief continues.[32]

The King's opposition to Horatio Walpole did not affect his relationship with Robert Walpole, who remained entrusted with both electoral (not Electoral) and parliamentary management. George himself did not take much of an interest in the mechanics of electoral returns and parliamentary patronage—he had ministers to do that for him, but he authorized expenditure and could take a direct role. Furthermore, George showed his views on contests in seats where the issue at stake was the strength of the government. In 1734, this included the triumph of the Pelham interest in the constituency of Lewes. George, 3rd Earl of Albemarle 'acquainted the King and Queen immediately with the good news, and they seemed to me to express a great and sincere satisfaction'.[33] This was understandable as it had been a close return, and the Pelhams only won by using the returning officers. Henry Pelham's victory in one of the two county seats for Sussex was also important.

Four years later, the appointment of Lord Vere Beauclerk as a Lord of the Admiralty obliged him, as a new place-holder, to stand for re-election for his parliamentary seat of New Windsor. Although the right of election lay with the inhabitants of the borough paying scot and lot (local rates), about 280 in total, and the constituency was therefore far from being a pocket borough under the control of a dominant patron, George was determined to have agreeable MPs chosen for what he saw as his borough. Beauclerk was not only in ministerial favour. His relative the 2nd Duke of St Albans was also conspicuously in royal favour, being both Constable of Windsor Castle and the Lord Lieutenant of Berkshire. In contrast, Richard Oldfield, the rival candidate, was backed by the Marlborough interest, including Sarah, the Dowager Duchess, who was the Ranger of Windsor Great Park. She noted George's determination to have Beauclerk elected, not least the King's remark in the Drawing Room, 'we have the returning officer', a remark repeated to indicate his interest and his partisan nature.[34] In the event, both candidates polled the same number of votes, leading to a double-return that the House of Commons, thanks to the ministerial strength, decided in favour of Beauclerk.

Thus parliamentary management by the ministry contributed to royal interests and vice versa. However, the dynastic interest was divided because of the political prominence of the electoral position of Frederick, Prince of Wales, particularly in 1741. He was able to deploy political interest in numerous constituencies, especially in Cornwall, of which the Prince was Duke. This was serious as the county was heavily over-represented in the House of Commons.

Caroline's influence was not as far-reaching as that of her contemporary Elizabeth Farnese over her husband, the idiosyncratic and very uxorious Philip V of Spain (1700–46), but it was considerable. Ministers, moreover, saw this influence as useful. Indeed, in 1736, Walpole got Caroline to press George against an alliance with Denmark and Sweden.[35] Close to Caroline, Walpole had claimed that Spencer Compton 'took the wrong sow by the ear . . . I the right',[36] when there was talk earlier in the reign about the popularity of George's mistress, Henrietta Howard, who had links with the opposition. George's favour for Henrietta had been seen as a sign that Walpole would not survive the change of monarch, but Walpole did not make the mistake of some ministers and courtiers of assuming that Henrietta was the power behind George as Prince of Wales. Indeed, after George became King, she enjoyed little power. Caroline's anger with whoever looked to Henrietta helped strengthen Walpole's position. Caroline allegedly turned against Chesterfield because she saw him win a large amount of money at cards which he deposited with Henrietta.

The relationship with Henrietta ended in late 1734, as George no longer found her attractive. The following year, she married George Berkeley, with whom she had a happy marriage. Instead, George turned to Mary Scott, Countess Dowager of Deloraine (1700–44), the governess of George's two youngest daughters, and a pretty woman who, however, was unable to hold George's interest.

Despite their disappointments about Henrietta, opposition politicians continued hopeful that Walpole's influence might decline if that of Caroline did. This became particularly important after Walpole's victory in the general election of 1734 as, under the Septennial Act, it would not be necessary to call another one until 1741 (unless the King died), and indeed none was called till then. In the mid-1730s, these opposition hopes focused on George's interest in his new mistress, Amalie Sophie Marianne von Wallmoden, with whom George began a relationship on his visit to Hanover in 1735. In contrast to Henrietta Howard, who was born in about 1688 and married in 1706, Wallmoden had been born in 1704 and married in 1727. She offered George youth and stability, characteristics which do not always go together, and, in 1736, he was reported as having promised her that he would return that year.[37] Indeed, George was highly attracted to Wallmoden,[38] and his long stay in Hanover that year—over six months—owed much to her. Horatio Walpole commented that George spending his birthday in London was not a way to 'satisfy the mob and tradesmen in England'. That December, William Pulteney reported:

> One Mrs Mopp, a famous bone-setter and mountebank, coming to town [London] in a coach with six horses on the Kentish Road, was met by a rabble of people, who, seeing her very oddly and tawdrily dressed, took her for a foreigner, and concluded she must be a certain great person's mistress. Upon this they followed the coach, bawling out, 'No Hanover Whore, No Hanover Whore'. The lady within the coach was much offended, let down the glass, and screamed louder than any of them, that she was no Hanover whore, she was an English one, upon which they all cried out, 'God bless your Ladyship', quitted the pursuit and wished her a good journey.[39]

Thus, Mrs Mopp reprised Nell Gwynn's patriotic claim under Charles II not to be French; a sentence that can be variously reordered without losing the meaning. When Wallmoden did arrive, the crowd cried 'Hanover whore' as a greeting.[40] George had a son, Johann Ludwig von Wallmoden (1736–1811), by Wallmoden, but he was not acknowledged because he was born before Wallmoden's divorce. The son, known initially as Monsieur Louis, became a Hanoverian general. He was to be unlucky in war, and was responsible for the surrender of the Electoral army when Napoleonic French forces attacked in 1803.

Despite George's keenness for Wallmoden, she did not challenge the Queen's position, and Caroline's power at Court remained readily apparent. Indeed, when George returned to St James's in January 1737, he was particularly nice to Caroline. Furthermore, although she had a role at Hanover, Wallmoden was not to play one in the British Court until after Caroline died. The Queen would not have accepted her presence and the ministry took the same view.[41] Nevertheless, she had to accept public knowledge of George's new relationship. Hervey cited two satires written, he alleged, by Chesterfield:

Great George escaped from narrow seas and storms
Now rides at large in Carolina's arms.
Bold Jonah thus, as holy writ will tell ye,
A whale received at once into her belly.

and

What! just escaped from Cleopatra's charms
To souse at once into your Fulvia's arms?
With equal violence of haste to run
From blooming twenty to fat fifty-one.
Was it for this the youth abroad was sent,
And so much gold unprofitably spent?
So travelled Hottentot, refined in vain,
Returns with rapture to his Cyutts [cabin] again.[42]

George himself seemed bored after his return from Hanover, and unwilling to leave the palace.[43]

Frederick, Prince of Wales proved a more serious irritation for the Queen. Having developed political links with opposition Whigs, he was increasingly seen as a 'Patriot Prince', and thus as an antithesis to a Hanoverian King. This was particularly marked in 1736, when opposition Whigs, self-styled 'Patriots', congratulated Frederick on his marriage to Augusta of Saxe-Gotha, claiming that the marriage had been forced on George and Walpole by popular demand. The ministry discovered that Frederick was encouraged by Frederick William of Prussia, which was not the way to win George's sympathy. Indeed, George refused to receive the new Prussian envoy, Baron Börck, which was a significant snub.

As a result of his marriage, George increased Frederick's Civil List allowance to £50,000 but, in early 1737, the Prince, who had substantial debts, demanded that this be doubled. He chose to do so by favouring an opposition motion to that end in the Commons, and, by so doing, slighted the willingness of George and Walpole to find the money for the young Court by also giving Augusta an allowance of £50,000. On 21 February (os), a group of peers accordingly carried a message from father to son:

His Majesty has commanded us to acquaint your Royal Highness in his name, that, upon your Royal Highnesses marriage, he immediately took into His Royal consideration the settling a proper joynture upon the Princess of Wales; but his sudden going abroad [in 1736], and his late indisposition since his return had hitherto retarded the execution of those his gracious intentions, from which short delay His Majesty did not apprehend any inconveniencies could arise, especially since no application had, in any manner, been made to Him upon this subject by your Royal Highness, and that His Majesty has now given orders, for settling a joynture upon the Princess of Wales, as far as he is enabled by law, suitable to her high rank and dignity, which he will, in proper time, lay before his Parliament, in order to be rendered certain, and effectual for the benefit of Her Royal Highness.

George set out his position in terms of his responsibilities to the entire royal family: '. . . His Majesty thinks a very competent allowance, considering his numerous issue, and the great expenses which do, and must necessarily attend an honorable provision for his whole royal family.'[44] Frederick, however, replied verbally, 'it is in other hands: I am sorry for it.'[45] The opposition, in the event, was unable to win parliamentary support in either house, being defeated in the Commons by 234 to 204 votes[46] and in the Lords by 103 to 40. Although Carteret's comparison in the Lords between Frederick and Edward, the Black Prince, a renowned fourteenth-century warrior, was risible, the political centrality of the issue was a noteworthy comment on the key role of the politics of the royal family. Edward Weston, an Under Secretary, commented that the matter 'ingrosses everybody's attention so much that little time is employed upon foreign business', while Robert Walpole wrote to Waldegrave:

> Your Lordship will not very much wonder that we have been behind hand of late in our foreign correspondencies, considering how fully we have been employed in our domestic broils and contests, the most troublesome I ever knew, and from the great objects of division, the most dangerous that could have been attempted.[47]

Such divisions within the royal family increased public interest in rumours about the Court. George and Caroline decided not to turn the Prince out of St James's, where the royal Court then was, but that summer there was a total breakdown in relations. The pregnant Augusta went into labour on 31 July (os) 1737, and Frederick insisted that she leave Hampton Court, where the royal Court was in residence, and go instead to St James's, where there were no preparations for her giving birth. Frederick did so in order to distance himself from his father, but this step infuriated his parents; George writing to his son on 3 August (os) that it was 'a deliberate indignity'.[48] This was not simply a matter of personal slight. Concerns about the legitimacy of the succession, which had been driven to the fore by false claims that the son born to James II and VII's wife, Mary of Modena, in 1688 was introduced into the bedchamber in a warming pan, ensured that Privy Councillors were supposed to be present at the birth of an heir apparent. Frederick indeed sent messengers, while en route to St James's, to summon Privy Councillors, but he was seen as irresponsible as well as neglectful of his duty to his parents. This irresponsibility extended to the lack of any prepared bed for the Princess's labour.

George and Caroline refused to see Frederick after Augusta, the daughter born that day, was baptized on 29 August (os), although, unlike the George William born to Caroline in 1717 during a similar rift (see pp. 46–7), she was to have a long life. On 10 September (os), Frederick and his family were ordered to leave St James's as soon as Augusta was well enough to do so. George wrote to Frederick:

> The professions you have lately made in your letters, of your particular regard to me, are so contradictory to all your actions, that I cannot suffer myself to be imposed upon by them . . . an evidence of your premeditated defiance of me, and such a contempt to my authority, and of the natural rights belonging to your parents . . . the whole tenour of your conduct for a considerable time has been so entirely void of all real duty to me, that I have long had reason to be highly offended with you.
>
> And until you withdraw your regard and confidence from those by whose instigation and advice you are directed and encouraged in your unwarrantable behaviour to me and to the Queen, and until you return to your duty, you shall not reside in my palace, which I will not suffer to be made the resort of them who are under the appearance of an attachment to you, foment the division which you have made in my family, and thereby weaken the common interest of the whole.[49]

The reference to Caroline was significant as was the stress on obedience and duty. Frederick left St James's on 12 September (os). He moved to Norfolk House, St James's Square, until, in 1743, he transferred to nearby Leicester House. George also banned anyone who held royal office from entering Frederick's presence, and withdrew the guard from his residences, a public display of the Prince's loss of favour. The echoes of the dispute between George and his father in 1717 were clear. This hostility between George and Frederick was maintained when Caroline fell ill, George sending a message on 11 November (os) 1737, 'in the present situation and circumstances, His Majesty does not think fit, that the Prince should see the Queen, and therefore expects he should not come to St James's.'[50]

Frederick now seemed securely in the opposition camp. Confident that the Queen's support for Walpole had been crucial, the opposition, however, were disappointed in their hope that the minister would fall after Caroline's death on 20 November (os) 1737 following painful surgery for a rupture. George, who had spent much time with her during her final illness, frequently sleeping at the foot of her bed, was conspicuously upset.[51] He also revealed a sentimental side when he ordered that one side of her coffin should be removed so that, after his own death, one side of his own coffin could also be removed, and their bones could be joined in death. The anthem 'The Ways of Zion do Mourn' was commissioned from Handel for the funeral. The entire episode is noteworthy as it indicates the sentimental side to George that it is too easy to forget. There is also a reminder of the emotionalism that seems to have been held in check by George's emphasis on order and duty. This was a preference that he appears to have thought important for others as well as himself, and this seems to have conditioned his attitude to his two sons.

Caroline's death led to a regularization of George's emotional life, although not as Caroline advised. On her deathbed, she had urged George to marry again, meeting the sobbing rejoinder that he would only take mistresses. The two sides of his British life—with Caroline and his sexual relationship with Mary Scott, who George complained 'stank of Spanish wine so abominably of late'[52]—were replaced when Wallmoden came to London in June 1738. This was a step taken with Walpole's advice, for the minister thought that George needed female guidance, and felt that Wallmoden, who had no links with the opposition, would suit his purposes, as indeed proved the case. In doing so, he also underlined the failure of Cumberland and Newcastle to use George's daughter Princess Amelia as a substitute for Caroline in her role as royal hostess, and one moreover through whom they could hope to influence George and persuade him to dispense with Walpole. Thus, the King's favours were linked to Court and ministerial factionalism. Indeed, Ossorio had claimed that Walpole and Newcastle had rowed over Wallmoden, with George playing a role in the dispute. The appointment of her relative Ernst, Freiherr von Steinberg as the new head of the Hanoverian Chancery in London was also significant.[53] There is, however, very little reliable evidence on such points.

In December 1738, George was depicted in the caricature 'Solomon in his Glory'. This showed the King on a couch with his leg over those of Wallmoden. He is dropping his sceptre as she rests her hand on his knee. A portrait of Caroline is on the wall, as is a mourning outfit for her. The caption, from *Proverbs*, was an ironic comment on George:

> Come let us take our fill of love until the morning. Let us solace ourselves with love; for the good man is not at home. He is gone a long journey, He hath taken a bag of money with him and will come home at the day appointed.

The theme in the caricature was of Caroline betrayed, a theme highlighted by the symbols of neglect and indulgence displayed around the lascivious couple. Wallmoden appeared as making advances, and George as self-indulgent, and as failing as a monarch.

Wallmoden's role was certainly acknowledged, as she acted as George's hostess at Court and had apartments at St James's and Kensington Palace. In February 1740, she became a naturalized British subject, being created Countess of Yarmouth for life the following month. Her husband, Gottlieb Adam von Wallmoden, divorced her that summer, but this did not arouse much of a response in Britain. Yarmouth was to be of some consequence in Court politics because of her access to George. Indeed, in 1756–7, during the Devonshire ministry, the twice-weekly levée presided over by the leading minister was held in her apartments. Hardwicke described the crowd there.[54] Yarmouth also discussed politics with foreign envoys.[55]

In some respects, Yarmouth matched the position of Melusine von der Schulenburg (1667–1745), who was George I's lover from at least 1691, having three daughters with him; they were passed off as the children of her sisters. Melusine, who was kind, well-educated, and from a prominent family, provided George with the calmness he did not find in his excitable and angry wife. When George became King, Melusine and their daughters came to Britain, and were installed at St James's Palace. Naturalized as British in 1716, she became Duchess of Munster in the Irish peerage that year, and Duchess of Kendal in the British peerage three years later. Yarmouth was a less conspicuous figure than Melusine had been, but, nevertheless, was believed to be influential. In the caricature 'The Scotch Patriot', published in May 1740, which depicted Argyll going into opposition, he is shown taking his leave of George and Yarmouth. The latter was George's mistress, but the degree of closeness and emotional support might make the modern term partner seem more appropriate, although that would be anachronistic if applied to her. By 1742, another caricature, 'The Court Shuttlecock', could represent the relationship as in difficulties, with Yarmouth, complaining 'Your Cockee my Love mounts rarely in Yarmouth', and Walpole's illegitimate daughter, Maria, declaring her willingness to replace Yarmouth. She was not in fact to do so, and the relationship between George and Yarmouth continued until his death, and was apparently a close companionship.

The political relationship between King and first minister was not disrupted by the death of the Queen nor by Wallmoden's rise. Instead, after Caroline's death, George, who appreciated Walpole's ability, promised his continued support. Opposition commentators had exaggerated Caroline's influence and importance to Walpole's position and, anyway, as George became older and increasingly irascible, he had become less easily led by his wife. Walpole, nevertheless, still had to be careful about George's views. In 1740, he angered the King by being opposed to his projected visit to Hanover, and had to write in very fulsome terms:

> Your countenance and goodness have been my only support in uncommon difficulties and under that protection I have been able to despise and defy all opposition, but the power of serving with success depends solely upon the proportion of credit and confidence you are pleased to give. When that is withdrawn or diminished, I shall become an useless and unprofitable servant.[56]

Despite bad attacks of piles after his returns from his 1735 and 1736 trips to Hanover, George himself stayed largely fit and healthy.

There were reports of ill-health, but some were from unreliably hostile commentators, such as the splenetic Sarah, Duchess of Marlborough, who, in January 1738, reported that George was near dead, and certainly very ill, adding 'so much changed in his manner, that he does everything he is desired, and signs what is brought him, without enquiring into it'.[57] A year earlier, John Couraud, an Under Secretary, had observed 'a slight aguish indisposition the King has felt by fits 3 or 4 days past',[58] and, although others suggested that the situation was more serious, there was no sustained illness.[59] George was certainly able to work hard. In 1739, he boasted 'no business ever stayed one moment for him',[60] a claim that was important to the dutiful King.

Royal support for Walpole was provided until the end of his ministry, and George indeed was a more consistent and loyal support than he was later to be for Newcastle, who was a key minister in the late 1740s and 1750s, although only First Lord of the Treasury in 1754–6 and 1757–62. George's backing for Walpole was seen for example in the disposal of army patronage, which was closely guarded by the King and employed to help Walpole. In 1736, William Pitt was sacked from his commission for opposing the government in the House of Commons. Sarah Marlborough remarked that March,

> It is said they don't intend to turn out anybody in the King's service who voted . . . for the Prince [of Wales] in either House. If they don't, I think that shows some fear, for Sir Robert in the House of Commons in the debate where it was taken notice of the shameful things they had done in turning out officers of great merit said that a minister must be a very pitiful fellow if he did not turn out officers who pretended to meddle with the civil government.

Two months later, however, Lady Irwin noted:

> The King two days ago turned out Mr. Pitt from a Cornecy [sic] for having voted and spoke in Parliament contrary to his approbation; he is a young man of no fortune, a very pretty speaker, one the Prince is particular to, and under the tuition of my Lord Cobham.[61]

George's attitude was crucial. Pitt had offended him by praising his heir and suggesting that Frederick's marriage to Augusta of Saxe-Gotha was due to the Prince and to public opinion, rather than to George. It was implied that George was mean, and more concerned about limiting the Civil List, by avoiding the necessary provision for a married heir, than with ensuring the succession by arranging Frederick's marriage. Pitt went on to advise the Prince to pursue his quarrel with George over his allocation under the Civil List in Parliament, to become a Groom of the Bedchamber to the Prince, and to attack his treatment over his army commission. The parliamentary attacks, in February 1737 and February 1738, were launched against Walpole, but George was obviously closely involved, and was also a target.

Willing to strike against Pitt, George, however, was determined to maintain his control of the army against all-comers, whether opposition politicians or his own ministers. Indeed, Horatio Walpole recorded in 1740 that his brother was snubbed by George:

> when he lets fall a word or two in favour of some officer, is told (that is between you and me) that he does not understand any thing of military matters, and by this means he has often the ill will of disappointments, which were not in his power to prevent . . . Sir Robert has very little to do in the military promotions; he recommends friends and relations of members of Parliament to be ensigns and cornets, but his Majesty himself keeps an exact account of all the officers; knows their characters, and their long services, and generally nominates, at his own time, the colonels to vacant regiments.[62]

'At his own time' meant that George would not be hurried to suit his minister and his political calculations. Nevertheless, George also helped Walpole with appointments to the army. In 1740, Sir James Lowther observed, 'Colonel Mordaunt has got a regiment, they give almost all of them to young colonels that are in the House.'[63] John Mordaunt (1697–1780), a Walpole loyalist, had indeed received army promotion. At the same time, Mordaunt was also a protégé of the King. The grandson of a Viscount, he was an equerry to George from 1737 to 1760, and was promoted by him through the ranks of general (Brigadier-General, 1745, Major-General, 1747, Lieutenant-General, 1754) and became a Knight of the Bath in 1749.

George's support for Walpole was not restricted to army appointments. In February 1740, Walpole told Dudley Ryder:

that he had the only confidence with the King, with whom he often talked freely. That the King often showed him letters and complaints which he had received privately against him . . . the King always then flew into passions against Sir Robert's enemies.[64]

George could relax with Walpole, and an angry Chesterfield was clearly thinking of George and Walpole when he told the House of Lords in 1740, 'Kings are generally for consulting with such as are of their own choosing, and these are so often such as have no dignity, privilege or right by their birth.'[65] In short, a lack of ministerial dignity could be unworthy of the King other than in serving base intentions. Intent on retaining control of the Commons, Walpole remained a commoner.

Walpole could not take George for granted, and the King could be very stubborn in resisting patronage demands, as in 1738 when he responded to Robert Walpole 'in a very dry and short way "that he would not do it, he had a person of his own to give it to".'[66] The following year, George did not want to appoint Robert Trevor as Envoy Extraordinary and Plenipotentiary at The Hague. Robert broke the news to his brother Horatio, Trevor's patron:

> It is impossible for you to leave the Hague before somebody or other is there to relieve you, and at this juncture it can be nobody but Mr. Trevor that can do the business, but this consideration will just now have no other effect upon the King, but to make him very angry with Mr. Trevor, and order us to think immediately upon somebody else.

Appointed Envoy Extraordinary in September 1739, Trevor wanted the additional appointment as Plenipotentiary, which would have given him more money and status, but found George resistant. Hanover was seen as a more appropriate setting for patronage requests as George was believed to be in a better temper there, not least because of 'the attention of the subjects to please'. Horatio was able to write in December 1740 that the King 'began to relent on your account, but complained of the great sums employed, in support of his foreign ministers'. Payments for diplomats came from the Civil List. It was not until the following July that Trevor gained the promotion he coveted.[67]

Similarly, Benjamin Keene, a protégé of Walpole, who was the Envoy Extraordinary and Plenipotentiary in Spain, was denied the promotion to Ambassador he sought until his second embassy there in 1749. This presumably reflected not simply George's determination to limit costs but also the fact that Keene was a commoner, albeit the eldest son of the Mayor of King's Lynn. He was not granted honorific promotion, the Order of the Bath, until 1754. In 1738, on another matter of patronage, the 14th Earl of Malton was informed that, although Walpole had pressed the King, 'he had the misfortune and concern to find that he could not prevail'.[68]

Clashes could lead to rumours of separation between King and minister, but they were far-fetched, as in the anonymous report sent in 1738 to Waldegrave, then envoy in Paris, which conveyed 'news . . . that His Majesty is grown so indifferent to Sir Robert that he has sent for his Hanover ministers to direct his councils and have his confidence; which they imagine may unite the two parties and hurt the establishment as neither of them would like a foreigner to preside as minister or director of his Majesty's councils in England.'[69] In fact, leaving matters to his first minister, George did not play a major role in the politics of the period other than by his important show of consistent support.

After the political crisis of 1733, George needed to devote relatively little attention to the political situation in Britain until 1739–40, because Walpole appeared in secure control. Indeed, following his victory in the 1734 elections, Walpole was able to maintain his position in the Commons until the aftermath of the 1741 elections. However, he was placed under increasing difficulties as a result of divisions within the government, in particular as a result of Newcastle challenging his foreign policy and patronage decisions. When he had the chance to do so, Newcastle hated taking responsibility, but the Duke likewise loathed playing second fiddle.

Caroline's death was not to provide an occasion for any reconciliation in the royal family. The ailing Caroline had herself pressed George to keep Walpole in power, and he did so.[70] Frederick sought to be the chief mourner at his mother's funeral, but George decided, instead, that Amelia should have this honour.[71] This was a sign of the prominence that Amelia was to have at George's Court, certainly after the last attempts to marry her off faded away in the 1740s. The Prince was not to gain the allowance of £100,000 that the King had received as Prince of Wales until 1742, and, until then, his active opposition was a major challenge to the stability of the government. This matched the situation in 1717–20, when George, as Prince of Wales, had been in opposition to his father George I; but, as a sign of changes in the political culture during the century, the antipathy between George III and his eldest son, the future George IV, in the 1780s, while still very important, did not compare in its political impact to that between George II and Prince Frederick, although it came close to doing so in the Regency Crisis of 1788–9, and would have done so had George III died then.

The dispute between George II and Frederick, Prince of Wales was not extraneous to the growing ministerial and political tensions of Walpole's last years as first minister. Instead, it served as a fundamental question-mark against the continuity of current arrangements. George's age further made this an issue. If, as yet, there was no sign that he was very ill, let alone close to death, the passing of the Queen had served to underline the transience of rulers. If her death had not resulted in a Court revolution, still less a governmental one, it was more than a passing intimation of change.

7

Turmoil and Crisis
1741–1746

Rivalries within the royal family, both narrowly and widely defined, posed key political problems at the beginning of the 1740s. The crucial rivalries were between George and his eldest son, Frederick, Prince of Wales, and between George and his nephew, Frederick II, the Great, of Prussia. Both were important issues, but, in the event, Frederick II came to the throne of Prussia in 1740 and launched that December what soon became a major European war, before his first cousin (who would never deserve the epithet great) could challenge his father at the general election of 1741.

George had hoped that the accession to the Prussian throne of Frederick II would transform the diplomatic situation, as Frederick, while heir, had been given money secretly by George in the 1730s. Had Frederick co-operated with his uncle, then Hanover would have been reasonably secure. As a result, without worrying about its vulnerability, George could have taken a more assertive stance in the international crisis created by the death, without sons in 1740, of the Emperor Charles VI, ruler of the Habsburg dominions (centred on Austria). Charles's eldest daughter, Maria Theresa, inherited his dominions, George, indeed, sought co-operation with Frederick on the basis of supporting the Habsburg succession, although his British ministers were concerned that the chances of co-operation were unduly limited by his determination to secure Hanoverian interests. To George, support for Maria Theresa was an opportunity for improved links with Austria in the hope that the latter would abandon the good relations with France that had prevailed since the end of the War of the Polish Succession.[1] The King sought to muster diplomatic support, pressing Ossorio, for example, on successive days on the need for a clear plan in the event of France trying to exploit Charles's death.[2]

Frederick chose, however, to follow an independent course, repaying his uncle's money and attacking Austria by invading the wealthy province of Silesia (now south-west Poland), beginning the War of the Austrian Succession (1740–8).[3] In response, an angry George told the Saxon envoy Utterodt that Frederick was a prince guided only by ambition and the desire for aggrandizement, that he negotiated everywhere for support for his aggression, and that, if Frederick's pretexts for the invasion of Silesia were accepted, no ruler could be secure in his German possessions. Indeed, George feared that France would seek to exploit the situation.[4]

Horatio Walpole, however, observed 'our master is divided between resentment and fears; he cannot bear to think of augmenting the territories of his Electoral neighbour [Prussia] on one side, and he justly apprehends that his own dominions should fall first a sacrifice should he stir on the others.' As Elector, George thus needed the security provided by allies. In January 1741, in response to Frederick's invasion, George planned action by Austria, Saxony, Hanover, the United Provinces and Russia, with British assistance.[5] The resources of British diplomacy were to be mobilized to thwart Frederick, and that at a time when there was already war with Spain, the War of Jenkins' Ear. This had broken out in 1739 as a result of the inability to sustain a settlement to Anglo-Spanish disputes over British trade to Spanish America. In March 1741, George told Ossorio that he was resolved to carry out his engagements to Maria Theresa.[6]

Frederick only wanted a short war, and, after defeating the Austrians at Möllwitz on 10 April 1741, consolidated his rapid conquest of Silesia. However, Maria Theresa refused to accept its loss and chose to fight on. As a result, Frederick, in June 1741, negotiated an alliance with France. Following this, France militarily intervened in Germany, its troops beginning to cross the Rhine on 15 August, as well as encouraging other claimants on the Habsburg inheritance to action, particularly Augustus III of Saxony and Charles Albert of Bavaria. Although, in the late 1720s, when opposed to Austria, George had been reluctant to back the Pragmatic Sanction, the agreement that left the Habsburg dominions as an undivided inheritance to Maria Theresa, he now saw it as necessary for European stability. This was in line with his agreement with Charles VI, by the Second Treaty of Vienna of

1731, whereas other rulers were willing to break their guarantees of the Pragmatic Sanction.

George sought to resist the new anti-Austrian alignment, worrying the British ministry that he wanted to put himself at the head of an army, and that he would engage himself more than they wanted. Ossorio reported that George only consulted his Hanoverian ministers,[7] while Newcastle was worried that George's concern about Hanover was leading him to press Sir Robert Walpole to downplay the war with Spain.[8] George's particularly lengthy stay in Hanover that year ensured that his views seemed especially significant. There was a strong urgency, but a lack of realism in his plans for an alliance against France and Prussia.

George's options, indeed, were greatly restricted because he had no military prospect of opposing a threatened French invasion of Hanover. The stress appears to have led George to a nervous collapse in July 1741, with George reported as in despair and as declaring that he resolved to sacrifice his life rather than survive the ruin of the Electorate.[9] A less over-excited Harrington, who was the only British minister to accompany George to Hanover, claimed 'there is no manner of doubt but that the measures His Majesty shall pursue, as King, will be revenged upon him, as Elector, unless timely care be taken to prevent it.'[10] There was no British military support for Hanover, not least because the British were engaged in the War of Jenkins' Ear, the Dutch were determined to remain neutral, Denmark and Sweden were pro-French, Russia was now involved in war with Sweden, and Prussia was scarcely going to provide Hanover with assistance. Clemens August, Elector of Cologne, did not accept George's request not to let French troops into the Electorate, and this was serious as he was also Prince-Bishop of Hildesheim, Münster, Osnabrück and Paderborn, each of which bordered Hanover. The British Whigs were prepared to accept, work with and seek to monopolize the Hanoverian royal family, but preferred to forget that they had to care for Hanover as well. They liked to exert an exclusive claim over George to which they were not entitled, and which George resented.

Indeed, under the threat of French attack, George was obliged as Elector, on 25 September 1741, to accept a neutrality convention, incorporated into the Neustadt Protocol of 12 October.[11] This led George to agree not to fight France and Prussia and to vote for Charles Albert, Elector of Bavaria, the French candidate for the Imperial throne, who was crowned Emperor Charles VII the following February. This vote was greatly disliked by George's British ministers, who correctly feared that Electoral measures would be interpreted as affecting British conduct both at home and abroad. They also felt that they had been both kept in the dark and let down. The Convention indeed hindered British attempts to create a pro-Austrian alliance in Europe, while, in Britain, it embittered discussion about foreign policy in Walpole's last parliamentary session as first minister, which opened in December 1741.

The Convention was also viewed as evidence of a ministerial failure to defend national interests. This was especially the case when (allegedly as a result of a secret clause, that did not, in fact, exist) the British fleet failed to prevent Spanish forces designed to attack Austrian-ruled Lombardy from landing in Italy. François de Bussy, the French envoy who accompanied George to Hanover in 1741, had indeed raised general British policy, specifically toward Spain in the Caribbean, but he found an unwillingness to commit Britain on the part of Harrington, who told him that Parliament would not accept any such arrangement. George insisted that Britain and Hanover were separate states,[12] and Jean-Jacques Amelot, the French Foreign Minister, noted that he had rejected a French attempt to extend the neutrality to comprehend Spain, stating that he was not the master in Britain, that to give his word would be useless, and that he would not be able to sustain what would offend the entire nation.[13] George's views were underlined in December 1741 when Newcastle informed Arthur Villettes, envoy in Turin, 'As to His Majesty's opinion how far the ambitious views of the House of Bourbon may be to be stopped the King can only say that nothing shall be wanting on his part towards it.' George himself pressed Charles Emmanuel III of Sardinia not to turn to France, and promised to get Maria Theresa in return to cede territory in northern Italy to him.[14]

Alongside concern about George's Hanoverian commitments, the bold hopes of gains from Spain in the Indies had proved abortive. Initially, there had been military success. In 1739, at the outset of the war, Vice-Admiral Edward Vernon, with six ships of the line, attacked the port of Porto Bello on the isthmus of Panama, which was defended by three well-sited fortresses. The British warships were becalmed alongside the first and, with a heavy fire, silenced the Spaniards. They then landed sailors and marines who climbed through the embrasures and took the surrender of the position. The other forts and the town then surrendered.

Vernon's success led to a wave of jingoism that encouraged the political commitment of military resources to empire and created high expectations about the prospects from action in the Caribbean.[15] In the volatile political atmosphere of Britain in the closing years of the Walpole ministry, the government felt it necessary to respond to these expectations, a necessity that had scant meaning for George, whose military experience and interest did not extend to amphibious operations. However, the situation was far less promising than was generally believed in Britain. Vernon had destroyed the fortifications of Porto Bello, for he was in no position to retain them. The following year, Vernon achieved little, but in 1741, before Hanoverian security had become a key issue, and, in part, making it difficult for Britain to provide military support for the Electorate, a major military effort was made in the Caribbean. This was launched against Cartagena, on the coast of modern Colombia. Supporting fortresses were captured in March 1741, and the fall of the town appeared imminent, but an assault on the hill fort which dominated the city failed and, after disagreements about the best way to launch another attack in the face of heavy losses through disease and a well-conducted defence, the troops re-embarked in April.

The unexpected failure led to bitter recriminations, with the army and naval commanders criticizing each other. The debacle helped associate the government with failure. Although head of the army, George bore no responsibility, as the failure was largely due to Vernon's volatile nature and to the problems this created for combined operations. In addition, Vernon, totally misjudging the strength of the Spanish position and the determination of the defenders, refused to land his seamen, and this helped ensure defeat. Later success with amphibious operations during the Seven Years' War (1756–63) was due not to an innovative strategy, but rather to greater resources and better co-operation between army and navy commanders.[16]

George's position was controversial because of Hanover, not his headship of the army. He was strongly associated with the Electorate, which he visited in 1740 and 1741, having not done so since 1736 much to the pleasure of the British ministers. Indeed, Sir Robert Walpole had opposed George's determination to go in 1739 and had prevailed on him to change his mind.[17] As Elector, George, as a result of the 1741 neutrality convention, was committed to a policy that was at variance with that of his British ministers. The central problem was one monarch, two dominions. It was a balancing act to say the least. In the caricature 'The Queen of Hungary Stript' (1742), George was depicted as sitting back and doing nothing to help Maria Theresa. He was identified by the phrase 'I have signed the Convention'. In January 1742, Hardenberg, the Hanoverian envoy in Paris, assured Fleury, the leading French minister, of the Elector of Hanover's good intentions, but refused to answer questions about the King of Britain. Amelot commented, in a letter intercepted and deciphered by the excellent British deciphering department (which was linked to its first-rate Hanoverian counterpart) that pushing the idea of one person having two jobs had given Fleury an impression of bad faith.[18] In 1744, the Dutch government was to complain of 'the perpetual dodging between the King's two qualities.'[19]

With Frederick the Great following an assertive, independent and destabilizing line, 1741 was a year of great difficulty for George. The breakdown in relations within the royal family was also particularly serious because Frederick, Prince of Wales was active on behalf of the opposition during the general election of that year. Although he saw himself as a leading political player, Frederick was very much in the hands of superior political intelligences and personalities, but the attitude of the heir to the throne was a decided advantage to the opposition.

The general election of 1741 was a major blow for the government. 286 supporters, 131 opposition Whigs and 136 Tories were elected, Walpole's majority falling from 42 at the end of the last Parliament to 19 owing to defeats in Cornwall and Scotland, in which respectively the opposition of the Prince of Wales and John, 2nd Duke of Argyll was important. Although the respective weight of opinion and patronage were difficult to weigh, it was also the case that there was a groundswell of opinion against the government.

The Tories and opposition Whigs combined effectively when the new Parliament met at the end of 1741, some of the former acting partly in response to instructions from the Pretender, while the latter were encouraged by the active opposition of Prince Frederick. When the House of Commons heard election petitions and double returns, a classic trial of strength between government and opposition, the ministry was put under great pressure because a few ministerial MPs refused to attend debates: Walpole was hit by the abstention, rather than the outright desertion, of some of his supporters. Having lost the Chairmanship of the Commons' Elections Committee on 16 December (os) 1741, the ministry lost three parliamentary divisions on the Westminster election petition. Foreign diplomats noted George's inability to have sympathetic MPs chosen even for Westminster, where he lived,[20] but this constituency was also a populous one that was no pocket borough under the control of a patron.

Faced with a mounting crisis, Walpole, during the 1741–2 Christmas recess, sought a reconciliation with the Prince of Wales. Frederick, however, refused to come to terms with George until his father dismissed Walpole.[21] The Prince's attitude encouraged politicians such as Wilmington and Lionel, 1st Duke of Dorset to believe that Walpole would fall, and that it would be better to bargain with the leaders of the opposition than with the minister, especially when the King was nearly 60. The Earl of Egmont noted that the failure of the attempted reconciliation 'has effectually undone [Walpole], it having fixed such members among the anti-courtiers who were wavering in their conduct upon suspicion that the Prince might be prevailed on to reconcile himself to his Majesty'.[22]

Walpole resolved to battle on, but the situation in the Commons continued to deteriorate. Hardwicke and Newcastle advised George that government business required Walpole's resignation. The government clearly had to be reconstituted, for control of Parliament to be regained, and that obviously involved the resignation of Walpole. On 2 February (os) 1742, Walpole decided to resign and, in the following day, Parliament was adjourned.[23]

Walpole's fall in February 1742 was the product of a political crisis but, far from ending instability, his departure from the scene was followed by turmoil. This affected George, but his position was in the event to be far more challenged in the 1740s by the vulnerability first of Hanover and then of the Hanoverian dynasty in Britain itself. The latter, caused by the Jacobite invasion of 1745, was the more dramatic of the two, but, in the event, was to be beneficial to George and the dynasty, because it led to a groundswell in patriotism. This patriotism, however, had earlier been challenged by the impact of George's policies as Elector, particularly of the Hanoverian neutrality of 1741.

The fall of Walpole, in the face of his inability to continue dominating the House of Commons, was a dramatic display of George's weakness, both politically and within the royal family. George, however, was determined to protect his former minister, and there was to be no repetition of the harrying of Anne's Tory ministers after the accession of George I; the latter, of course, had backed this as he regarded the ministers as having betrayed Hanover in 1713. Indeed, Walpole was created Earl of Orford on 9 February (os) 1742 as a very public display of royal approval which also allowed Walpole to sit in the Lords. His illegitimate daughter Maria Skerret was made a countess, and he received an annual grant of £4,000. When, in seeking to establish an acceptable new ministry to replace that of Walpole, George offered William Pulteney office, he made the condition that Walpole should be 'screened from all future resentments'. Pulteney rejected the condition, but assured George, via Newcastle, that he was 'by no means a man of blood'.[24] George's continued favour for his former minister was readily apparent. He wept when Walpole resigned and 'begged to see him frequently'. When Orford visited Court in July 1742, 'The King spoke in the kindest manner to him at his Levée, but did not call him into his Closet as the ministry feared he would, and as, perhaps, the old ministry expected he would.'[25]

George also played a direct role in the composition of the new ministry, for example keeping a prominent Tory and sometime Jacobite out of the Admiralty Board:

> A list was drawn up. Amongst them Sir John Hynde Cotton was put down, upon the scheme, as was before said, of placing the administration upon the broad bottom. This list was presented to the King. He struck out Sir J.H. Cotton with his own hand. This alarmed all people to a high degree. The seeds of a vehement and formidable opposition were sowed anew.[26]

George alone was not responsible for the reconstitution of the government as an all-Whig ministry, based on taking some of the opposition Whigs into office but not the Tories, yet his view on the subject was central. An investigation of the distribution of secret service funds also highlighted the importance of the Crown, when Nicholas Paxton, Solicitor to the Treasury, and John Scrope, Secretary to the Treasury, refused to testify against Walpole. They argued that they were accountable only to George as the money had been paid by the King's special warrant. The change of government also led to an ostensible reconciliation between George and Frederick. The latter gained a larger allowance, but not the affection of his distant father, who took care not to speak to him. George was willing to hold grudges, but, in the case of Frederick, there were many reasons to do so because the Prince was scarcely trustworthy.

Care was necessary in the handling of George, as Richard Grenville

MP noted after his patron, Richard, 1st Viscount Cobham (who was also Pitt's patron), accepted office in the summer of 1742. Employing a comparison that reflected the continued weight of conventional assumptions, of which the application to George is also indicative, Grenville wrote to his naval brother, Thomas:

> Lord Cobham bid me tell Mr. Haddock that if either of his sons were for the army, everything in his power should be done, and swore by God he'd jump over the moon if possible to serve him. However, things must subside before the new servants can have any great weight. None of us should like to have coachmen, stewards, chamberlains, cooks etc. enter our house by force, and turn out those old ones we have long had confidence in. They must at least convince us that they have put our estates, kitchens, stables etc. into better order than the old ones kept them, before we should appoint every postilion, scullion etc. by their direction.[27]

George's political preferences remained an issue in part due to the degree to which, after his fall, Walpole was believed to retain considerable influence with the King. This was a position similar to that which John, 3rd Earl of Bute was reported to hold with George III after his resignation in 1763. Indeed, it was always simpler to castigate royal views by blaming them on a supposedly evil adviser. In the caricature 'The Screen' (1743), the Crown is shown as the source of patronage, with the King offering 'cockades for boys at £300 a piece', while Walpole flourishes. Walpole certainly exercised considerable influence on George from his retirement until his death in March 1745. George, sensibly, sought and valued his advice, referring to his 'consummate judgement in the interior and domestic affairs of this kingdom'. Indeed, in November 1744, he pressed Walpole to come again to London in order to give advice more easily.[28]

Walpole's influence with the King remained important in large part because of the ministerial rivalry of the period, and, in turn, played a role in that rivalry. Wilmington had replaced Walpole as First Lord of the Treasury in 1742, a blow to Walpole's influence. However, the new First Lord died in 1743 and Walpole's former protégé Henry Pelham, Newcastle's younger brother, then beat Pulteney for the post. Wilmington's death was a significant change in the composition of the political world as far as George was concerned as he had been one of the politicians he knew best. George himself was more concerned about foreign policy than the Treasury, and supported Carteret, an old rival of Walpole, who in 1742 in the reconstitution of the ministry, became Secretary of State for the Northern Department, the department that dealt with relations with the German states. Carteret, who knew German, had served as a diplomat and as Secretary of State, and appeared a highly competent choice for the post.

Newcastle, who remained Secretary of State for the Southern Department, however, was determined not to yield ministerial primacy and policy control to Carteret, who was aligned with Pulteney. This created a fundamental tension in the ministry, and one that inevitably involved the King, not least because Newcastle was prepared to thwart George on this point. Walpole told Sir Dudley Ryder, the Attorney General, that 'the Pelhams and Chancellor [Hardwicke] treat the King in an impudent manner, not submissive enough, though the King piques himself on not having anybody to dictate to him.'[29] The last remark was an accurate view that reflected the minister's long experience. Walpole knew that George had to be worked round.

Looked at differently, there were more frequent and serious ministerial impasses than in the late-1730s, and this increased the role of the King. He was more important as arbiter, sounding board, defiant 'no man', and the central pivot point of government. Furthermore, George was more experienced than he had been earlier in the reign, both in terms of his options and with regard to his knowledge of the individuals and issues involved. The shadow of his father was now long passed.

Carteret was strongly committed to an active policy of direct opposition to France on the Continent and George personally associated himself with this. By the spring of 1742, the Austrians had recovered from the disasters of the previous year and had advanced into Bavaria. This turn in the tide made it possible both for George to abandon his neutrality as Elector, and to discuss Britain invading France in concert with Charles Emmanuel III of Sardinia, who was to be encouraged by gaining territory.[30] British intervention seemed necessary in order to consolidate the Austrian recovery and the British ministers supported a more vigorous anti-French policy on the Continent. In 1742, after Walpole fell, troops were moved to the Austrian Netherlands (Belgium), which France had not yet attacked.

The following year, despite Prussian diplomatic opposition, George in person led an army into Germany, where French armies were still operating. This march in some respects imitated Marlborough's march to Blenheim in 1704. On 27 June 1743, George, in command of an army of British, Hanoverian and Austrian units, clashed with a larger French army at Dettingen near Mainz, winning a victory that owed much to superior British musketry. The French had laid a trap: one part of their army, under the Duke of Gramont, was deployed in a strong position behind the Dettingen stream, blocking the British route, while another part threatened the British rear. Nevertheless, instead of holding his position, Gramont advanced, only to be driven back in defeat. A British participant reported:

we left the camp of Aschaffenburgh (provisions being prodigiously scarce) with an intent of coming to Hanau. The French who were encamped opposite to us, did the same, passed the river at Dettingen, and waited for us on the plains near that place. They played their cannon on us before we could come up to them, and killed great numbers. Whole ranks were swept off by my side, but, God, be praised I was not in the least hurt; about 12 o'clock we came up with them . . . attacked the French with great fury, and after a terrible firing of near half an hour, the French ran away. They then brought up their second line, which, after we had given them a huzza, we fell on and beat back in about half an hour. After this they presented us their third line in most beautiful order . . . upon which, after giving him three huzzas the English marched up with surprising resolution; but such a panic ran through the French at seeing our first line still able to oppose their third, that they turned about and retreated over the river with great expedition . . . Between the first and second attack we breathed a little, while the English horse attacked the French cavalry; but I am sorry to tell you, after the first line they all ran away, and broke through our foot, but however the foot rallied immediately and received the French horse guards or Gendarmes (who were pursuing our horse) with the greatest bravery . . . the fury of their onset we could not withstand so they broke our ranks and got through; but our men immediately closed and turned about, and with assistance of a regiment of Hanoverians who were in our rear, the French horse being between both we killed them in heaps . . . This engagement with the cannonading, lasted from a little after nine in the morning till after four in the evening . . . . Our regiment has suffered as much as any. I had my right and left hand men killed twice by my side, and was myself shot through the hat, which I thank God was all I suffered. The King came to the head of us after the battle, complimented our Brigadier on the behaviour of his regiment, and made us his bodyguards that night.[31]

An account of the cavalry engagement written by Cornet Philip Brown makes clear the problems faced by the British cavalry:

upon their [French] advancing to attack General Honeywood's and General Ligonier's horse we marched forward to meet them sword in hand, at the same time their cannon ceased, and they flanked us on the left with their foot, then we engaged and not only received but returned their fire. The balls flew about like hail and then we cut into their ranks and they into ours. Major Carr whose lieutenant I am was on my right. His skull cap turned two musket balls, but he received two deep cuts by their sabres. Cornet Allcraft who was near me was killed and the standard which he bore was hacked but he saved it. Captain Merriden on the right of the major was killed. Captain Smith on the left was wounded and his lieutenant Mr. Draper killed. In the centre squadron Captain Thomson was dismounted, trod under foot by the horses and his lieutenant shot through the thigh. I did not receive the least hurt, but my left hand and shirt sleeve was covered in blood which must fly from the wounded upon me. Providence was greatly my kind Protector for though I was in the midst of the battle I was not in the least hurt; had not the English foot come to relief we had been all cut to pieces, the enemies arms being nine deep and we but three. Afterwards we rallied again and marched up to attack them again, but before we were ordered the enemy had retired.[32]

Brown's account captured the confusion of a cavalry engagement and also the need to co-ordinate cavalry and infantry successfully in battle. Lieutenant Leonard Robinson of the 3rd Hussars wrote to his wife 'our regiment is cut to pieces'.[33]

This was the first victory over the major French force since Malplaquet in 1709, and one won without the butcher's bill of very heavy casualties on that fearful day. In 1743, the reputation of the French army was at a high state, thanks to its successes in the War of the Polish Succession

(1733–5) and in the 1741 campaign in Germany. Furthermore, there had been no British naval triumphs over France yet in the 1740s and the effect of Vernon's victory over the Spaniards at Porto Bello in 1739 had been dissipated by the total failure of the Cartagena expedition in 1741. As a result, Dettingen was initially greeted with both relief and joy, in a celebration of valour that owed much to spontaneous delight. Many church bells were rung and congratulatory newsprint was in plentiful supply.

Much of the praise focused on George. Thomas Sherlock, Bishop of Salisbury claimed, 'the King's personal behaviour at Dettingen had such an effect on the people, that a little prudent management would have given his friends a great superiority.' In London, according to Thomas Birch, Dettingen led to a 'tumult of joy', but the impact was also felt in the provinces. Newcastle was not one to expect to receive bad news from a steward in such a context, but he would have been pleased to hear from Nottinghamshire:

> The middling sort of freeholders here are greatly pleased with the success at Dettingen and say it was all owing to His Majestys being there, that now they do not grumble so much to pay 4 [shillings] in the pound as they did, and drink his Majesty, the Duke [Cumberland] and the rest of the brave fellows abroad.[34]

There was no capitalizing on the victory, however, Political and military indecision, and serious differences of opinion over military options, combined with the effects of poor weather and disease, and the absence of an adequate artillery train, ensured that George was unable to make an impact on France's well-fortified eastern frontier. There was certainly nothing to match the determination and unity of command that John, 1st Duke of Marlborough had offered from 1702 until 1711 in the War of the Spanish Succession, although he had only breached the eastern frontier in 1708–11 with considerable difficulty. This failure led to dissension and disappointment. John, 2nd Earl of Stair, who was difficult by instinct and reproachful by habit, resigned his command, and went on to criticize Hanoverian influence on the army. His memorial to that effect was printed.

Much anger now focused on George, who was criticized for allegedly showing favour to his Hanoverian troops at Dettingen at the expense of the British, not least by wearing the Hanoverian sash. The caricature

'The Confectioner General Setting Forth the H-n Desert [for Dessert]' presented George as a selfish coward. His Hanoverian troops are shown as inactive observers of the battle, the sash of the Order of the Garter, marked Poor E-g-d, lies around George's feet, while he wears the yellow sash of Hanover; he sheathes his sword, and declares 'Nolo Prosequi' [I do not wish to pursue]. In case the message is unclear, 'Plague of all cowards' is the most readable comment from a participant. George was called the Confectioner because he preserved his Hanoverian troops. The description also meant that he was not a true soldier. The choice of the sash was regarded as indicating George's primary loyalty. Anger contributed to the discussion of a parliamentary ban on royal travel, taking up an idea also advanced in 1737.[35] Criticism of George, making him 'as black and as odious to the people as possible', reached to the far corners of the land.[36]

Participants in the battle were less critical, and saw evidence of George's favour for his British troops. By the time George returned to London in November after the end of the campaigning season, there was a revival of the initial enthusiasm. The novelty of a King returning to the capital as a conquering hero was joined to victory over the hereditary foe, an enemy moreover that patriots had spent the years of the Walpole ministry decrying. Optimism also owed much to the fact that this was the first campaigning season in the year. Church bells rang out, Handel did his stuff, and bonfires and illuminations lit the night sky.[37]

Although the controversy earlier in the year had tarnished the impact of Dettingen politically, the French had been driven from Germany, repeating Marlborough's success in the Blenheim campaign of 1704. This did not prevent French attempts to pretend that they had been victorious. Furthermore, alongside criticism of Dettingen, it is important to note that Marlborough's campaigns had in their own day been controversial, particularly his later ones, not least the butcher's bill of Malplaquet. Jonathan Swift, in his pamphlet *The Conduct of the Allies* (1711), argued that Marlborough and the Whigs had fought on for their own self-interest. The controversy surrounding Dettingen replicated that around other battles as well, not least the victory at Minden in 1759 in which the British cavalry failed to charge.[38] For George, the key point was that the army on which he had lavished so much attention since 1727 had performed extremely well. This was particularly impressive given the fact that no British monarch had won comparable success in battle for centuries. More recently, William III was defeated at Steenkirk

(1692) and Neerwinden (1693), and George I had not led a British army into battle.

The aftermath of Dettingen brought ministerial tensions to a height. These concerned Orford (Walpole), who, in seeing Carteret as a threat to political stability, identified George's Hanoverian ambitions as the political faultline. To Orford, there was a need for Whig unity against the Tories, and he advised that the threat from the Jacobitism of the Tories had to be driven home to the King:

> the king must, with tenderness and management, be shown, what he may with reason depend upon, and what, he will be deceived and lost, if he places any confidence and reliance in. The king . . . may be convinced that the Whig party will stand by him, as they have done, through his whole reign, if his majesty does not surrender himself into hands, that mean and wish nothing but his destruction, and want to be armed with his authority and power, only to nail up his cannon, and turn it against himself. Upon this ground, you will be able to content with Carteret. He gains the king, by giving in to all his foreign views; and you show the king, that what is reasonable and practicable, can only be obtained by the Whigs, and can never be hoped for by any assistance from the Tories. He promises, and you must perform . . . you must expect to meet the king instructed, and greatly prepared in favour of the points which Carteret has in view to drive.[39]

Controversies over favour for Hanover helped, however unfairly, to weaken, by extension, the foreign policy and strategy with which Carteret was associated. Attacks on Hanover became a staple in 1743. Thus, the caricature 'An Actual Survey of the Electorate, or Face of the Country whereon Hanover Stands' depicted Hanover on George's face and hat, adding 'The real value of a thing/ Is as much money as 'twil bring.' Carteret was put under considerable pressure in Parliament in the winter of 1743–4, with William Pitt launching powerful attacks in the Commons on the government for pro-Hanoverian policies.[40] That George was personally committed to the measures for which Pitt criticized the Commons' Address to the Crown helped make the issue more serious. Nevertheless, the proposal to refrain from thanking the King for his speech opening the session was rejected as unacceptable. Five days later, in unsuccessfully moving to address George to discontinue the payment of Hanoverian troops, Pitt argued that government policy was threatening royal popularity, 'that it was no ways premature but most parliamentary when His Majesty is on the brink of losing the affections of his people to endeavour to stretch out a friendly arm to deliver him from the grasp of an infamous minister'.[41]

The reference to losing the affections of the people was a serious insult to George. It was also argued that George's concern with Hanover was leading to an abandonment of British interests. Parliamentary attacks were matched by public agitation, especially in the press but not only there. In 1744, 'Orator' Henley, an independent and often eccentric preacher on all topics, advocated the medical-political benefits of tar water, 'It might be used for Court holy water to put St James's in mind of the navy and the privateers and clear their eye-sight of the film of Hanover.'

Money was an issue with the Hanoverian army, for the Electorate was poor and, as Elector, George did not have the funds to support a major war effort. He was therefore dependent on British financial support. This issue, however, was intertwined with a more general sense of George as mean and avaricious, a point even made by those George favoured such as James, 2nd Earl Waldegrave who knew him reasonably well. Money was seen as a key to his position on many issues, as with the rejection of a marriage of his younger son, William, Duke of Cumberland, with Luise (Louisa), daughter of Christian VI of Denmark, because the Duke required an adequate settlement. He did so on the advice of Orford, because this was seen as the best way to persuade the King against the match, which Cumberland did not want.[42] Cumberland never married. Had he had a Danish marriage then this would have been a double marital link alongside that of his sister Louisa with Crown Prince Frederick of Denmark.

George was apt to retain a keep sense of anger over the attacks on Hanover, and he was inclined to personalise the issue. This accentuated his already powerful dislike of Pitt, and also affected his view of John, 4th Earl of Sandwich, another vociferous opposition Whig, who attacked the alleged Hanoverian impact on British policy in the House of Lords in 1744. When Sandwich came into office, George snubbed him, and he was happy to dismiss him in 1751.

Public pressure accentuated ministerial division, while the strain was increased by the ebbing of success in the war. Hostilities were formally declared in 1744, in response to the French invasion attempt that March, a scheme thwarted by a serious storm in the Channel which dispersed the French fleet. This attempt by the French, on behalf of the Jacobites, led to an upsurge in loyalist propaganda. Lancelot Allgood, a Northumberland landowner, wrote to the Lord Lieutenant:

> Your Lordship may be assured that the gentlemen, clergy and freeholders in this part of our country retain a just impression in their minds of the fatal consequences of any invasion or rebellion, wherefore His Majesty may be fully satisfied of our inviolable attachment to his sacred person and government.

The choice between rival kings and kingships was the issue. Richard Tucker reported government propaganda in action, in the shape of the charge to the Grand Inquest in Dorset given by the judge, who dwelt on the dangerous consequences if 'James III and VIII' became King, 'as the family have been supported and bred up at the charity of France and nursed in the politics of that country they will be under such obligations there that this nation must become a province of France.'[43]

The immediate crisis created by the invasion attempt was short-term, but ministerial and political dissension continued. George wished to sustain Carteret in office. He was the minister most ready to support the King in German politics, and one who, unlike most others, also knew German. Royal favour, however, could not prevent the Pelhams from criticizing Carteret; indeed it encouraged the criticism. When a smiling George told their ally Lord Chancellor Hardwicke, in January 1744, that 'Ministers are the Kings in this Country', Hardwicke replied, 'If one person is permitted to engross the ear of the Crown and invest himself with all its power, he will become so in effect; but that is very far from being the case now, and I know no one in your Majesty's service that aims at it.' This did not fully answer George's point, as he was replying to Hardwicke's argument that the King would benefit from taking the measures necessary to ensure parliamentary unity.[44] Nevertheless, the Chancellor was correct to argue that if the monarch allowed himself to be manipulated by a favourite, then the latter would become the key figure. In the absence of such a course (and, despite opposition claims, George was never reduced thus to being a cipher), it was necessary for the King to address the problem of his dependence on others for parliamentary management, the point at issue in his discussion with Hardwicke.

The possibility of independent action by George and Carteret was thwarted when, under pressure from the Pelhams, who were concerned about what had happened on the 1743 trip to Hanover, George agreed not to go abroad in 1744. This meant that he would have no chance of commanding the British army which was to be deployed that year in the Austrian Netherlands, achieving little against the French. George was accused of seeking to dispose of eastern France like the objects in his garden at Herrenhausen,[45] but the changing fate of operations made such hopes empty, not least because Frederick the Great resumed hostilities with Austria. George's anger put a strain on his relations with his ministers, but they were put under more acute pressure by Newcastle's demand that Carteret be dismissed.

An unwilling George turned for support to Chesterfield and John, 1st Earl Gower, leading opposition figures, but they also refused to serve with Carteret, unsurprisingly so as they were critics of the pro-Hanoverian policy associated with the minister. The King also sought advice from Orford, via John Selwyn, but Orford urged him to part with Carteret. With the strains of parliamentary attacks imminent as the session neared, the minister resigned on 24 November (os) 1744, his career a victim to his own lack of political following, but also to the unpopularity of policies seen as pro-Hanoverian.[46] In the resulting reshuffle, a 'broad bottom' ministry was created by the Pelhams, including former opposition figures such as Chesterfield, Dodington, Bedford and Sandwich. The caricature 'A Very Extraordinary Motion' showed a supine George being forced to take in ministers being carried toward his mouth by the Pelhams. Pitt as Secretary at War, however, was a minister too far, and a resentful George refused to accept him in this post.

Carteret's resignation was an undoubted defeat for George. He had attempted to maintain his independence and to call upon whom he wished for advice; and the Pelhams had called him out upon this breach of what they saw as the ministerial deal. How could they be his servants in Parliament, if they were not in reality his ministers? In this crisis, George had his limited political mobility reduced to virtually no mobility (he was still able to thwart Pitt) by political collusion. The Pelhams had blackmailed him by refusing to serve unless he accepted their terms, and he had had to submit. However, he could then await them falling out with each other, dying, or retiring. George, after all, was the constant, while they were ephemeral. Nevertheless, he needed managers, and there were few to choose from. 1741–6 were very tough years for George, but he exerted his influence as best he could and was not just a cipher for the Pelham interest. The delicate balance of constitutional practice was certainly challenged by the events of the era. George overplayed his hand, and was to do so even more in 1746, but the Pelhams also did so in 1744–6. George was indeed the pivotal player.

George's temper continued as volatile as the political situation. Indeed, he railed against the Pelham interest. Ministers could expect complaint or abuse, and George continued to hanker after Carteret in office. Lord John Russell published in 1842 a conversation that took place between George and Hardwicke in January 1745. Typically, he noted but did not detail, 'much discourse on foreign affairs', which, in fact, took a great deal of the time when ministers met the monarch, but he did recount:

> *The King*—I have done all you asked of me. I have put all my power into your hands, and I suppose you will make the most of it.
> *Chancellor*—The disposition of places is not enough, if your Majesty takes pains to show the world you disapprove of your own work.
> *The King*—My work! I was forced; I was threatened.
> *Chancellor*—I am sorry to hear your Majesty use those expressions. I know of no force; I know of no threats. No means were employed but what have been used in all times—the humble advice of your servants, supported by such reasons as convinced them that the measure was necessary for your service.
> *The King*—Yes I was told that I should be opposed.
> *Chancellor*—Never by me, Sir, nor by any of my friends.[47]

In 1745, however, George cheered himself up by visiting Hanover, setting off in May on what promised to be a longer trip than his 1743 visit to Hanover. Unexpectedly, this visit was to be cut short, as on 23 July (os) Charles Edward Stuart, the elder son of 'James III and VIII', reached Eriskay in the Western Isles. He had sailed from France intent on raising a Jacobite rebellion in Scotland. By 17 September (os), Edinburgh had fallen to James.

On 30 July (os) 1745, in response to news of Charles Edward's landing, Newcastle had already pressed for the return of George from Hanover. In the event, George was less speedy in deciding to return than the Lord Justices, the ministers left in control in London, would have liked. The ministry also wanted troops moved from the British army in the Austrian

Netherlands, but its commander, George's second son, William, Duke of Cumberland was mistakenly confident that the forces in Scotland would be able to defeat the Jacobites. He replied to Newcastle, 'I am surprised to see this romantic expedition revived again. But I don't doubt but that Sir John Cope [commander of the forces in Scotland] will be able to put a stop immediately to this affair.' Cumberland instead sent Lieutenant-General John Ligonier to meet George on his way to London at Utrecht and to press him on the dangerous situation created by French advances in the Austrian Netherlands. Ligonier succeeded, George deferring the transfer of the British troops. This was symptomatic of his preference for military over civilian advice in what was a military issue, and that was more understandable because this was wartime and there was also a fast-moving campaign in the Austrian Netherlands. George decided to rely in Britain upon Dutch units prevented from acting in the Austrian Netherlands by a parole agreement with the French, units that were to be moved across the North Sea.[48] These Dutch units, however, were correctly regarded as less effective.

George did not appreciate the seriousness of the situation in Britain until the advancing Charles Edward outflanked the royal forces in the Highlands, and it was not until 4 September (os) that orders were sent for the immediate dispatch of the ten best British battalions in the Austrian Netherlands to Britain. George's delay, in part, reflected advice from Carteret, now Earl Granville, who was still influential with the King, and the opinion of his ally the Marquess of Tweeddale, the Secretary of State for Scotland, about the seriousness of the situation there. Sir Dudley Ryder, the Attorney General, recorded in his diary on 15 September (os) 1745 that Tweeddale and his allies were claiming that the Jacobites were deserting and would soon be suppressed. Carteret wanted to focus military efforts on the Continent, and had little time for Newcastle's anxieties. If George was guilty of a fundamental failure of perception, this was a failure that was widely shared. At the same time, his inability to respond rapidly was in part a product of an inappropriate choice of advisers, at least an inappropriate choice as far as this crisis was concerned.

The crisis escalated after Charles Edward comprehensively and rapidly defeated the government army under Cope near Edinburgh at Prestonpans on 21 September (os) 1745. Cope was a long-serving officer who had enjoyed the patronage of James Stanhope and whose career had flourished under George II. He had become a colonel in

1732, a brigadier-general in 1735, and a lieutenant-general in 1743. Cope indeed shared in the glory of Dettingen where he had commanded the second line of the cavalry. He became a Knight of the Bath after the battle. However, like George, he had no experience of command against irregular forces and was routed at Prestonpans in a battle that developed much faster than he had anticipated. A Highland charge, the formation unbroken by the fire of Cope's infantry, led the latter to flee in panic a few minutes after the first impact of the charge. The Jacobites lost about 25 men, Cope about 300, but Cope's army was destroyed, with at least 1,500 men taken prisoner. Although cleared by a court martial, Cope never commanded troops in action again.

Charles Edward invaded England in early November, advancing via Carlisle, which fell after a short siege, as far as Derby, which was entered by the Jacobite forces on 4 December (os). At that stage, the two governmental armies in the field, led by Field Marshal Wade in the North-East and by Cumberland in the Midlands, had both been out-manoeuvred, and Charles Edward was closer to London, for the defence of which a third army was being hastily assembled on Finchley Common.[49]

George, nevertheless, did not panic as James II and VII had done in 1688. Instead, he provided firm and confident support for the war effort, which focused on Cumberland (now recalled from the Austrian Netherlands), in whom he had great faith. In a conspicuous display of confidence in popular support, that was also a prudential response to the need to ensure the defence of London, George in October reviewed the City of London's militia units in St James's Park. These were not the usual type of troops he reviewed, but the crisis had led to a reliance on non-regulars. George himself was threatened by the Jacobites. In response to the Privy Council reward for anyone taking Charles Edward into custody, the Prince declared George an outlaw and offered a reward for his arrest.[50]

There was a great upsurge in anxious loyalism, as Charles Edward's success in Scotland led to fears that George would be overthrown. Richard Finch, a London tradesman, in a letter that reiterated the theme of loyalty to Crown and constitution, claimed that:

A native of London who went abroad before this rebellion began and knew the discontents of the people before would scarce credit the zeal, affection and loyalty, which appears everywhere all over the nation, on behalf of the King, and the Protestant religion; to the degree that smaller matters seem to be cancelled; the newspapers every day full of pathetic incitements to fight for our king and our liberties . . . Our most gracious King and our excellent constitution were never so greatly the love and delight of all ranks and orders of men as at this time.[51]

In practice, the response across the country was far more varied, which helped to explain the determination shown by the dynasty's supporters to obtain support. This significantly focused on opposition to James, particularly to his Catholicism, rather than on George's virtues and value, although both the latter were stressed. At least, thanks to his Protestantism, George was acceptable, and, as with the invasion scare in 1744, there was an outpouring of loyalty, for example from the Dissenters, who had much to lose from George's overthrow. There were also more prosaic reasons for being pro-Hanoverian, not least the fear that a Jacobite restoration would lead to the annulment of the National Debt. The rallying to the Crown was welcome, but, ultimately, it was military success that was crucial, as George understood. This success was to bring to an end a dangerous sense of flux. After Cumberland's victory at Culloden in 1746, the Hanoverian monarchy was to be stronger and its legitimacy largely unchallenged. The association in the '45 of the Stuarts with Catholicism, autocracy and France helped bolster Hanoverian popularity, especially since France and Jacobitism were again closely linked in invasion schemes in 1744–6. The royal family was seen as central to the Protestant establishment, with 'God Save Great George our King', the basis of the later National Anthem, being sung. There was a conscious echo, in their defence of the Protestant establishment, of William III's role as royal warrior in 1688–90 in securing this establishment by expelling James II and VII from the three kingdoms: having overrun southern England, William had gone on to command in Ireland, most conspicuously at the battle of the Boyne in 1690.

Throughout the crisis, nevertheless, political tensions between monarch and ministers continued, with George still resentful of the Pelhams and ready to listen to Granville (Carteret), with whom he was still linked, in part through Lady Yarmouth. In September 1745, George failed to persuade Harrington to form a new ministry that would have enabled him to dispense with the Pelhams. Once the Jacobites had retreated, the political differences reached a new height, with the King rejecting pressure to take Pitt into office, as Newcastle wanted both in order to broaden the ministry, and to lessen opposition attacks in the Commons. George treated the demand as an insult, and one that underlined why he disliked the Pelhams. The King also continued to take advice from Bath (formerly Pulteney) and Granville.

Meanwhile, the Jacobite threat ebbed. The Highland chiefs were disappointed by the lack of the support promised them by Charles Edward: both assistance from English Jacobites and the absence of a French landing in southern England. After bitter debates in Derby, the chiefs forced Charles Edward to turn back and he began his retreat north on 6 December (os). Government troops sought to block the retreat, but were unsuccessful. Once back in Scotland, a Highland charge was again decisive in giving the Jacobites victory at Falkirk on 17 January (os) 1746. The government troops were also affected by indifferent leadership and a lack of fighting spirit.

Falkirk, however, was to be the last Jacobite victory. Charles Edward was short of money, and the dynamic of Jacobite success had been lost. The inexorable nature of the deployment of resources by the British state, once its cohesion was not challenged by losing the initiative, was readily apparent in the preparations made by Cumberland who built up a large army in Aberdeen, ready for the final showdown.

Meanwhile, back in London, George's lack of support for the Pelhams had provoked a political crisis. They forced his hand when, with their supporters, they resigned their posts in the government on 10 and 11 February (os) 1746. Philip, 2nd Earl Stanhope noted 'the immediate occasion of all this hurly burly was the peremptory negative which our cousin William Pitt's demand of the Secretaryship at War met with in the Closet.' Others, however, did not present George as causing the crisis in this fashion. Hardwicke claimed that the resignations did not proceed 'as some will perhaps tell you, from the King's having refused to make a certain gentleman Secretary at War. That is a trifle in comparison of other things and was quite over and the King's pleasure entirely submitted to.'[52] Even Newcastle stated that the claim that the resignations proceeded from a determination to force George to take Pitt in as Secretary at War was inaccurate, and was spread by the Pelhams' enemies, presumably in order to present them as disloyal, arrogant and aggressive. Instead, he saw the resignations as arising from the Pelhams' determination not to continue in office if they lacked royal support.[53] John Tucker, who had accepted office in 1744, claimed:

The generality of mankind who see only the outside of things ascribe all this to the refusal of Mr. Pitt to be Secretary at War but that point had been given up these 10 days. The true source is the countenance given to Granville and Bath, who have generally opposed whatever has been proposed by the other party and obstructed all their measures but the affair which immediately concluded towards this resolution was a proposition in Council to carry on the war with the utmost vigour on the Continent even though the Dutch should not declare war, which was opposed with one vote by all the Pelhamites.[54]

By withholding his confidence from his ministers, George had undermined their position in Parliament. But, in also provoking their desperate resignation at a time of war and rebellion, this left George with little room for manoeuvre.

The collective resignation was a major challenge for parliamentary monarchy. The constitutional guidelines that sought to define the relationship of Crown and Parliament, such as the Act of Settlement of 1701, were vague, providing scant guidance for most political eventualities, and were dependent upon mutual goodwill. There was as yet no received understanding of such central issues as the collective responsibility of the Cabinet, the particular responsibility of the departmental head to both King and Cabinet, the special role of the first minister, and the notion that the King should choose his ministers from those who had the confidence of Parliament.

The resignations, however, were of short duration. Bath and Granville failed to form a new administration, crucially being unable to find a manager of Commons' business. The weakness of the new ministry was also indicated when the City of London withdrew a loan offered to the government. The major financial interests had close links with the Pelhams, and, in wartime, there was a desperate need to keep loans flowing to the government. Bath and Granville had not appreciated how many politicians would resign with the Pelhams, and found themselves unable to recruit a sufficient number of supporters, a situation that was exacerbated by the unpropitious wartime circumstances.

Within forty-eight hours, Bath and Granville, proved feckless in their politics, had abandoned the attempt, forcing George to turn again to his former ministers, although not without some bitterness, particularly towards Harrington who pushed conditions for his return to office.

Newcastle reported on a conference between the King and Henry Pelham, 'wherein the chief resentment was showed to Lord Harrington, and that in the strongest and bitterest manner, and hints flung out that, if we would give him up, everything else should be done'. The King also had to respond to his failure to establish the new ministry, which was apparent to all, both the political world and the public. As ever, the working constitutional practice was organic and changing, and pressure, if not force, was a shaping factor. George had to admit in public what he had tried to deny in private: that he was led by parliamentary men and had to respond accordingly. George was forced to give posts to those they wanted to bring in, in order to strengthen the ministry, Pitt in short: a conspicuous display of the new political order. The Pelhams also successfully demanded the ejection of Bath from the Cabinet and the end of Granville's influence. Despite being able to keep Pitt from the Secretaryship of State, George seemed beaten, even more conclusively than when he had had to part with Walpole in 1742 and Carteret in 1744. He was described as 'fatigued and perplexed'.[55]

In his sixties, George's time seemed past. The glory he had briefly won at Dettingen in 1743 was swiftly forgotten, and that at Culloden three years later was Cumberland's, while the Prince of Wales appeared the rising figure in politics. The King, it was said, had declared, 'he was now resolved to be quiet and let them do what they thought fit . . . that it signified nothing, as his son, for whom he did not care a louse, was to succeed him, and would live long enough to ruin us all.'[56]

8

The Rule of the Pelhams?
1746–1754

With the failure of Bath and Granville, George appeared defeated. The ministers who had triumphed maintained control until March 1754, when Henry Pelham unexpectedly died. Throughout this period, George was in the background as far as the conduct of domestic politics were concerned. In part, this reflected the extent to which his self-imposed political rules ensured limitations upon his effective action. He did not want to turn to the Tories to support the ministry. Their opposition to British commitments to Continental power politics alienated him, and he continued to suspect some of them of Jacobite sympathies. George also wished to employ favourites, especially Granville (Carteret); yet, from bitter experience, he now knew the Old Corps Whigs led by the Pelhams, who were implacably opposed to those favourites, to be essential. With a parliamentary majority, George could possibly have cleared out the Old Corps, as George III was to do in the early 1760s; as it was, he remained dependent on the Old Corps in Parliament.

The King's preference for using, and ability to use, favourites, as well as his official ministers, had been stomped upon by the Pelham group. As a result, George was largely to concentrate on foreign policy and to continue to concede the management of domestic politics to his ministers. He had long done so, but now did so on different terms. George, nevertheless, remained at the heart of the practice of the constitution. This practice, and thus the constitution, was forming, and formed by, the continued interpretation of roles and parameters. An open-ended process, this interpretation was both greatly influenced by the role of individuals and a major theme of political debate.

Unable to dominate the ministry, George sought to circumvent it in policy terms. Thus, in the mid-1740s, he pursued a secret anti-Prussian foreign policy, operating through the Hanoverian government and the British envoy in St Petersburg, John, 3rd Earl of Hyndford, in a way that contradicted the anti-French emphasis of the British ministry. This compromised the wish of the ministry to focus Russian attention on opposing France, rather than as George wished, Prussia, and also thwarted the hope of winning over Frederick the Great after the end of the Second Silesian War with Austria (1744-5).[1] There was also tension, that culminated in 1747, over how far British policy in the United Provinces should entail support for the Orange interest, and how far it should lead to continued backing for their republican opponents. In 1745, Frederick the Great asked his envoy in London whether he should regard the King of England as one or two people, in short whether Britain was not, through the King, a party to Hanoverian moves.[2]

Yet, it was also possible for George to affect policy more directly. This was seen from the outset when Pitt was taken into office in the reconstitution of the ministry after the Bath-Granville interlude. George loathed Pitt for his earlier public criticism of pro-Hanoverian measures. As George was firmly opposed to his being Secretary-at-War, Pitt was, instead, appointed Joint Vice-Treasurer of Ireland, a lucrative sinecure but scarcely a key office, and certainly one that did not require contact with the King. Two months later, the able Paymaster General, Thomas Winnington, died, a victim of medical practice in the shape of excessive bloodletting. Pelham suggested that Sir William Yonge, the sickly Secretary-at-War, take the post and thus make way for Pitt, but George declared that 'that fellow should never come into his Closet'.[3] Being Secretary-at-War would lead to business meetings with the King, not least as a result of George's interest in army matters. As a result, Pitt became Paymaster, yet another lucrative post that did not involve access to the Closet. Yonge was given Pitt's sinecure, and Henry Fox became Secretary-at-War. Pitt would therefore handle army finances, while Fox dealt with George on military matters. A protégé of Sir Robert Walpole, Fox was, from 1741 to 1761, MP for New Windsor, a constituency in which George took a considerable interest. He was also familiar with him as Surveyor-General of Works from 1737 to 1743.

Contemporaries were in no doubt of George's influence. Pelham writing, 'It is determined, since the King will not hear of Pitt's being Secretary at War, that he shall be Paymaster.' At Court, George displayed clearly who was in or out of favour. Not one to change his opinion of individuals easily, George did not hesitate to snub Pitt in public, Henry Harris writing in December 1750 'Saturday was a devilish dull day at Court . . . The Paymaster General not spoke to, scarce looked at, upon this thin occasion.'[4] Thus, George's attitude was central to the machinations to keep Pitt in government but out of the Closet. Another former critic of George's commitment to Hanover, John, 4th Earl of Sandwich, found, in 1747–8, that as an envoy, paid from the Civil List, support for his expenses were rejected by a hostile George, Newcastle noting, 'The negative was then so strong, that nothing was to be done.'[5]

At the same time, however determined George might be, he was constrained by constitutional and political realities. In March 1748, Newcastle wrote to Cumberland:

> I am afraid they have a very imperfect notion, in Holland, of our constitution, and of the method of granting supplies in Parliament, by what the Greffier proposes . . . vizt. that His Majesty would be pleased to advance this money to the Republic, for a short time, out of the money granted for the supplies of this year: whereas your Royal Highness knows that there is not one shilling granted by Parliament, without its being appropriated to some particular use.[6]

George was also dependent on others for information, and there was a perception that this dramatically reduced his options. On 2 December (os) 1747, Hugh, Earl of Marchmont, a placeholder, made notes of a conversation with Chesterfield, who was then a Secretary of State. Neither was keen on the Pelhams, and each had been in opposition and was therefore repeating the standard view of George as manipulated. This view had been taken as read for years, but that did not necessarily make it any the less accurate. Chesterfield reported being told by Cumberland:

> that the state of Scotland was very bad, that he believed the King's ministers there did not serve him well . . . and that it would continue so till the King had resolved to be King of Scotland, which was what the [3rd] Duke of Argyle insisted upon being . . . He [Chesterfield] then told me that on the Duke of Newcastle telling the King of the President's [Duncan Forbes, Lord President of Court of Session] illness the King said he would be a loss for on the whole he was a good man, though he had errors, and that if he died he supposed

Areskine [James Erskine] must be the man. To which the Duke of Newcastle said, To be sure, there was no other. I said I was heartily sorry to hear it; that it was a mortal blow to the King's interest for Areskine had been a notorious Jacobite . . . I then told him of Dr. Lee and Mr. Nugent having spoke to my brother of coming into the Prince's service and my fear of its being misrepresented to the King by the low German people about the Prince. He said he would mention it to the King if I liked.[7]

Yet, although the failure of the Bath-Granville ministry in February 1746 was an abrupt lesson in ministerial politics, it nevertheless entailed compromise for George, not subordination. If he could not sustain Granville as Secretary of State in 1744 and 1746, the latter was weak because his very position and prospects had depended totally on George: he had no other political backing. There was no comparison to the situation in 1717–20 when George I had backed Stanhope and Sunderland against political attack (see pp. 45–51).

Furthermore, in 1746, Cumberland's crushing victory over the Jacobites at Culloden revived the royal mood, John Maule MP noting on 24 April (os), 'I never saw anybody in such glee as the King was this day at the Levée which was much crowded. He complimented the Duke of Argyll upon the behaviour of the Argyllshire men',[8] this Argyll, Archibald, the 3rd Duke, being the brother of John, the 2nd Duke, who had been a favourite of George as Prince of Wales, before falling out with his government.

Cumberland had advanced on Charles Edward's base at Inverness, and the latter failed to contest his advance until the last moment. Then, with an underfed and underpaid army, Charles Edward attempted a night attack on Cumberland's camp. This advance was mishandled and then abandoned before any attack could be mounted. In the subsequent battle of Culloden on 16 April (os) 1746, the terrain suited Cumberland's defensive position. Cumberland also outnumbered his opponent, 9,000 to 5,000, and the Jacobites were outgunned. The circumstances were not suitable for a Highland charge, not least because Cumberland's numbers permitted defence in depth, while his artillery thinned the Highlanders. The general rate of fire was increased by the level ground and the absence of any serious disruptive fire from the Jacobites, while the flanking position of the royal units forward from the left of the front line made Culloden even more of a killing field. Many factors led to confusion amongst the Jacobites: the slant of their line, the nature of the terrain, which was partly waterlogged, the difficulty of seeing what was happening in the smoke produced by the guns, and the independent nature of each unit's advance.

The results of Culloden, not least the heavy Jacobite casualties, marked the military end of Jacobitism as a serious force. Charles Edward's idiosyncratic and undisciplined behaviour in the following years greatly lessened foreign support, so that the Jacobite movement ceased to be of major importance in diplomacy or international relations. Charles Edward's conversion to the Church of England on a secret visit to London in 1750 did not lead to any rallying to the Jacobite cause, and the Elibank Plot of 1751–3, a scheme for a coup in London involving the kidnapping of George, was betrayed.

Determined to see the capital sentences on Jacobites carried out,[9] the King was a keen supporter of the restoration of order in Scotland. The major new fort at Ardersier Point near Inverness, built after Culloden in order to help prevent an invasion of Scotland via the Moray Firth, was appropriately named Fort George. It never heard a shot fired in anger, but that does not imply that the fort was without value, for it discouraged any attack by this route. In practice, the navy acted as a guarantee of national security, but it was necessary to have a second strand. The nature of this was a matter of controversy. George and Cumberland were keen to rely on regular troops, while some politicians, especially in opposition, emphasized the role of the militia.

Order was also backed in another direction when, in 1747, George supported the restoration of Orangist control in the key Dutch provinces of Holland and Zealand, a measure in which the threat of force played a role in overthrowing anti-Orangist provincial governments. George had always been closer to the Orange interest, which tended to be more anglophile than the 'republican' party, and this tendency had been strengthened by his eldest daughter Anne's marriage to William IV. In 1747, the crucial issue was whether William could become stadholder of the two provinces and whether war would be formally declared between the United Provinces and France. The relevant correspondence indicates clearly that George took an assertive line, and was happy to maintain a squadron of warships in Dutch waters even against the advice of the Admiralty. In 1747, Newcastle wrote to Cumberland, then back in command in the Low Countries and a source of reports for the King[10]:

I am recommended by His Majesty to send your Royal Highness the enclosed copy of a letter, which I received yesterday from the Lords Commissioners of the Admiralty, advising the recall of Commodore Mitchell with his squadron from the coasts of Zealand. His Majesty would have your Royal Highness mention this to the Stadholder, as what the Lords of the Admiralty are extremely desirous should be done . . . but the King would by no means, especially at this time, recall this squadron, without giving previous notice of it, and hearing what the Prince of Orange, and the Dutch ministers might hope to say against it.[11]

The commitment to order was characteristic of George's views. Order and stability were clearly linked in his mind, and they were seen as making states more desirable allies. This was seen in George's attitude to Poland, an instructive issue as the rule of Poland by the Elector of Saxony in certain respects matched that of Britain by George as Elector of Hanover. In 1755, Robert, 4th Earl of Holdernesse, the Secretary of State, instructed the British envoy, 'The King laments the distracted state of that kingdom . . . lay the foundations for a sincere reconciliation between the Saxon ministers, and those chiefs of the Polish nobility who have thought themselves slighted or ill-treated.'[12]

In Britain, George and his new ministry were drawn closer together in 1747 by the changing attitude of Frederick, Prince of Wales. The latter's move away from uneasy support for the government, and towards opposition, played a major role in leading the Pelhams to hold the general election in 1747, a year earlier than was necessary under the Septennial Act, because they hoped that this would deny the Prince sufficient time in which to organize support. Frederick's revived support for opposition, which reflected his frustration with his position, accentuated and darkened the King's animosity.

After the contested returns had been settled, the ministry had a majority of 144.[13] Success in the election strengthened both George and ministers. Frederick's defeat avoided humiliation for George, but also ensured that the ministry appeared vindicated, as Walpole had been in 1727. As a consequence, challenges to ministerial stability in the late 1740s did not focus on Parliament. Instead, divisions within the ministry over foreign policy proved the key issue. Alongside the mass of diplomatic correspondence, much about the politics of policy is obscure, but, repeatedly, the evidence suggests that it was the attitude of the King that was crucial. That was certainly believed by contemporaries, and this, indeed, was an aspect of George's power. Chesterfield, for example, told Marchmont in February 1748, the month in which he ceased to be a Secretary of State, that Newcastle lacked the support of George's German advisers and:

> that to gain favour the Duke of Newcastle had given himself up to prosecute the King's favourite scheme, the war; that he had told the King that by doing so he ruined himself, his head was at stake, but he would sacrifice all to carry on his project; that the King hated him and laughed at him behind his back, but this was such a favourite scheme, from the narrowness of the King's views, his hopes of acquiring something in Germany by conquest which Lord Granville [Carteret] had set before him to gain him and the real benefits to Hanover of £800,000 a year for his troops.[14]

The remarks at the end referred to George's hope for territorial gains for Hanover and the money paid to support its army's participation in the Allied cause.

The British ministers were brought round to accept the view that Britain's central role in the War of the Austrian Succession with France must go on, but then became determined on a speedy peace as a result of Dutch inability to resist French advances. In 1747, French victory over Cumberland had been followed by the siege and storming of the leading Dutch fortress, Bergen-op-Zoom, and, in 1748, the French successfully besieged the major Dutch fortress of Maastricht. Cumberland was in no position to relieve it and William IV made Dutch weakness clear, contradicting what he had earlier told George.[15]

Peace now seemed urgently necessary. Thus, George's 'system', if the continuation of the war to the benefit of Hanover is to be understood in this light,[16] collapsed because of exogenous factors, rather than any inability to maintain control of the ministry. Indeed, the previous year, Robert Trevor had been recalled from his embassy in The Hague because he wanted peace. Chesterfield's removal as Secretary of State in February 1748 was attributed to his support for peace and George's for war. However, French advances made peace a necessity.

George also had to face unwelcome pressure from within government for closer relations with Prussia. These were pushed again in 1747 by Pitt and Horatio Walpole, and in 1748 by Henry Legge who was appointed envoy to Berlin, although he was not to last long in this post. Horatio Walpole argued that ill-will toward Frederick the Great bred a resentment that forced unnecessary costs upon Britain.[17] This policy clashed, however, with George's hostility to Frederick, a hostility that owed much to Hanoverian jealousy of, and concern about, Prussia, whose gains of Silesia (1741) and East Friesland (1744) ensured that Prussia had clearly become the major North German power. This was particularly so in comparison with Hanover, which had gained nothing from the war or in compensation for these Prussian gains. Rather than turning to Prussia, possibly by pursuing the idea mooted at the time for Prusso-Hanoverian co-operation in secularizing North German prince-bishoprics, George and Newcastle preferred to maintain the alliance with Austria. Chesterfield claimed in 1747 that:

> he believed that the King of Prussia might be brought to get us a good peace, or if France refused he would have her interest; that our King would not send him a minister calling him a fripon and wished he was Cham [Khan] of Tartary [the Crimean Tatars]; that he, Lord Chesterfield, had told the King he wished so too but as he was King of Prussia the more he was a fripon the more necessary it was to have a minister who was a spy at his Court; that with all this he could not prevail and the King of Prussia treated this as an intended neglect.[18]

The end of the War of Austrian Succession in 1748, with the preliminaries of the Treaty of Aix-la-Chapelle signed on 30 April and the definitive treaty on 18 October, lessened immediate concern about the security of Hanover. This created more international and domestic options for George at the same time as peace made it urgently necessary to improve the international situation, so that, in the likely event of another war, circumstances would be more favourable. The peace terms brought Britain no gains, and the return of Louisbourg on Cape Breton Island to France earned particular criticism as the fortress was seen as the guard of the St Lawrence River and, therefore, the guarantee of French Canada. Captured in 1745 by the Massachusetts militia supported by the Royal Navy, it was hoped that the fall of the fortress would be followed by the conquest of Canada but, instead, it was returned in order to secure French withdrawal from the Low Countries. During the last stages of the war, France's foreign trade had been greatly harmed by the British navy, her economy by a poor harvest, and her finances by the costly conflict. The French were also concerned by the advance of a British-subsidized Russian army towards the Rhine.

George, although disappointed about Hanover's failure to make any gains while Prussia, in contrast, retained its acquisitions, was ready to see the peace as a matter for congratulation. In his eyes, the French had been stopped from overrunning Western Europe, and thus Dettingen had a wider and continuing significance, a point made by the triumphal arch erected at Göttingen to celebrate his visit there in 1748. Dynastic success was also registered in France's public expulsion of Charles Edward Stuart. George was closely associated with the celebrations in London and insisted that the *Music for the Royal Fireworks* by Handel should be performed in the 1749 celebrations by an orchestra that included many martial instruments and no violins. The sound of drums and trumpets was welcome to the King.

George took advantage of the new international situation during his trips to Hanover in 1748, 1750 and 1752, trips that reflected his affection for the Electorate, although they led to criticism, for example by the Tory newspaper *Old England* on 12 November (os) 1752. That year, reflecting the widespread conviction of George's preferences, Giovanni Zamboni, a longstanding diplomatic agent in London, reported that it was widely believed that George would spend the remainder of his life in Hanover. The visits attracted British visitors to the Electorate. William, 4th Earl of Essex found 'a great many English' in Hanover that year.[19] George's visits also led to a stepping up in the diplomatic tempo, not least because the turnaround time for messages to foreign courts from Hanover was far faster than when the King was in London. The central position of the King was shown publicly in a lack of importance of the ministers left behind in London that led some foreign envoys who did not accompany George to Hanover to request permission from their Courts to return home. This also ensured that other rulers, such as Frederick the Great in November 1754, were keen to be informed if George was going to Hanover.[20]

The ministerial viewpoint about the political system was expressed by Henry Fielding in his pro-government newspaper the *Jacobites Journal* in its issue of 26 December (os) 1747:

> an Administration composed really of all the great men, whose
> abilities of any kind made them worthy of any place in it; supported

by both Houses of Parliament, and, as appears by the last election, by a vast majority.

More pertinently, and urgently, the role of the King, and the need felt by the ministers to manage him, was captured in a letter from Henry Fox to the diplomat Sir Charles Hanbury Williams:

> The Duke of Newcastle, Mr. Pelham, the Duke of Bedford, have all agreed that you should go to Turin, Sir James Gray to Poland, and Mr. Villettes to Venice. The Duke of Newcastle proposed it to the King, who approved of it, but added that the Czarina [Elizabeth] having desired it, it was necessary a minister from him should go to Warsaw *now*, and unfortunately you are the only one who can . . . when you are at Hanover you must, if you would act discreetly, behave as one who is trying to be well with, and agreeable to His Majesty rather than as one who may presume he is already so, which last I fear is not your case.

In order to help, Fox had 'begged' Lady Yarmouth to assist Hanbury Williams, and indeed Newcastle saw her as responsible for royal views on embassies.[21]

More generally, the ministry responded to George's views, leading Frederick the Great to claim in 1753 that George governed Britain absolutely.[22] After the Granville/Bath failure to create a new ministry in 1746, an implicit bargain between King and British ministers had helped to bring governmental stability in the latter stages of the War of the Austrian Succession, and it was to be sustained in the post-war years. This bargain rested on a degree of mutual understanding and co-operation, in which Newcastle showed a willingness to back George as a standard-bearer of Continental interventionism and an opponent of Prussia.

This willingness led to a policy focused on a German league designed to ensure the passage of the Imperial Election Scheme —the election of the Habsburg heir, the future Joseph II, as King of the Romans and, therefore, next Emperor—with this league to be supported by British subsidies. Furthermore, George wanted an alliance system intended to deter Frederick the Great from fresh adventures, and also to protect the Austrian Netherlands from being overrun by the French again, as it had been in 1745–8. The unhelpful Austrian response was seen as provoking to both George and 'the Nation',[23] but this deterred neither the King nor his ministers, although Newcastle presented himself as under acute difficulties due to the extent to which George was 'so provoked'.[24] In November 1751, Newcastle, writing to Robert Keith, the envoy in Vienna, about the Austrian attitude to the maintenance of the Barrier forts that protected the Austrian Netherlands, noted 'how earnest the King is to have an happy end put to this affair'. That month, George also wrote to Prince Charles of Lorraine, Governor of the Austrian Netherlands, about his keenness for good relations between Britain and the Austrian Netherlands.[25]

An alliance system was necessary because Hanover, like the Austrian Netherlands, was vulnerable, the average strength of its army in the early 1750s being no more than 21,000 men. Under royal impetus, awareness of Hanoverian vulnerability greatly affected British diplomacy, although, added to severe opposition criticisms, there were serious concerns from within the government camp. Henry Pelham was anxious about the cost, while Horatio Walpole pressed George against peacetime subsidy treaties to foreign rulers, before attacking them in Parliament.

Nevertheless, in 1753, Newcastle, who was on message from George's perspective, argued that the Austrian troops should be so disposed as, 'in case of an attack, from the King of Prussia, on His Majesty, a very considerable diversion be immediately made', adding 'His Majesty thought no time was to be lost in knowing what assistance he might expect from Russia in case of an attack.' The threatening situation on the Continent made clear the need, and Frederick stoked the flames. In January 1751, he told the French envoy in Berlin that, if war broke out, he would invade Hanover in order to capture the Electoral treasury, and that, if he failed to seize it, he would impose, under threat of burning everything, a massive daily levy until the treasury was delivered. Two months later, the Prussian Foreign Minister said that, in the event of war, Prussia would use a conquered Hanover as a source of supplies.[26] Frederick was regarded as personally hostile to George, and the opposition newspaper *Old England*, in its issue of 1 August 1752, was being mischievous when it suggested that, as a Protestant, George should support Frederick as the next King of the Romans. Hanover was indeed to be rapidly conquered when first attacked: by the French in 1757. Frederick saw George's influence as in part dependent on his ability to persuade Newcastle to support him:

I hope Pelham maintains his position, but I fear that when George II goes to Hanover he will be able to lead the Duke of Newcastle further than the British ministers would like him to go and that, once the decision has been taken, these ministers will be obliged to applaud it.[27]

Support for the King's views was carried further because George's position strengthened in 1751, as a consequence both of ministerial differences and of the death of the Prince of Wales. Newcastle's concern to rout his ministerial rival, John, 4th Duke of Bedford, Secretary of State for the Southern Department, in which he succeeded in 1751, was important, as he needed royal support to this end, and indeed he benefited from Lady Yarmouth's backing. Already in 1750, Harrington had failed to get a new post when he was moved from being Lord Lieutenant of Ireland, in large part due to his lack of favour with George who had seen him as acting a particularly unreasonable part in 1746 when the King was forced to part with Granville. Harrington was no longer thought well enough to handle Ireland, and Newcastle, instead, proposed him for the sinecure post of General of Marines, only to meet with a firm response from George, who was prone to harbour grudges. Newcastle's description of this to his brother captures George's bluntness and his clear and direct manner:

He said, he would do nothing, he would not be troubled about it here [Hanover]. That as to the General of Marines, he should not have it if *he* could hinder it, and at last said, 'He deserves to be *hanged* and I am ready to tell him so.'[28]

The Cabinet was divided in the winter of 1750–1, with Newcastle opposed to Bedford and Sandwich. Newcastle demonstrated his value to George by emphasizing the common interests of Britain and Hanover, a theme that matched the Duke's political alignment which included a close relationship with Gerlach Adolf von Münchhausen, the leading Hanoverian minister, and that helped strengthen Newcastle's credit with George.[29] Complaining of Prussian conduct in 1751, Newcastle wrote 'one sees the affectation of distinguishing the King from the Elector'.[30] The previous year, Newcastle rejected the Dutch proposal that, instead of George paying half of the intended joint subsidy to the Elector of

Cologne, he pay two-thirds—one-third as King and one-third as Elector, claiming that it was

> contrary to all practice for His Majesty, in the same act, to enter into any engagements in two different capacities; and in the instructions the King has been pleased to give to Baron Steinberg, there is not, as I apprehend, any particular description of the capacity in which His Majesty proposed to be engaged.[31]

George was also by now irritated anew by Pitt who demonstrated his independence in 1751 by calling, against Pelham's wishes, for a parliamentary inquiry into the conduct of Lieutenant-General Philip Anstruther as Lieutenant-Governor of Minorca in 1733–47. Anstruther, an MP, had apparently used his sweeping powers to feather his own nest and deny justice to those he disliked, but the issue also enabled Pitt to criticize the Secretary-at-War, Henry Fox, who had come to the support of Anstruther. Pitt's vim over the subject, which was debated in the Commons in February, March and April 1751, was reported to have greatly offended the King, who would not have welcomed parliamentary attacks on an officer, and thus on Cumberland, the Captain-General. He asked Fox 'with whom it was that Pitt meant to ingratiate himself? Was it with Lord Egmont?',[32] a key adviser of the Prince of Wales.

This indicated George's concern that opposition to him was in part motivated by the reversionary interest, while the latter, in turn, inspired opposition. To George, this was a frustrating nexus, and a disturbing one because intercepts revealed links between the Prince and Prussia,[33] which had long sought such a relationship. The Prince remained in impotent opposition, although this very opposition challenged the likely longevity of the current political situation, and thus its stability. In 1750, the year in which Gaston, Duke of Mirepoix, the French envoy, referred to Frederick as inclined to disagree with his father in everything,[34] Frederick indeed would have become King had George lived only as long as his father had done.

George, however, was far from failing. Instead he continued to make his views clear on both political and family matters. In March 1751, this came out when the Admiralty rejected a proposal from the Board of Trade to dispatch two warships to help strengthen the imperial presence in Nova Scotia, where there was concern about French intentions. The

Board of Trade then presented a memorial which Bedford took to the King. Horace Walpole reported:

> The Duke of Bedford said to the King, 'Sir, this paper is too long for your Majesty to read, but I will tell you the purport of it: It is a project of the same faction [Pitt and the Grenvilles], who have endeavoured to increase the navy this year: I have desired your Majesty's servants to meet at my house next Wednesday; I believe they will not think it proper to come into this proposal'. 'No', replied the King, 'they are the most troublesome impracticable fellows I ever met with; there is no carrying on the measures of government with them'.[35]

Later that year, George rejected George, 2nd Earl of Halifax's request that he be made a third Secretary of State, for the Colonies, or, as head of the Board of Trade, that he be admitted to the Cabinet (unless American affairs were discussed), as well as have a higher salary, and be permitted right of access to the Closet. George was not only keen to save money, but was also uneasy about any widening of membership of the Cabinet, rightly so as it might have threatened the effectiveness of governmental action.

The unexpected death of the Prince of Wales on 20 March (os) 1751 transformed the dynastic situation by weakening the reversionary interest. Having been ill for two weeks, with a pain in his side, the Prince died suddenly after being pronounced 'quite safe' by his doctors. A burst abscess in one of his lungs, possibly the result of an old sporting injury, was held responsible. The death was a striking reminder of the unpredictability of high politics in a system still dominated by the attitudes and affairs of the ruling dynasty. Frederick's demise was followed by the collapse of his political interest, by his widow, Augusta, turning to the King for support, and also, that June, by a 'quiet revolution at Court'.[36] This was a major change in the ministry in which Bedford and Sandwich were replaced with less fuss than other such changes under George. Pitt wanted to succeed Bedford as Secretary of State,[37] but George and Newcastle preferred to have Robert, 4th Earl of Holdernesse appointed. Aside from experience as a diplomat, he was a peer without political weight, and was therefore unlikely to resist the views of George or Newcastle. George was more positive, as Holdernesse had been a Lord of the Bedchamber since 1741 and, according to Newcastle, he was chosen at the King's behest, although George stipulated that Holdernesse was not to be shown the intercepted diplomatic correspondence and that he should only handle the business of his province (the Southern Department). As Newcastle was a pliant Northern Secretary, the situation now seemed most satisfactory for George. According to Horace Walpole, George was influenced by the fact that Holdernesse's mother was a distant relation, a second cousin, once removed.[38] Newcastle emphasized that the decision was very much that of George. He wrote to Pelham from Hanover in September 1750:

> if this change is ever made, as it solely arises from the king, so it shall, for me, end with him. That is, as the king cannot reproach me with having said one word to him, since I have been here, relating to the removal of the Duke of Bedford . . . as therefore, if it is done, it arises singly from his Majesty himself; so the successor shall be his own choice. [39]

The return of a more quiescent Granville (formerly Carteret) to the government, as Lord President of the Council in June 1751, also reflected George's influence. This brought Granville back into the milieu of government, although without a key post. George had already had Granville, although then out of place, elected to the Order of the Garter on June 1749, a conspicuous show of support: he was installed at Windsor in July 1750. Granville's career is poignant for the larger story of the royal support of servants, and the accompanying reluctance to accept dictation by Commons' managers.

George had thus survived his eldest son. This was a result not only of the fatal crisis in the latter's health in 1751, but also of George's generally robust health which had consequences both for the length of the reign and for the conduct of government during it. It is instructive to assess the implications for British history, Anglo-Hanoverian relations, and George's reputation, had he died earlier, and to appreciate that contemporaries had to consider these possibilities. George (1683–1760) lived only slightly longer than his paternal grandfather, Ernst August (1629–98), and shorter than his maternal grandfather, George William of Celle (1624–1705), but had he lived only as long as his father, George I (1660–1727), George II would have died in 1750. George's benign genetic inheritance, which was also seen in the longevity of his sister Sophia Dorothea (1687–1757), contrasted with the fate of his eight children. Only one, his unmarried daughter Amelia (1711–86), lived to be fifty and, aside from George William (1717–18), who died as a baby, the boys died in their forties: Frederick (1707–51) and William, Duke of Cumberland (1721–65); and the girls more variously: Anne (1709–59), Caroline (1713–59), Mary (1723–72) and Louisa (1724–51), the last after an abdominal operation. Prior to his death, William had already had 'a violent pain in his side and a fever' in November 1751, after falling from his horse while hunting,[40] and a stroke in 1760. George was very alarmed by William's illness in 1751, seeing the country as in danger of being 'left to nothing but a woman [Augusta, Princess of Wales] and children'.[41]

Resistance to disease was not the sole factor to consider in noting George's longevity. The avoidance of accidents was also important, not least because he was exposed to possible danger on his trips to Hanover. For example, George's return in January 1737 from his 1736 trip to Hanover proved hazardous, and he had a risky, lengthy, storm-tossed passage before he landed at Rye. Winter storms combined with the timing of the parliamentary session to ensure that George went to Hanover in the late spring.

If George was advised by his doctor not to go to close the parliamentary session in 1749, that was a rare occurrence. Nevertheless, the sensitivity of the issue of his health was indicated that year when Sir Dudley Ryder, the Attorney General, was willing to consider prosecutions to deal with the opposition attempt, brought to his attention by Newcastle, to create a sense of uncertainty by suggesting that the elderly George was ill:

> As the publication of such false news of His Majesty has a tendency to disquiet the minds of his subjects, hurt public credit, and diminish the regard and duty which they owe him, I think the doing it with such views is an offence punishable at Common Law, and for which an indictment or information can lie. And the frequency of such publications is evidence of such wicked designs.[42]

At the same time, action had to be considered within a legal framework, which, as Ryder noted, created problems. The very character of his advice reflected the position of the monarch within a society not only where there was a system of laws that constrained governmental power but also where there was an ideology of constitutional and legal observance. Three years earlier, there had been rumours about George's health, Alexander Hume Campbell writing from London,

> The King has been very ill and is not yet well. The Birthday [celebrations] is put off and I fear he is worse than they will tell. People suspect bad and avow their apprehension from his successor's character . . . those who know will not tell but by pretending he is perfectly well, which is not truth, make people believe him very bad.

Several days later, it was rumoured that George was dead.[43]

Death or serious illness, such as that which affected his grandfather, Ernst August, in his last years, or his eldest grandson, George III, would have led either to the earlier succession of his heir or to regency arrangements. The latter would have had serious implications. As an ill old man, Ernst August transferred the business of government to his eldest son, the future George I. An equivalent transfer for Frederick, Prince of Wales, in opposition from 1736 to 1742 and from 1746 until his death, would have created major political problems, although he might have matured into accepting his father's ministers, as did George II, and also George IV as Prince Regent.

Frederick's death brought Prince George back into the orbit of his grandfather, for George II did not extend to his daughter-in-law or his grandchildren the loathing he had shown for his troublesome eldest son. Rejecting advice that she continue her late husband's role in opposition, Augusta sought the King's protection for herself and her children, and he extended it, going to see her on 31 March (os), refusing to sit in the chair of state, and, instead, sitting by Augusta on the couch and comforting her. The King urged Prince George and his brother Edward to be brave, obedient to their mother, and to deserve the fortune they were born to. The entire episode saw the King at his best. Often hot-tempered and clumsy in personal relationships, he had a fundamental integrity and warmth. Four days later, George again went to see Augusta and settled with her the education of the children. Newcastle noted, 'Everything passed extremely well at the interview; the King continues to be perfectly satisfied with the Princess, and is in raptures with the young prince, who, he says, has taken a liking to him.'[44] In November 1752, George gave Augusta the Queen's place at the ball on his birthday, a conspicuous honour. George was lenient in his treatment of Augusta and the grandchildren, possibly even too lenient in light of what was to be the battle over the education of the Prince. George himself, as Prince of Wales, had endured the separation of his children at his father's behest, and this was not to recur. George, instead, allowed Augusta great latitude, although he kept her finances on a short leash.

Had George died soon after the death of Frederick in 1751, the position would have been made more complex by the vocal public concern about the attitudes and intentions of Cumberland, whose unfortunate reputation for ruthless ambition prefigured that during the reign of William IV and in the early years of Victoria of George III's fifth son, Ernest, Duke of Cumberland (from 1837 King of Hanover). Had George II died, there was concern that the role taken by Cumberland in the regency would have been to the detriment of Augusta and of the young Prince's interests. In the event, the provisions for the regency that George recommended to Parliament proposed Augusta as regent and guardian, while Cumberland was to be simply President of the council appointed to advise her in the event that she became regent, a decision Cumberland accepted, stressing that he was submitting to the plan because George commanded it. Augusta was allowed to exercise certain key royal powers—the creation of peers, the appointment of judges and the dissolution of Parliament, but only with the advice of the council, the members of which she could not dismiss unless the majority agreed. During the debate on the legislation, Bath wept when he mentioned the possible event of George's death.[45] Indeed, many of George's contemporaries, and those who had been influential in his early years, were already dead. Henrietta Howard (1688–1767) survived, but Argyll (1678–1743) and Wilmington (1674?–1743) were dead. George's youngest daughter, Louisa, also died in 1751.

The debates on the Regency Act, the key legislation of the 1751 session, are an instructive commentary on the continued political importance of the Crown and of related constitutional issues. The King's careful scrutiny of the Regency Bill is indicated by a draft in Newcastle's papers with the Duke's comment, 'May 3rd 1751. NB. This draft of the Regency Bill was this day sent to the King, and His Majesty was pleased to approve it, with one remark only upon the form of the oath to be taken by the Council of Regency.' George's concern calls into question the dismissive view of Horace Walpole that George 'had been made to believe that this Act against his own son [Cumberland] was of his own direction'.[46] A more searching remark on royal influence was made by the Tory MP Sir John Cotton who criticized the clause that allowed George to name four members of the council in his will. Aside from Cumberland, the other nine members were ex-officio. The King, however, was concerned with power rather than constitutional precedent. When Hardwicke disagreed with him on the amendments to the praemunire clause in the Regency Bill, George replied 'that is a distinction only for lawyers to make'.[47] Such a view was typical of the King's robust attitude.

So also was the conversation with Fox which captures the flavour of royal views, not least in the mixture of self-righteousness and brisk and baffled probity that his grandson George III was also to express. George II asked Fox whom he would have made Regent, earning the response that he would have preferred Cumberland:

> The King replied, 'My affection was there'—but avoided talking on the impossibility. He assumed to himself the chief direction of the bill; and added, 'I have a good opinion of the Princess [Augusta], but I don't quite know her'. He then spoke largely and sensibly on the restrictions, and gave reasons for them. 'That a council was necessary for her, even in cases of treason; women are apt to pardon; I myself am always inclined to mercy; it is better to have somebody to refuse for her. As to the power of peace and war, I never would declare either without consulting others. And as to the objection of the Council being irremovable, who knows it will be composed of the present people? It will be the ministers I shall leave: had you rather have those I shall leave, or have the Princess at liberty to go and put in Lord Cobham or Lord Egmont? What did you say against the bill? do you like it? tell me honestly?'. Fox answered, 'If you ask me, Sir, no. What I said against it, was, because what was said for it, was against the Duke'. The King told him, 'I thank you for that: my affection is with my son: I assure you Mr. Fox, I like you the better for wishing well to him. The English nation is so changeable! I don't know why they dislike him: it is brought about by the Scotch, the Jacobites, and the English that don't love discipline; and by all this not being discouraged by the ministry.'[48]

The emphasis on discipline was characteristic of George and reflected a consistent strand in his social and political views, one that related these views to a moral strand that made sense of his own experience and interests. For his grandson, the equivalent theme was integrity.

In practice, Cumberland, although hostile to his troublesome brother Frederick before the latter's death, was a man of integrity and, in particular, duty, with, like his father, a keen sense of appropriate behaviour. Cumberland made no real attempt to build any political interests outside his army, although he pushed a militarized idea of empire that was important to the development of an aggressive imperialism.[49] The Duke, indeed, was, in the 1760s, to prove a useful ally to his nephew, and Cumberland's early death in 1765 robbed George III of a valuable source of advice.

George II was still healthy, particularly so for his age. In 1753, Frederick the Great thought him unlikely to want war because of his advanced age and the absence of an adult successor, but, two years earlier, when Lady Anson saw George in the Drawing Room, she noted 'the King looks extremely well'. In 1752, Newcastle remarked 'I never saw the King in better health or in better years',[50] a claim corroborated by others.

Healthy and also of note: although George was essentially prepared to leave domestic politics to his ministers, he was concerned about foreign policy. In 1751, Mirepoix, the French envoy, reported that George was indifferent to ministerial intrigues and left his ministers with control over domestic matters and government patronage: being concerned, instead, essentially with Hanover and also with his jealousy and fear of Frederick the Great. Also that autumn, Newcastle had found George willing to talk on a confidential basis about foreign affairs, but 'totally silent upon everything at home'.[51] Ministers remained concerned with the royal mood, Newcastle writing to his brother from Hanover in 1752, 'I gave the King a general account of your letters—He is in extreme good and reasonable humour;—willing to hear, and disposed to do what is right.'[52] Newcastle humoured George by allowing him to be rude without complaint and by answering back courteously, if firmly, and this proved the basis of a successful working arrangement. The Duke's willingness to go to Hanover in 1748 was both a testimony to the importance of accompanying the King there and a sign of his determination to try to win George's favour. Less accommodating politicians who were seen as overbearing, such as Bedford, were less welcome to the King.

The correspondence of the Pelhams scarcely suggests that George was a cipher. Documents, of course, have to be read with care. To read, unexpectedly in State Papers Domestic for 1752, an instruction, from Newcastle, as the Secretary of State with George in Hanover, to his counterpart in London, to complain to the Spanish government beginning, 'His Majesty is so much concerned for the interests of his trading subjects in the West Indies',[53] is suggestive, but it does not necessarily mean that George indeed was greatly concerned. Signs of bellicosity may be more indicative, as when Newcastle wrote that year that George 'extremely approves the directions for fitting out, with the greatest expedition, a stronger squadron for the coast of Africa, than the French will have there'.[54] The emphasis on the King in diplomatic correspondence with British envoys was far more than symbolic. In 1753, Newcastle wrote to Robert Keith, envoy in Vienna, about George's concern about criticism of his opposition to giving his guarantee of the Austro-Modenese treaty:

> The King has no objection to the being a party to the treaty; provided that can be done without His Majesty's becoming guarantee of it; and indeed it was for that reason, that it was objected to. But, if it be expressed in such a manner, as to leave no room for any future demand of the King's guaranty; His Majesty will agree to the inserting of his name, as a party.[55]

Occasional anger served as an abrupt reminder of the need to handle George with care, and was also an aspect of a rudeness that some commentators found frequent. George, for example, was regarded as being very rude to British aristocratic visitors to Hanover in 1750. This took up the theme of rudeness shown in the 1730s when he turned his back at Court on aristocrats of whose politics he disapproved. Such brusqueness did not accord with fashionable assumptions of gentility, but George had no wish to star in a new-fangled novel about sensibility. His manners were very much those of a different generation.

Anger and a concern with authority were combined in 1752 when George lambasted Newcastle in Hanover on an espionage matter and also about the acquittal in London of a printer which the King 'said he had read, set out in the newspapers: he run into one of the usual but strongest declamations against our laws, that punished nobody; against our informations from the intercepted letters, which told us nothing, for without His we should know nothing', the 'his' being a reference to interceptions of post going through the Electorate which were indeed impressive: at Celle, the posts between Paris and Berlin, Copenhagen, St Petersburg and Stockholm were intercepted and deciphered. Newcastle commented on George's concern about:

> this spirit in the juries and the City [of London] which the King had flattered himself was almost entirely spent, and at an end; and indeed there were great appearances of it. From thence His Majesty fears that quiet which he thought himself sure of, is not so certain, and that he may still be more obliged to follow the advice of his ministers, than he had of late thought himself.

George, in contrast, was 'extremely well satisfied' with the 'strong direction' of the Lord Chief Justice in the case. The Lord Chancellor, Hardwicke, assured Newcastle that the acquittal was not due to opposition to the government nor to dissatisfaction with George.[56] The Jury Act of 1730 was one that had divided the ministry, but most ministers had then supported it.

George's concern in 1752 also reflected his clear commitment to order. The following year, in the royal speech opening Parliament, George said that he was appalled by the rise in murders and robberies. The speech was written by the ministers, but the King had to accept it. To George, politics was an aspect of order. In 1748, the King expressed the fear that the Dutch 'spirit of sedition' would spread to England. Similarly, in Ireland, George responded to disaffection in 1753 by issuing an order that earned the criticism of Horace Walpole:

> Lord Holdernesse, by the King's command, wrote to the Chancellor of Ireland, telling him, that the King had sent the Duke of Dorset [Lionel, 1st Duke] to govern them, because he had pleased them so much formerly, and because he had the good of Ireland so much at heart: that His Majesty wondered at any man taking upon himself to answer for a nation; and that he expected that all who loved him would support the Lord Lieutenant . . . Thus the absurdity of the memorial was balanced by the haughtiness of the mandate.[57]

Thus many of the attitudes attributed to George III as constitutional novelties had been anticipated under George II.

The episode relating to the acquittal of the printer in 1752 indicated George's attention, even when in Hanover, to events in Britain. This was seen for example in his response to Parliament. George was mindful not only of the need for management, but, also, of parliamentary views. When, in January 1751, Parliament took action against Westminster electors of Jacobite tendencies for showing contempt to Parliament, George praised the parliamentarians involved, among whom Henry Fox was prominent, saying to Newcastle, according to Horace Walpole, 'They are not like those puppies who are always changing their minds! Those are your Pitts and your Grenvilles, whom you have cried up to me so much. You know I never liked them!'[58] In December 1753, Henry Fox found him 'too full of yesterday's debates to say anything to me on Lord Kildare's subject this morning'.[59] Four years later, William, 2nd Viscount Barrington, the Secretary-at-War, reported to his friend Newcastle, 'the King was perfectly informed yesterday of every circumstance which passed on Monday in the House of Commons; all which His Majesty heard with the greatest pleasure and approbation.'[60] George's knowledge also related to rumours of ministerial cabals. In 1755, in the Closet, George was reported as challenging Fox with accusations of intriguing against the Pelhams.

George was no alarmist, however, about the prospect of his heir becoming a crypto-Tory. In late 1752, there was a clash over the Prince's education, with George Lewis Scott, the Sub-Preceptor, and Andrew Stone, the Sub-Governor, accused by their supervisors, Thomas Hayter, Bishop of Norwich, and Simon, Earl Harcourt, of being quasi-Jacobites pushing unwelcome Tory views. This controversy caused Harcourt and Hayter, who produced no evidence for this claim and were believed by neither the King nor Newcastle, to resign that December. The King had already been critical of Hayter, and he reassured Augusta that he did not believe Harcourt. The latter was succeeded as Governor by James, 2nd Earl Waldegrave, a socially adroit courtier who enjoyed considerable favour with the King.

George was furious about this issue being brought into public and Parliament. He could not understand the public interest and fascination with what he thought private family matters. He could not recognize that royal family matters could never be private, but were instead public business: George resented and did not understand this trend. His Hanoverian background was obvious here, and George could not see that for monarchs there was no such thing as a private sphere. Instead, life was conducted in a fishbowl. In March 1753, Andrew Stone reported that George had told Pelham that he saw Bedford's unsuccessful motion on this topic in the Lords 'to be as personal a thing to himself as ever was brought into Parliament'.[61] To George, such matters were simply inappropriate for the public domain. This reflected a degree of naïveté about sensitivities on such points, but also a concern with the dignity of monarchs that was typical of his rank.

As the education of the future King became controversial, however, relations between Augusta and George became poor. In large part, this was due to the need for money. George imagined that he had a strong need for it, which was not correct at this period, while Augusta, with nine young children to support and the debts of her improvident husband an incubus, felt cheated. This was not least because George had not given his grandson the revenues of the Duchy of Cornwall, which indeed were properly only for the monarch's eldest son. Augusta also felt that the ministry was failing to look after the interests of Frederick's former servants. George, however, was scarcely going to reward former opponents, who included those who had lent money to Frederick in order to fund his opposition to his father's ministers.

The Prince was clearly affected by his mother's anger, and his relations with his grandfather deteriorated. The Prince's assumptions about the internal dynamics of the royal family contributed to the sense of lost rights and misuse of power that affected his response to the political system. This response was partly shaped by the idea of a virtuous, impartial and powerful 'Patriot King' advanced by Bolingbroke in his influential *The Idea of a Patriot King* (1749).

Nevertheless, despite differences with the young Court and also difficulties sometimes with his ministers, the situation in the early 1750s was favourable to George. The government supported his views on foreign policy and British backing was a guaranty of Hanoverian security. George was reasonably content. Indeed, in 1754, his response to Pelham's untimely death on 6 March, aged 59, was to say that he had hoped to finish his days in peace, but that he now saw clearly that it was impossible to do so.

9

Last Years
1754–60

The present critical conjuncture of affairs, and my constant
inclination to have the advice and assistance of my Parliament on
all important occasions, have made me desirous to meet you here
as early as possible.

Beginning of George II's speech to Parliament,
13 November 1755.

Visiting London in 1754, the Count of Gisors, a very well-connected,
and somewhat brash, French aristocrat, found George, then elderly by
the standard of contemporary European monarchs, particularly Louis
XV, still playing an active role in ceremonial and social events and terms.
However, looking to the French example, Gisors was far less impressed
by the King's political position. Gisors spoke to George at the palace,
which he thought horrible, and they both attended a masked ball, where,
according to Gisors, most of the women present were whores. Gisors
was also unimpressed by George's position, claiming that, in any other
state, the King's mistress would share his power, a perspective that owed
much to the situation under Louis XV, where Madame de Pompadour
presided, whereas in Britain, in contrast, her equivalent shared his lack
of power. According to Gisors, George was also unable to award a
colonelcy to one of his favourites.[1]

In fact, although she did not seek to play a key social role, the
Countess of Yarmouth had considerable influence, while George was
the central figure in army patronage, a reminder of the extent to which
commentators could err. Furthermore, far from George's position

contrasting totally with that of his French counterpart, Louis XV's freedom of manoeuvre was considerably constrained by the nature of domestic politics, including the commitment by the *parlements* to their sense of their privileges.[2] Nevertheless, although George was still active, commentators had to address the point that, in light of his age, he could easily die soon and was very likely to die before too long.

In the meantime, however, the political situation seemed under control, with the Pelhams providing both effective management in Parliament and support, through British foreign policy, for the Continental stability that George sought and which he thought essential to Hanover's interests. Furthermore, on the death of Henry Pelham, the First Lord of the Treasury (a reminder of the role of sudden death in British politics, which had also been seen with the deaths of Stanhope in 1721 and Sunderland in 1722), George's views on ministerial choice prevailed. Pitt did not gain the Secretaryship of State vacated by Newcastle's replacement of Pelham at the Treasury, a replacement that reflected the political importance of the latter ministry as well as Newcastle's frenetic determination to retain control. George had made it clear that he did not want Pitt, who, in turn, referred to 'the weight of the irremovable royal displeasure'.[3] The Secretaryships, particularly the Northern one held, before he transferred to the Treasury, by Newcastle, which had responsibility for diplomatic relations with the German and Baltic courts, Russia and the Netherlands, required royal favour. The monarch played a crucial role in the conduct of foreign policy, and George did not wish to have to deal with Pitt personally in the Closet in any circumstances.

The decision, instead, for the successive promotions to Secretaryships of Holdernesse in 1751 and Sir Thomas Robinson in 1754 indicated George's determination to have ministers with whom he could deal easily, as well as a preference for courtiers and men with diplomatic experience, over managers of the Commons. Holdernesse had been a diplomat and a Lord of the Bedchamber, while Robinson moved from being Master of the Great Wardrobe to the Secretaryship. This background to senior government posts exemplified the importance of the Court. Furthermore, Robinson's long service as envoy at Vienna from 1730 to 1748 ensured that he was particularly knowledgeable about the German politics that concerned George. Robinson had worked for George over Mecklenburg, East Friesland and other issues.

George was knowledgeable about diplomacy and expected others to share his competence. In 1755, Holdernesse wrote to Hanbury Williams, 'I am expressly commanded by the King to recommend the utmost caution to you in giving anything in writing at the Court where you reside: as there are instances of very improper uses having been made of even very innocent papers.'[4] This was an instance of the accumulated experience George had acquired and could deploy, an experience greater, and certainly more wideranging, than that of his ministers.

In place of Pelham, Newcastle sought to entrust the management of the Commons to Henry Fox, but Fox refused to accept the task when he discovered that the Duke intended to retain full control of all government patronage and to manage the forthcoming general election: that would have left Fox with responsibility, but without the power to give substance to his management. The politically weaker Robinson, in contrast, proved more pliable. Indeed, Pitt 'once said that the King might as well have sent his jack-boot to govern the House of Commons as Sir Thomas Robinson',[5] an image that captured the sense of George as autocratic.

Robinson, however, was not up to the growing political problems that stemmed from the outbreak of hostilities with the French in North America in 1754 as competing views about the frontier there led to military clashes in the Ohio Valley. The King, in the speech opening Parliament on 14 November 1754, declared:

> It shall be my principal view, as well as to strengthen the founda-
> tions, and secure the duration, of the general peace, as to improve
> the present advantages of it, for promoting the trade of my good
> subjects, and protecting those possessions, which make one great
> source of our commerce and wealth.

Such hopes, however, were increasingly redundant in the deteriorating state of Anglo-French relations, but George was unwilling to have the more vigorous and politically potent Pitt succeed Robinson. Newcastle told the Sardinian envoy that only Pitt was able to manage the Commons (by which he meant that he feared Pitt's opposition there), but that he had failed, despite very great efforts, to get the King to talk to Pitt, as George detested him. The envoy commented that he did not know what Newcastle could do unless George changed his mind, although he also noted Newcastle's certainty of royal support.[6]

Instead of Pitt, the position of *de facto* chief government spokesman in the Commons next went to Fox, a politician seen as able to deliver the necessary leadership and one whom George respected. Throughout, George took a close interest in politics, corresponding, for example, with Fox via Yarmouth. It was George who saw Fox on 2 December 1754 to try and win him over to support the government. The detailed negotiations on the ministry were then entrusted to Waldegrave, a choice that reflected George's overseeing, but this did not end George's role. To him, delegation did not mean walking away from a situation. Thus, having seen Fox on 3 December, Waldegrave saw the King next day. George sensibly insisted that Fox should put his views in writing, telling Waldegrave that he had to 'explain himself in the clearest manner', an attitude in keeping with George's emphasis on straightforwardness. Those involved saw royal wishes as both a substantive matter of government and a key issue of political tactics. Robinson, on 12 December 1754, presented George as victorious:

> Our affairs in Parliament have been a little disturbed, by the private views of some ambitious gentlemen, who have been desirous of more power, than the King intended to give them. But these matters are subsiding. One of the gentlemen [Fox] having submitted; and the other [Pitt] being left to meditate upon it.[7]

George's attitude was certainly seen as crucial by foreign envoys, with his confidence in Robinson appearing especially important.[8] Fox had wanted to have his Secretaryship at War turned into a third Secretaryship of State, but this was not to be. Instead, he was allowed to join the Cabinet in December 1754. This, in part, reflected Newcastle's continued support for Robinson, and tension between Newcastle and George increased as the Duke thought the King overly favourable to Fox who had close links with Cumberland.

In 1755, Holdernesse, then accompanying George to Hanover, reported to Newcastle about an audience at Herrenhausen: 'The King entered much into conversation upon parliamentary and party matters and said you had promised to write me word at a proper time, how *some people* stood affected to his measures.'[9] Robinson had proved a minister well-suited to a political system of courts and cabinets, but not to one in which Parliament played a major role, and parliamentary management could be difficult. In 1755, Newcastle, therefore again sought to strengthen the ministry. This required royal support, as Newcastle was only too well aware. On 18 April, he drew up a memorandum:

> To represent to the King the present state of the House of
> Commons, the difficulties attending this session, and the im-
> possibility of operating another without some solid settled
> consistent plan, especially considering the present situation . . . that
> it is by no means proposed to engage His Majesty to anything, but
> only to learn upon what terms His Majesty may have the assistance
> of those who may be of use to his service.[10]

Newcastle tried to win Pitt round to act as Commons' spokesman for
the ministry, but the protection of Hanover was not a priority for Pitt,
and, as George did not want Pitt as Secretary, and especially not as
Secretary for the Northern Department, Newcastle turned again to Fox,
a step encouraged by the latter's threat to join the opposition.[11]

Personnel issues were related to complex questions of policy and
these constrained George's options. The vulnerability of Hanover
ensured that he did not want war with France, but the deteriorating
situation in North America limited his options and George claimed that
France had negotiated in bad faith.[12] Hanover was indeed vulnerable to
attack in what was a fast-deteriorating international situation. Although
conflict between Britain and France had broken out over the Ohio
country in 1754, full-scale war was not declared until 1756. However,
alongside the concern that it could break out, there was a specific worry
that France might attack Hanover in order to put pressure on Britain,
including counteracting any British gains in North America. It was
assumed that this would also involve an attack by France's ally Prussia,
to which Hanover was particularly vulnerable.

In response, the British government sought to strengthen relations
with Austria and its ally Russia, each of which bordered Prussia and
was in a position to put military pressure on it. George was associated
with this policy, which had indeed been a significant theme in his views
since the early 1730s. To him, the empire that counted was the Holy
Roman Empire and not the British empire, although, alongside his
continued interest in Hanover, he became more concerned about the
latter during the course of the war. Already, in June 1755, Holdernesse
had written 'entre nous' to Newcastle, that 'the King seemed overjoyed
at the probable success of his measures in America',[13] a reference to the
decision to deploy more troops there and to attack French positions,
in short to a militarization of policy, which was frequently George's
instinctual response.

Attempts were made by politicians (and subsequently have been by scholars) to lessen the tension between European and imperial goals in British foreign policy, and to argue that they were fundamentally compatible. This was indeed the argument Pitt made from 1758, but it does not capture George's attitude at this stage. He saw a clash in commitments, and, despite his interest in North America, clearly favoured the European dimension. Such a clash was particularly apparent in the mid-1750s. Nevertheless, when the war went well, George was to press for the conquest of Canada from the French.

George's role might appear marginal if the focus is on the crisis for the British empire in North America, but that is mistaken as George's determination to keep attention directed to Europe influenced both British policy and politics. Holdernesse underlined George's determination in a letter to Hanbury Williams, who had been appointed envoy to St Petersburg, 'I am particularly commanded by the King to press your departure, as every day may be of the utmost consequence in the present critical state of Europe.' Similarly, a Cabinet meeting recommended that the Austrian envoy be informed 'that His Majesty has lately given the strongest orders for concluding, forthwith, the treaty with Russia, and greatly augmented the terms hitherto offered, both with regard to the preliminary subsidy, and to the sum to be allowed for the Russian troops, when in motion',[14] the last a reference to the wish to deploy Russian troops in order to put pressure on Prussia. George was regarded by Frederick the Great as having a great predilection for Austria, as well as considerable concern for Hanoverian interests and views. Ironically, this concern, a concern that was also to influence Newcastle's views, was to help lead to an alliance with Prussia.[15]

There was even, in response to the crisis, a revival of Jacobite hopes, although their claims of support in Britain were misplaced.[16] Rumours about Jacobite prospects helped underline the importance of showing 'the unanimity of the nation in support of the King', for which Parliament provided opportunities.[17]

On 10 January 1755, George told the newly arrived French envoy, Mirepoix, that he sought a continuation of peace, but he also spoke to him with warmth about the situation in North America. Characteristically, George presented this in terms of honour and obligations, with the monarch appearing in the traditional light of a defender of his subjects. He told Mirepoix that, in response to repeated complaints from the colonists, he could not dispense from providing them with the protection he owed them. George claimed that he had no intention of expanding his possessions, but he stated that he could not accept that others should infringe the territorial rights of his subjects; an approach that Mirepoix declared was shared by Louis XV.[18] George, therefore, very much took the government's view.

Mirepoix claimed in correspondence that George did not care much about the colonies and did not want war, but that he had no intention of trying to improve the situation for Hanover by making concessions over North America, and indeed had no power to make such a suggestion, which was an accurate account both of George's position and of his views.[19] There were suggestions that George was capable of taking initiatives without consulting the government, but these related to less central issues, such as the choice of the new envoy to Paris.[20] In the event, Newcastle told Mirepoix that George had ordered him to consult with the French envoy on the new appointment.[21]

George was in line with the development of government policy in the growing crisis over North America, and British diplomatic instructions were not simply using the Crown as a fiction. Holdernesse wrote in January 1755:

> These repeated insults of the French, which, in their consequences, would end in the ruin of His Majesty's colonies, induce the King to send two regiments to America, together with some ships of war, and to give orders for raising more forces within the colonies ... though the King is determined to maintain and defend the just rights of His Crown and People, His Majesty will use his utmost endeavours, that these disputes with the Crown of France, may not be productive of consequences fatal to the general peace.[22]

In this context, the decision to go to Hanover proved particularly controversial. George spent as much time as possible in the Electorate, and in 1755 Horace Walpole remarked that 'His Majesty was never despotic but in the single point of leaving his kingdom' in order to go to Hanover. Newcastle was reported as in despair about the journey, which he thought both ill-advised and dangerous, the latter because Hanover was exposed to attack from France's ally Prussia in the event of war breaking out between Britain and France. The French indeed sounded Frederick the Great that summer on such a possibility.[23]

Later that year, the well-informed Sardinian envoy, Count Viry, then with George in Hanover, attributed the King's illness to distress at leaving his beloved Electorate, on what indeed proved his last visit. George had certainly been able to spend a long time during that visit on his favourite activity of reviewing troops. Richard Potenger, an Under-Secretary, noted of the reviews, 'His Majesty we had the satisfaction of seeing there in very good health and spirits, and able to pass many hours of the morning on horseback and on foot without being fatigued.'[24]

The visit certainly ensured that George became the focus of diplomacy, not least because he was accompanied by Holdernesse, a pliant Secretary of State. The latter's correspondence made much of George's views. Thus, in May, the envoy in Vienna was informed about the King's reply to a paper presented by the Austrian envoy:

> His Majesty adopts the general principle laid down by the Court of Vienna, that the assistance the allies are to give each other ought to be mutual and reciprocal, and not *unilateral*. The King feels the force of the argument made use of by the Court of Vienna as to the dangers to which they are exposed by the neighbourhood, and the enmity, of the King of Prussia, and of all the consequences derived from it . . . The King has, long ago, foreseen, and endeavoured to find a remedy to the evils, which may result from the power of His Prussian Majesty.[25]

Ministers saw support for Hanoverian issues as crucial. In 1755, Newcastle wrote to Holdernesse, 'I am sure you will take a lucky moment, when *we* are in good humour, to lay the letters before the King . . . His Majesty must see the regard we have had to His German dominions',[26] the last a typical attempt to ingratiate himself that was at once as, Newcastle so often was, petulant and pleading. The Duke must repeatedly have tried George's patience.

Hanoverian security became a more important issue not only because of the prospect of war with France over North America, but also because, in this emergency, Austria proved an unhelpful and ungracious ally. This weakness in the British and Hanoverian defensive system led George to take a more direct diplomatic role and approach Prussia. Newcastle had proved the key player in the Imperial Election Scheme of the early 1750s, but George was the central figure in dealing with Hanover's vulnerability. This was scarcely surprising, as Newcastle had little to offer. Indeed the Duke's advice indicated why George felt he had to act if he was to avoid being left in a parlous position. Newcastle informed Holdernesse in July 1755:

> As the King is very wisely of opinion, that it is absolutely necessary, that something should be substituted, in lieu of what is now become impracticable; that it may, in these circumstances, be most advisable, that His Majesty's views (as far as they relate to the Continent) should for the present be confined to the security of his own dominions there; in which the King need not doubt having the assistance of this country, from justice, gratitude, and the declaration of Parliament.[27]

Three months later, Newcastle informed Horatio Walpole that:

> this whole summer has been employed by myself, and my Lord Chancellor, in representing to His Majesty the impossibility of engaging in a general plan for the Continent, or supporting in our present circumstances a war there. His Majesty has very graciously adhered to that advice.[28]

In practice, the likely costs of war with France limited what could be done for the Continent, a firm limitation of George's position as Elector and one he had little influence over as King.

Ministers resented George's trips to Hanover, especially that in 1755. That April, John, 2nd Earl Poulett found no support when he tried to persuade the House of Lords to address the King against his forthcoming trip to Hanover, in what indeed was a period of international and domestic uncertainty, not to say instability, but the King was aware that his ministers privately shared Poulett's views:

> The King was asking at Court today, what was to become of Lord Poulett's motion? And being answered, dropped for want of a second, he asked the Duke of Newcastle, why *he* had not agreed to second it, as he had frequently expressed his wishes for his (the King's) staying at home. The King lately asking the Lord Chancellor whether he did love now and then to visit his seat in Cambridge-shire; the Chancellor answered, *Yes, but not in term time.*[29]

Poulett was forbidden the entrées at court, a serious public snub, and denied Court office, but, by avoiding the public criticism of the King that would have pushed matters to an embarrassing climax, the ministers were able to maintain their critical stance about George's trips. Mirepoix, therefore, was correct in claiming that the ministry would have preferred it if George had stayed in Britain. Indeed, according to Mirepoix, George was determined to visit Hanover even if there was war, although such a course was regarded as unacceptable by some commentators. Frederick the Great was an ally of France and a Prussian attack on Hanover was thought likely in the event of war being declared between Britain and France. It was therefore suggested that if George did not go abroad this would be a sure sign that the country was indeed on the eve of war.[30] Equally, by going abroad, George could further negotiations that might help bring Hanover security in the event of war. That was Frederick the Great's accurate view of George's objective.[31]

Mirepoix, who argued that George displayed more vigour in ensuring that he got to Hanover than in furthering peace,[32] claimed that, whatever Regency powers George left to ministers in London, it was not possible that the Regency, in his absence, could address policy with the necessary energy or resolution, either to settle differences or to determine the pace of events abroad.[33] As relations deteriorated, the Cabinet certainly sought George's views on the orders to be given to the fleet, specifically to open hostilities, as well as permission from the King to break off negotiations with France if the ministers judged it appropriate.[34]

The major amount of fuss caused in the spring of 1755 about George's trip, fuss that was far greater than that in 1748, 1750 or 1752, reflected the sensitivity of circumstances, but also the extent to which the Hanoverian commitment, in the shape of the King's presence, had taken on new-found power as a way to combine both popular and ministerial anxiety. Poulett's motion indeed was printed as a six-page pamphlet. This anxiety helped condition the subsequent response to the Hanoverian neutrality in 1757.

The potential role of the King in British politics was seen as an opportunity by Antoine-Louis de Rouillé, the French Foreign Minister, who sought to avoid war with Britain. Indeed, he observed that George's journeys had nearly always been the occasions for very active negotiations.[35] Rouillé suggested to Mirepoix that George declare to Parliament that, at the same time that the ministry took vigorous measures to support its claims, it would neglect nothing to prevent a new conflict by a friendly negotiation. To Rouillé, such a declaration would only displease those who sought an unjust war.[36] His suggestion testified not only to a grasp of the tactics available to the government, but also to a realization of the nature of parliamentary monarchy, and of the potential within it to use the Crown in order to make important announcements. However, the possibility of negotiations in Hanover were cut short by the British attack on French warships convoying reinforcements to Canada, an attack that, in part due to fog, had only very limited success. On 19 July 1756, Bussy had an audience with George at Hanover, but already the letter recalling him as a result of this attack was on its way.[37]

The linkage between domestic politics and foreign policy was a key issue throughout George's reign, and one that was of particular interest to him, although, to George, Hanoverian concerns were not foreign policy. Ministers could hope that international issues would make the King pliable, perhaps fortunately as they must have involved endless juggling and strain. In July 1755, Newcastle confided in Hardwicke:

> I think both the King and my Lord Holdernesse very properly combine *our home situation*, with the foreign one, and in order to support the one, His Majesty possibly might be brought to consent to whatever your Lordship and I should propose with regard to the other.[38]

The deteriorating international situation, however, exacerbated governmental tensions and rivalries, not least between Newcastle and the axis of Cumberland and Fox. Nevertheless, Newcastle's failure to win Pitt's support, which he presented as a way to help George as Elector,[39] led him to turn to Fox, who saw the King on 26 September and was appointed Secretary of State for the Southern Department and Commons' Leader. This, however, was only to be a stopgap and did not lead to stability, as Fox's relationship with Newcastle, who kept him from the control of patronage, was distrustful. Moreover, Pitt, dismissed as Paymaster, went into angry opposition. George and Pitt, the one stubborn, the other self-obsessed, bore much of the responsibility for this move, but there was a tendency to present the King as manipulated by the ministers. It was easier to criticize ministers than the King. This was also the case with Henry Legge, the Chancellor of the Exchequer, who went into opposition at the same time. Lady

Harcourt had commented in June 1755, 'Legge is extremely ill-treated by all that faction, and even by the King himself, who they influence strongly against him.'[40]

Pitt created difficulties for the ministry in the Commons by his bitter attacks. The government was weakened by Admiral Byng's humiliating failure in May 1756 to relieve the British garrison in Minorca, which had been besieged by a French expeditionary force. As a result, Minorca fell. That October, Newcastle, despite the large size of the government's majority in the House of Commons, resigned when he was unable to persuade Pitt to serve under him in the ministry. The forthcoming parliamentary session seemed more dangerous to the Duke with Pitt in opposition, not least because Fox felt unable to stand up against Pitt. George was furious with Fox, Richard Rigby noting:

> His Majesty is wondrous angry, talked of his insatiable ambition, and the many favours he had granted him, and the much greater degree of power than ever he meant to have granted him . . . The event ended in the King's sending back to Mr. Fox, and putting it to his honour and conscience if he would desert his service at this critical time.

One of George's gripes was that Fox had pressed for the raising of 'so young a peer as Lord Ilchester [Fox's elder brother] above so many ancient barons'.[41] The combination of rank and lineage was an issue that greatly concerned George. Compared with George III, he was uneasy with peerage creations, although George III was cautious in such creations until 1784. Instead, he had a blood-right notion of rank. The extent to which George was seen as Mr Angry was reflected in Fox's reflection 'The King has carried his displeasure to me beyond common grounds.'[42]

The crisis was linked to tensions in the royal family. In 1755, Augusta and Prince George thwarted the King when he tried to arrange a marriage between the Prince and Sophie Caroline of Brunswick-Wolfenbüttel, a proposal that reflected the King's attempt to improve relations with Prussia. Sensitivity over the political leanings of the young Court, that of Prince George, helped lead to tension between it and the government when Prince George came of age on 4 June 1756. Wishing to weaken links between Augusta and her son, the Prince, the ministers suggested that George offer him an allowance and invite him to live at

Court, 'the only proper place in the King's opinion for the heir apparent to the Crown, of His Royal Highness's age',[43] but the Prince, who was wary of the King, accepted the first, not the second.

He also asked that Augusta's favourite John, 3rd Earl of Bute, who was acting as an adviser, if not surrogate father, for the Prince, be appointed his Groom of the Stole, a measure uncomfortable to both George and Newcastle because of Bute's links with Pitt, links that appeared to threaten the present ministry and its policies. George also emphasized his duty of care for his grandson, 'That the Earl of Bute being entirely unknown to the King; His Majesty cannot resolve to place him, at present, in the first station about the Royal Highness; where His Majesty is desirous of having one, with whose qualifications for so material an employment His Majesty is himself acquainted.'[44] Prince George was unimpressed. In July 1756, Newcastle sought to persuade Bute to abandon his interest in the Groomship in return for a pension [annual payment] from the King, but Bute was not interested.

That October, with the government weaker after its Minorca failure, Bute became Groom of the Stole, when George yielded to advice from Fox who thought that this concession would make parliamentary management easier. The royal message agreeing the appointment made the political nature of the decision clear, including the remark 'if the King shall be assured by his Royal Highness that these marks of His Majesty's indulgence and condescension will meet with such returns of duty and gratitude to the King as His Majesty has reason to expect'.[45]

Again, the theme was duty as a means to ground relations, but, from George II's perspective, this duty was not shown. When Fox resigned in October 1756, because he was not fully consulted about the composition of the young Court, a sign of his exclusion from the disposal of patronage, George reproached the minister for making him appoint Bute. The King, indeed, who yet again lacked the charm to derive benefit from either necessity or his office, rather gracelessly refused in person to give the golden key of office to Bute. These personal clashes were not tangential to the wider current of developments, but, instead, reflected and contributed to a sense of uncertainty. This made the political situation volatile. Pitt's links with the young Court, for example, made Pitt appear a more desirable ally to Newcastle, while, in April 1757, Hardwicke argued that 'no solid plan of administration' was possible unless the young Court was included. Newcastle replied that 'the King's aversion to Leicester House will make any junction there most difficult.'[46]

The serious military and political crisis that marked the start of the Seven Years' War with France (1756–63) ensured that Newcastle's failure to create a strong ministerial combination to the King's liking eventually forced George's hand on the composition of the ministry, although this failure was understandable given both the political circumstances of the period and the extent to which there was no real prime ministerial system. The crisis of war limited George's ability to compose his own ministry, but also exposed the weakness of the politicians of the period.

The King gave Fox authority to form a Fox-Pitt ministry, only for Pitt to reject the idea. Fox's nephew Henry Digby complained that Pitt 'seemed rather determined to conquer than assist the King', a view with which George concurred. He allegedly told Fox, 'if you go to the Tower, I shall not be long behind you'. Fox sought to rally support against Pitt, and made it clear that the King was behind him:

> His Majesty does not care to admit Mr. Pitt as a conqueror. He therefore desires the advice of your lordship together with that of the most distinguished peers and commoners in or near London, in order to offer such terms to Mr. Pitt, as at least ought to induce him to assist, and will inevitably put him in the wrong to his King and country if he does not . . . It is by Lord President's and the Duke of Devonshire's desire, as well as by the King's order, that I write to your lordship.[47]

William, 4th Duke of Devonshire, however, helped effect a compromise, in which Pitt came into office but without all his demands being met.

George had to accept a Pitt-Devonshire ministry, albeit one that was to be shortlived. In this ministry, Pitt had initially sought to replace Holdernesse at the Northern Department, but an angry George opposed the change, not welcoming the prospect of Pitt taking responsibility for handling relations with the German powers. Personal animus played a role, as George did not wish to see Pitt, but he was also concerned about professionalism, telling Fox:

> What a strange country is this! I have never known but two or three men in it who understood foreign affairs: you do not study them—

and yet here comes one man [Pitt] and says he has not so much as read Wiquefort [Abraham de Wiquefort, a key writer on diplomatic procedure], has all to learn, and demands to be Secretary of State! Indeed he has proposed Sir Thomas Robinson too, who does understand foreign affairs, but then Mr. Pitt insists on taking the province which Sir Thomas understands.[48]

Pitt had to compromise on the Secretaryship.

As, despite all the bluster, royal wishes were very important, Pitt took the Southern Secretaryship, receiving the seals on 4 December. On 26 November 1756, Holdernesse had written to Andrew Mitchell, the envoy in Berlin, that he had been instructed by George to inform him that there would be no change in policy and that Parliament would 'determine His Majesty upon the means of carrying these salutary views into execution'.[49] Pitt, nevertheless, ensured that the King's speech opening the parliamentary session in December included the promise that Hanoverian troops would be sent back from Britain to the Electorate. They had been brought over to help confront the threat of French invasion, but their presence in Britain was an unpopular step, and one for which the King was unjustly blamed. Opposition commentators knew how to develop such issues to make political points. The royal speech, written by Pitt, also promised that 'the succour and preservation of America cannot but constitute a main object of my attention and solicitude'. The speech praised 'a national militia', which contrasted with George's favour for regular troops.

George was no friend to the Pitt-Devonshire ministry, which was anyway harmed by Pitt's acute gout, by Devonshire's lack of experience and drive, and by a general failure to retain the political initiative. The fall of this ministry therefore can not be explained solely in terms of an effective ministry unreasonably overthrown by the Crown, however much this view was to be propounded. In early 1757, the King approached Newcastle, making clear his desire to dismiss the ministry. This set in train a course of complicated negotiations in which Cumberland played a major role. Newcastle recorded on 5 March,

Lord Waldegrave came to me yesterday by the King's order, given him by the Duke, to direct me immediately to see Mr. Fox, or to send Lord Waldegrave to him; and to order me to send my thoughts to the King by Lord Waldegrave, with regard to the future administration; which the King would have gone about forthwith.[50]

The reiterated reference to the King's wishes was very noticeable. In response, Newcastle reported that he was 'considering whether a plan of administration may not be formed which may have a prospect of success for the King's affairs, and of ease, and satisfaction to His Majesty; and, in that case, he will most readily take his share in it, if it shall be His Majesty's pleasure'. However, Newcastle privately confided that he was worried that he would be 'exposed to the indignation of the King'.[51]

The ambivalent relationship between the two men, and between politician and monarch, was captured on 16 March 1757 when Newcastle wrote to the King that he could not serve at the present, and that 'your royal countenance and protection [was] my great and only support whilst I had the honour to be in your Majesty's service, my comfort and pride when I am out of it'.[52] George himself not only followed the negotiations closely, but also the debates in Parliament, so that, for example, William, 2nd Viscount Barrington, the Secretary-at-War and formerly, as Master of the Great Wardrobe, a holder of Court office, could write to Newcastle the same day, 'the King was perfectly informed yesterday of every circumstance which passed on Monday in the House of Commons; all which His Majesty heard with the greatest pleasure and approbation.'[53]

George was clearly informed of news both by verbal report and from documents. On 26 March 1757, for example, Waldegrave gave the King Newcastle's reply to George's request for a plan of administration, Andrew Stone reporting, 'The King read it very attentively, and returned it to Lord Waldegrave. His Majesty showed no marks of surprise, or anger; said "The plan was very imperfect; and that he might have hoped for something more satisfactory from your Grace".' George asked Waldegrave if he knew the view of William, Lord Mansfield, the Lord Chief Justice. The letter was instructive for the comments on the King's mood:

> The King then complained, in general, that 'Everybody thought of themselves, and did not enough consider what he was obliged to go through'. Lord Waldegrave thought the King seemed rather

233

dispirited, and low, when first he went into the Closet; and that he
continued so, during the whole audience; but without any emotion,
or passion of any kind.[54]

Forbearance had clearly become the characteristic of George's personality. He was correct to argue that others thought only of themselves,
which was clearly George's view of British politicians, and it is unsur-
prising that he was often low and sometimes angry.

The negotiations led to Pitt's dismissal on 6 April 1757. Cumberland
had not wished to leave Pitt in a senior position when he went abroad
to command the forces defending Hanover against a likely attack, and
George, who was criticized for being overly dependent on the Duke's
views,[55] thought this a reasonable view. It was not simply the primacy of
military considerations that led George to accept the Duke's argument
that he must have confidence in the ministry, but those considerations
were important to him. George also disliked Pitt's arrogant brother-
in-law and ally, Richard, Earl Temple, the First Lord of the Admiralty.
Indeed, Devonshire told Hardwicke that pressure for ministerial
change arose because the King 'was so offended with my Lord Temple
that His Majesty could not bear the sight of him'.[56] The variation of
motives offered by contemporaries is reminiscent of the situation with
Granville's failure in 1746 (see p. 192).

Pitt's dismissal, however, produced a lengthy political crisis, while
moves were made to form a new ministry. As in 1746, George was party
to a political crisis in the midst of war, although, in his eyes, this crisis was
necessary in order that the conflict could be more effectively pursued.
George wanted a Newcastle-Fox ministry, but Newcastle thought that
only one of himself and Pitt could work. George, who took an active
role in discussions with politicians,[57] found this unacceptable and sought
to create a Waldegrave-Fox ministry, a welcome option to the King, not
least because Waldegrave was a trusted courtier. This solution, however,
was weakened by Fox's weakness as a Commons leader and was
unacceptable to Newcastle, leading him to encourage Holdernesse to
resign. Others threatened to follow, suggesting a repetition of the 1746
crisis. This ended the option of such a ministry.

A Newcastle-Pitt alliance was finally secured in July 1757. George
had told Devonshire, 'as to Pitt he had not so much objection to
him but he thought him too impracticable to act with anybody',[58] a
reasonable assessment of Pitt's intractability, not to say megalomania.

In June 1757, George had pressed Newcastle not to co-operate with Pitt:

> I pray you to consider my promise to Fox. If Pitt will come in with a great number of followers, it is impossible you can direct the administration, and I know that by inclination he will distress my affairs abroad, which are so enough already. I shall be glad to see you on Monday, and with a resolution to come in and support my affairs.

That Pitt returned to office in the Newcastle-Pitt ministry was not, however, a complete defeat for the King. Pitt was not Northern Secretary and finally had to accept office in a government committed to supporting the defence of Hanover, a qualified royal victory. Nevertheless, in 1757, this support did not yet involve British troops. Meanwhile, George secured for Fox the lucrative post of Paymaster General, a post he very much wanted, while Devonshire became Lord Chamberlain, a conspicuous sign of royal approval for his deft removal from the political scene.

Indeed, the crisis throws considerable light on the general issue of royal power, and the more specific problem of Hanover, although, like all crises, it was also a unique period. Foreign policy pushed the royal role to the fore, and even more because the King was concerned and very well informed about Continental power politics to an extent that was far greater than his interest in trans-oceanic disputes. Thus, in 1755, Holdernesse wrote from Hanover: 'it was in order to re-establish some kind of confidence [with foreign powers] that His Majesty ordered me to take Brussels and The Hague in my way hither.'[59] Such an emphasis on royal instructions was frequent.

Personality was a key element in the 1756–7 crisis. The serious political problems were exacerbated by Newcastle's insecure, frenetic and over-anxious character. He had only been willing to return to office if George and all the branches of the Royal Family (i.e. including Cumberland) supported the government.[60] Although that caveat sounds reasonable, Newcastle's insecurity made it very difficult for him to accept support without feeling fresh anxieties about its strength and/or duration. George, in contrast, could be explosive, but he was generally steadier and more phlegmatic than the Duke. In this, he also contrasted with Pitt. George's steadiness becomes more impressive when contrasted with the attitude of his ministers. Moreover, the deficiencies of his ministers helped ensure that George's role was crucial. He was the sole constant in the era. Nevertheless, the political and ministerial situation was seen as more volatile because George was perceived as vulnerable as a consequence of his supposed backing for Hanover. Waldegrave stressed this point:

> That the whole weight of opposition rested on a single point, his Majesty's supposed partiality to his Electoral subjects, which would at any time set the nation in a flame; and that being thought an enemy to Hanover was the solid foundation of Pitt's popularity.[61]

As far as his attitude to the other ministers and his confidence in dealing with George were concerned, Newcastle lacked both the personality and the position to sustain the political structure that his paranoia dictated: a concentration of decision-making and power on his own person. He could not be a second Walpole, not least because he was not in the Commons, and this created problems for George. Newcastle was not strong enough to take and, more crucially, bear responsibility for decisions, and his anxiety led to indecisiveness. Newcastle wanted strong colleagues able to take such responsibility, and, for that reason, operated best with Walpole, Pelham and Pitt. Yet he also wanted his colleagues subordinate and could not psychologically accept his own dependence on them; he was weak, but did not wish to acknowledge this weakness, and George was well aware of his limitations. George was not close to Newcastle, and this was a major source of the Duke's anxiety. Newcastle knew that reliance on the full favour of the King was the only thing that could make business go forward. This lack of closeness was also a help to George, as he did not feel personally committed to the Duke. Indeed, he said: 'I shall see which is King of this country, the Duke of Newcastle or myself.' The Duke, in contrast, referred to: 'those who now possess the King's confidence, but never will have that of the Public', a distinction that was a challenge to the position of the Crown.[62]

It is pertinent to draw out general conclusions. Newcastle was an individual example of a more general weakness. The Old Corps Whig political system could not cope with failure. The absence of a reliable party unity on which government could rest left politicians feeling vulnerable to attack. Thus, Pitt in opposition was an obvious threat, for he was a Whig able to exploit adverse developments. This exacerbated

Newcastle's anxiety. Controlling neither Crown nor Commons, Newcastle sought to be a crucial intermediary between the two, but this was an unstable basis for political control.

Despite George having accepted Pitt into office, royal views were still crucial. These related to place as well as policy. As Newcastle noted in June 1757: 'The two great difficulties that seem to arise in forming a plan of administration with Mr. Pitt and his friends are first the King's promise of the Pay Office for Mr. Fox ... Secondly the difficulty of removing My Lord Winchelsea and reinstating the other Lords of the Admiralty'; the Duchess of Newcastle subsequently added 'The King insists upon Mr. Fox's being Paymaster, and keeping the Admiralty as it is and says he will yield in everything else.' Fox indeed kept the Paymastership, although Lord Anson, Newcastle's ally, returned to the Admiralty.[63]

Pitt had angered George by his criticism of the degree to which British policies favoured Hanover, and that was central to George's concerns. In 1755, Rouillé, the French Foreign Minister, presented an attack on Hanover as a way to counter French naval weakness compared to Britain, while the French envoy in Vienna was confident that George would not expose Hanover, for which his attachment was well known.[64] Concern about the threat to Hanover from France and Prussia led to the Anglo-Prussian Convention of Westminster of January 1756, guaranteeing the respective possessions of George and Frederick the Great, as well as German neutrality. This was intended to supplement, not replace, British alliances with Austria and Russia, each of which had in part been designed to lead to pressure on Prussia.

Turning to Frederick reflected George's quest for security for Hanover and his perception of the state of these alliances and, in particular, his anger with Austrian policy. An ambivalence towards Austria ran through his reign from the outset, and it was certainly apparent in 1755. Without specifically mentioning Oudenaarde in 1708, it is clear that the vulnerability of the Low Countries to French attack was an important consideration to George, not least because it would weaken the role that Austria might take in protecting Hanover against Prussia. In May 1755, there was a noticeable tone of complaint: 'every measure the King is taking with the different powers of Europe must be at a stand until Her Imperial Majesty shall come to the necessary resolution of sending, without loss of time, a strong reinforcement into the Low Countries.' With clear-cut reproach, the envoy in Vienna was accused of going native. He was informed that the King could not see why he referred to the Austrian government as having a good disposition, 'when you see a refusal, on the part of the Court of Vienna, of coming into the only measure in which His Majesty's interest is concerned'.[65]

Instead, however, of supplementing the alliances with Austria and Russia, the Convention of Westminster, ironically, helped lead to the collapse of these alliances and to the Diplomatic Revolution in which France allied with Austria, and Britain with Prussia. Frederick the Great launched the subsequent Seven Years' War in Europe by attacking Austria and its ally Saxony in 1756, to the consternation of George, who, correctly concerned about the consequences, did not want the war to widen. He was also to be envious of Frederick, at least of his victory over the Austrians at Lobositz on 1 October 1756.

Frederick's attack on Saxony and Austria led to a major war in Europe, one in which France and Russia came to the aid of Austria, and put Hanover, as the ally of Prussia, in a very difficult situation. The Hanoverian government's hope that it would be possible to secure neutrality for the Electorate and its allies—Hesse-Cassel, Wolfenbüttel and Prussian Westphalia—was rendered fruitless by the determination of France to attack Prussia from the west. Furthermore, Hanover was a hostage for British policy.

The Electorate reaped the failure of the British diplomatic strategy when, in 1757, French forces rapidly overran it. Cumberland, with the 'Army of Observation' of Hanoverians and allied German forces, was defeated by the French at Hastenbeck on 26 July. The situation rapidly deteriorated. On 8 September, the outnumbered and outmanoeuvred Cumberland signed the Convention of Klosterzeven, disbanding his army and leaving the French in control of Hanover.[66] Frederick the Great, attacked by Austria, France, Russia, Sweden and the forces of most of the Holy Roman Empire and under great pressure, could not defend Hanover as well, and the range of the opposing coalition made Hanover particularly vulnerable.

Like the neutrality convention that George was obliged to accept as Elector of Hanover in 1741, Klosterzeven revealed the limited value to Hanover of its ruler's great-power diplomacy. The emptiness of such a policy without significant military force (and, in 1756, the army had been increased to 27,146 men) had been displayed, and, unlike in 1741, this time Hanover had been conquered with all the attendant destructiveness of war. Although George had earlier benefited from, and fostered, the willingness of Carteret and Newcastle to support an active Continental diplomacy, which entailed the creation of an international system that would guarantee Hanover, the weakness of both policy and arrangements was revealed in 1756–7. Ironically, Hanover's place in great-power diplomacy, instead, stemmed from its vulnerability and its consequent use by other states to try to affect British policy, most obviously in 1757, and this was the very opposite to what George had intended. Rather, however, than seeing this as a gross failure of imagination on his part, it is clear he had no alternative at this stage. If Frederick had proved an unpredictable ally, at least Hanover had been spared the Prussian conquest that had seemed a prospect if the pre-war Franco-Prussian alliance was maintained. Indeed, George's policy in the 1750s in many senses was a matter of learning from his problems in the 1740s. This was true not only of his foreign policy, but also of his management of ministerial politics.

At the same time, the crisis of 1757 indicated the extent to which there was no ready measure of success in evaluating George as international player, in large part because he had to focus on goals and define policy in response to the complex and shifting circumstances of German politics, more particularly the interaction of Austria, Prussia and Russia. The relationship of Hanover, and indeed Britain, with these shifting circumstances was far from clear. In 1756–7, which was one of the highpoints of crisis in George's reign, both in foreign policy and in ministerial politics, it was possible to argue that he was correct to support Frederick the Great because the threat to Prussia from the states arrayed against it led by Austria, France and Russia, was a grave challenge to George. This was true both of George's position as Elector, which would be affected by any blow against the Protestant cause, and by the strengthening of Imperial authority, and of his position as King, which would be affected by any success for the French alliance system and any deterioration in the balance of power. However, it was, and is, equally possible to claim that the challenges outlined were exaggerated and, indeed, that George should not have found himself a member of the weaker alliance.

This understandable lack of clarity over interests and goals ensured that the overrunning of Hanover by the French in 1757, and the negotiation of a neutrality convention, could be seen from very different points of view. The Convention was certainly presented as a betrayal of George's alliance as King with Frederick the Great. George told Newcastle that the Convention was:

directly contrary to his orders. The King was pleased to say, that his honour and his interest were sacrificed by it. That His Majesty had been by it given up, tied hand and foot, to France. That he did not know how to look anybody in the face, that he had lost his honour. Often saying that Providence had abandoned him. He hoped this nation would not forsake him, but support him and the King of Prussia.

George wrote to Frederick to tell him that he could not help him as Elector, but that he would do so as King. This provided the basis for British commitments: to keep Prussia in the war which was seen as a key goal for Britain in order to divert French efforts, Hanover had to be supported. In this interpretation of policy, George's position as Elector was benign.[67]

The real damage that Hanoverian neutrality could in practice do to Hanover or Britain, however, was unclear. It should not be assumed on the basis of simple assertion that neutrality was dangerous, and this was true for Hanover as well as for Britain. The benefit that either could gain from rejecting neutrality and allying with Prussia, the weaker power in the conflict on the Continent, was highly uncertain, particularly for Hanover, but the danger of such an alliance, especially for Hanover, was readily apparent. Linked to Austria, France had far more to offer German princes than she had done since 1741, and the best position for Hanover, and therefore for Britain, was neutrality for the Electorate. The different policies of George and his British ministers can therefore be questioned. That, however, is not to say that he necessarily made (or was persuaded to make) the wrong choices nor, indeed, that the value of the choices made can be readily established. Instead, such questioning simply returns George to the contemporary context of controversy. Neutrality, however, was not an easy option: other European powers did not see George's roles in Britain and Hanover as separate, as George and the British politicians saw them, and therefore it was understandable that they used pressure on Hanover to seek to influence British policy.

And so the French occupation of Hanover led George to consider negotiations with Austria for neutrality for the Electorate, a measure rejected by Pitt as likely to wreck Britain's alliance with Prussia and as posing the danger that Frederick would leave the war. Pitt indeed pressed George hard for the rapid disavowal of the Convention, refusing, in October 1757, to pay the Hanoverian troops while they remained inactive. The crisis led to a marked display of George's embarrassment and fury. Angered by Cumberland's failure to protect Hanover, a failure that reflected the strength of the French army, and by his agreeing to the disbanding of his army, George treated his son in a humiliating fashion when he returned to London, leading the latter to resign all his military posts. George also criticized Cumberland to Newcastle, telling the latter 'a scoundrel in England *one day* may be thought a good man *another*. In Germany it is otherwise. I think like a German.'[68]

Cumberland had been his favourite, but with him, as earlier with Frederick, Prince of Wales, and subsequently with George, Prince of Wales, George II showed his inability to handle difference and his own resulting disappointment. Under a codicil of 6 October 1757 to his will, George took away a large legacy he had left to Cumberland under the original will of April 1751. In another codicil of 1759, he left his son a third of the sum that had been allocated for George's daughters. Duty as ever was the theme. George expected service from himself, the politicians and from Cumberland, and could not fathom anyone who would not do their duty: that earned his wrath.

Cumberland's failure touched off a crisis of political acceptability and accountability in both Hanover and Britain. Convinced that Hanover had become a target for France because of the latter's war with Britain, the Hanoverian *Geheime Rat* (ministerial council) in the autumn of 1757 debated its support for the maintenance of the personal union with Britain.[69] However, Hanoverian neutrality was more sensitive an issue in British politics in 1757 than it had been in 1741, because Britain was now at war with France, the war was going badly, and the Byng debacle the previous year had created a sense that failure arose from a lack of will and that the resulting feeling of betrayal had to be assuaged. George had been keen to see a lack of determination punished in 1756, but now this was a prospect that threatened the royal family. In October 1757, the *Monitor*, the most influential London newspaper, and one that tended to favour Pitt, declared:

> The country which supplies the Crown with the sinews of war, has a right to inspect into the conduct, and to demand satisfaction, of those who dare to give him bad advice: by which the blood and treasure of the nation shall be misapplied or squandered away; and the glory and interest of the Crown and kingdom be diminished and injured.

George indeed considered himself replacing Cumberland in command of the army, but was persuaded by the ministers that this would not be wise, and agreed to let Ligonier become Commander-in-Chief. This represented a linkage of political and governmental structures as Ligonier, MP since 1748, now gained a seat in the Cabinet. His favour with George also led to his being raised to the Irish peerage, but that also showed the King's caution with peerage creations. Ligonier, who was of Huguenot origin, was not to be raised to the British peerage until the following reign.

That winter, Pitt played a major role in securing a political settlement that tied the defence of Hanover to British direction and identified it with the more popular Prussian alliance. He proposed that Britain pay the entire cost of the 'Army of Observation' and in 1758 won support for the dispatch to Germany of British troops which were designed to assist this army. Landing in Emden that August, the British forces saw action the following year. The dispatch of this force was an important concession to George, although it also fixed Hanover as a principal in the war, ending the option of neutrality, and leaving Hanover vulnerable to renewed French attacks. Nevertheless, provision for protection of Hanover was part of the settlement of domestic political differences, and this reflected George's importance.

At the same time, Britain's military commitment to the Continent created practical problems for the ministry that required the King's help, not least facilitating the supply of the British troops and also dealing with joint operations with allies. Thus, in June 1759, Newcastle was delighted to report that George very much approved a letter he and Holdernesse had drawn up, adding 'As a proof of the King's approbation, His Majesty ordered My Lord Holdernessse to carry the letter to Mr. Reiche (of the Hanoverian Chancery in London); and to direct him to prepare a draft of a letter, from the King, to Prince Ferdinand, exactly agreeable to *that*.'[70] Prince Ferdinand of Brunswick (Brunswick-Wolfenbüttel) was the commander of the army in which the British expeditionary force was fighting.

This army was to win a major victory over the French at Minden on 1 August 1759, with the British infantry playing the key role in the battle. Their courage and fire discipline was responsible for success. Six battalions defeated sixty squadrons of French cavalry by, having misunderstood orders, advancing across an open plain, and then repulsing two charges by French cavalry. Most of the cavalry casualties were caused by musket fire, but those who reached the British lines were bayoneted. These charges were followed by a French infantry attack that was stopped by British cannon fire, and then by another French cavalry attack, which concentrated on the flanks and rear of the British infantry, only to find the rear ranks turn about and fire their deadly muskets. Again the French charged home, but relatively few reached the British lines and they were stopped by the British bayonets. A subsequent infantry attack on the British stopped under cannon fire. The French did not fight well—their planning was poor and their artillery out-gunned, and the British cavalry failed to cement the victory by charging, but the battle showed what the British infantry could achieve and was a triumph in north-west Germany, an area dear to George's heart.

Born the same year as Cumberland, but a fourth son of a poorer German prince, Ferdinand made his name in Prussian service in the War of the Austrian Succession and in the early stages of the Seven Years' War, before replacing Cumberland in command of the allied forces in western Germany. There is a parallel between the differing military reputations of Frederick the Great and George II, and those of Ferdinand and Cumberland. In each pair, the former was seen as taking a more glorious role.

Despite the commitment of British troops and money to the war in Germany, George in 1759 was so driven by anger at what he saw as the neglect of Hanover that he advocated a division of his succession that would leave Hanover separate and independent. Indeed, Hanover had taken blows intended to hit Britain, and the French army fought on vigorously in Germany in order to try to limit Britain's trans-oceanic gains in any future peace settlement. Characteristically, George's anger rose from disappointed hopes for aggrandizement. He questioned Newcastle about the prospect of Hanover gaining territory as a result of the war, only to meet with the response that there would be a return to the pre-war territorial status quo in Europe in the eventual peace. George then let rip:

> after expressing great dissatisfaction with us, our ingratitude in doing nothing for him, who had suffered so much for this ungrateful country. To which I took the liberty to reply that this war had been most expensive to this nation; that it would increase our national debt 30 millions; that it would be impossible for us to retain all our conquests at a peace; and that whatever advantages

the Electorate should gain would be thought, by everybody, to be so far a diminution of what might have been retained for this country; and that *that* was the *point*; and the apprehension of all his servants. His Majesty then said, since you will do nothing for me, I hope you will agree to separate my Electorate from this country . . . pass a short Act of Parliament that whoever possesses this Crown shall not have the *Electorate* . . . *George* [Prince of Wales] will be King; and his brother [Edward, Duke of York] Elector.[71]

This was temper speaking, as well as resentment about the damage done to Hanover by foreign occupation. George did not pursue the issue of separation, although, nevertheless, he was keen to gain Hildesheim and Osnabrück. Had George had only daughters, then a division would indeed have occurred when he died, as women could not accede in Hanover, but, in the event, George had, through Frederick, four grandsons in the male line. A female succession did not occur until 1837, when his great-grandson, William IV, died, and Victoria succeeded to the British, but not the Hanoverian, throne. In the late 1750s, any changes in the Hanoverian succession would have required the approval of both Emperor and Empire, which was scarcely likely while George, as Elector, was defying both.

Minden was a key battle in a war in which, by the close of George's reign, British forces had smashed the French navy (at the battles of Lagos and Quiberon Bay, both in 1759) and also captured much of the French empire, most dramatically Québec in 1759, becoming the dominant European power in South Asia and North America. George was proclaimed in verse for British victories, and indeed war patriotism helped the Crown to keep the nation moving forward. The Reverend Samuel Pullein took time from his publications on silk cultivation to write the poem 'On the Taking of Louisburgh', which was published in *Owen's Weekly Chronicle* on 9 September 1758, as well as in the *Gentleman's Magazine*. Pullein saw the capture of the fortress, which was believed to be the key base in the French outer-defences of Canada, as a decisive moment in world history, and the war as part of a struggle against tyranny and superstition presided over by the unlikely figures of the elderly George and the sickly Pitt:

> Hail Western world! begin thy better fate,
> Hence let thy annals take a happier date . . .

George, feared in arms, beloved for gentle sway,
And Pitt, the vestal guard of freedom's ray;
Prompt to consummate heaven's supreme decree,
They give the mandate, and thy realms are free . . .
Thus liberty, released by heroes hands . . .
gives the new-known worlds a second birth . . .
When the fated ages shall have run
And shown new empires to the setting sun,
Each rising era shall its date restrain
To Pitt, and Liberty, and George's reign.

Montreal and the French forces in Canada followed in 1760, and John Pingo's medal *Canada Subdued* (1761) showed George's head on the reverse. Indeed, the progress of the conflict helped ensure that George II became, in the eyes of many Britons, more British and less German. This was paradoxical as he remained greatly concerned about Hanover, but 1756–60 was the longest period in the reign when he did not visit the Electorate, and this helped to lessen public concern about Hanoverian influences. In his last years, indeed, George prefigured his grandson, George III's, position in the 1790s and, even more, 1800s by increasingly appearing as a national symbol. As far as George II was concerned, the association of George with Britishness repeated that seen in 1745–6 when George as the opponent of the Jacobites was a symbol for a national identity directed against traitors, Catholics, Scots and the French.

The direct contribution of the, by then, elderly King to victory in the Seven Years' War was, in fact, limited, but he was keen on victory. Mirepoix, who had reported, in 1755, that George did not want war and cared little about the colonies,[72] was guilty of the common fault of diplomacy: offering an overly favourable account from the perspective of his superiors. Even when in Hanover in 1755, indeed, George had remained closely interested in British foreign policy, as war with France neared, while, once victories had been won in the Seven Years' War, the King was keen to retain any conquests made. After news arrived of successes in the 1758 campaigning season, George was convinced, as he told Pitt, 'that we must keep Cape Breton, and Canada' (the latter as yet unconquered), as well as regain Minorca by exchanging it with a yet to be conquered Martinique. Newcastle, who had to secure the finances for victory, thought both men unrealistic.[73] In late 1759, after far more victories had been won over the French, Pitt was willing to negotiate with France, but George wanted to fight on in order to obtain the best peace possible for Hanover.

The two men also differed over reinforcements for India, where the French were contesting Britain's position. Robert Clive, the British commander there, sought assistance from Pitt, finding a ready response, whereas George wanted the troops sent to Germany to keep French forces from Hanover.[74] George never had any particular interest in India, in contrast to his grandson, George III, who had views on the structure and content of British rule. In part, this reflected the expansion of the British position, which occurred too late in George II's reign to transform his views and, indeed, was overshadowed by news from Europe and North America. Under George III, the British presence in India became far greater.

The ability of Pitt to direct resources to trans-oceanic goals was a consequence of the way he, Newcastle and George operated parliamentary monarchy in the late 1750s. Once the Newcastle-Pitt ministry had been established in 1757, Newcastle was pleased by relations between George and Pitt, seeing them as crucial to the stability of the ministry. He informed his ally and protégé Charles, 2nd Marquess of Rockingham: 'The King is quite civil, and behaves very well to him, and indeed he deserves it, and His Majesty is satisfied. I have laboured all I can do to produce the good humour, and I have succeeded, and I must do them justice they have done their parts well.'[75]

George presented himself as a necessary part of the process, making compromises, such as his acceptance of Pitt, in order to secure goals. In 1757, he told Baron Haslang, the long-serving Bavarian envoy, that the reference to religion he had made in the royal speech to Parliament, which might offend Catholic envoys such as Haslang, had to be seen in the context of his domestic position. What he meant was that he had to say what would please the 'people' in order to get them to pay more readily for the measures of the government.[76] This was a shrewd response to the circumstances in which he found himself, for George was able to see the dichotomy that shaped his position and to act as was necessary for domestic politics, as well as in the interests of foreign policy.

The importance attributed to Yarmouth, however accurate, was, indirectly, another testimony to George's role. As George's confidante, she was alleged to have recommended at least three peerage creations in return for bribes, and was used as a way to convey ideas to George, as in February 1747 when Chesterfield prepared the King for his resignation by first telling her. That same month, Chesterfield testified to Yarmouth's influence by mentioning the sensitive issue of George's relations with Frederick, Prince of Wales, and, in noting its limit, also underlined her influence,

> his hopes of acquiring something in Germany . . . even Lady Yarmouth could not be heard upon it; that she kept all the credit she had with him and he would hear her when she talked of not pushing his son too far but showing him some indulgence, only answering that she was always speaking for that puppy; but when she even mentioned the danger the Electorate was in from the continuance of the war he fell into a passion and would not hear any more.[77]

In 1753, her queenly behaviour was noted by a Hungarian student visiting Hanover.[78] In October 1756, Yarmouth pressed Fox not to resign, while Pitt went to see her to forward his plan for a ministry nominally headed by Devonshire. Two years later, Pitt told her that, if the Habeas Corpus Bill was not passed, that would compromise his relations with his ministerial colleagues. In 1767, Robert Wood, one of Pitt's Under-Secretaries, was simply recycling an old myth when he claimed that Pitt had had 'the total direction of the old King under Lady Yarmouth and by her means',[79] an argument that drew on the accounts of Caroline's influence and that exaggerated that of Yarmouth.

The importance of the demonstration of royal favour was shown in 1759–60, when, after initially refusing, George allowed himself to be bullied by Pitt into awarding the Knighthood of the Garter to the latter's difficult brother-in-law, Earl Temple.[80] This was a reluctant, but necessary, step, and one that showed that George was far from alone in being concerned about status and rank. Indeed, his values in this respect were those more generally of landed society. Moreover and more generally, George had to accept that his inability to determine the composition of the ministry had consequences in legislative and policy terms. Yet George's attitude of acceptance was crucial to the success of parliamentary monarchy, and, during its first century after the Glorious Revolution, he helped to make it work in the longest period of individual rule.

He also helped keep government up to scratch. Expecting high standards, George was intolerant of excuses and often impatient. In

1757, he was angry about the lack of urgency in preparing for conflict shown by his Hanoverian ministers, Holdernesse writing, 'I never saw His Majesty more concerned than at the accounts received of the dilatory proceedings at Hanover.' The following year, Newcastle noted regarding British money for Hanover, a key area of royal concern, 'His Majesty wanted this money to be sent away in twenty-four hours. I told him this holiday time nobody was in town, no office open. That caused very severe reflections.'[81] What to some was a fussy concern with forms was also a determination to insist on standards, and a belief in regulation, not to say regimentation, that reflected George's military proclivities. Robinson noted of a Council meeting held in February 1757 to discuss the draft of a royal message to Parliament, 'The King was impatient while we were assembled and sent to know when we should have done.'[82]

Pitt used Newcastle to change George's mind, while George and Newcastle benefited from Pitt's ability to manage Parliament. There were clashes, nevertheless, as in early 1758, when Pitt tried to force George to replace Andrew Mitchell as envoy in Berlin, threatening to resign over the matter.[83] This dispute captured the problems posed by royal power. Berlin was a crucial embassy, and Pitt had to take responsibility for carrying government business through the Commons, but envoys were the personal representatives of the King. More generally, as a result of the ambiguity of the constitution, there was a tension between the parliamentary aspect of government—ministers taking responsibility for the successful management of Parliament—and the departmental one, where different spheres were focused on the Crown.

A serious clash within the ministry involving George occurred in 1758 over the Habeas Corpus Bill. This made it compulsory for a judge to grant habeas corpus where a man had been wrongly detained because of the Press or Recruiting Acts. Such a measure was popular with the Tories, but opposed by most of the ministry on the reasonable grounds that it might make recruitment more difficult. The Bill received its third reading in the Commons on 24 April, passing without any division, but it was blocked in the Lords in May and June, as a result of ministerial action, with Newcastle speaking against it. George attacked the Bill in the Circle. Pitt's pressure on his colleagues over the issue angered George, and his threats that the defeat of the measure would create difficulties for the ministry proved abortive. The Bill failed and Pitt had to accept this product of a George-Newcastle alignment.

The politics of government led to an inherently unstable situation that Pitt, like other ministers before and after, found frustrating, although George's favour for him increased in 1759–60 because he was willing to press for the continuation of the war in order to drive the French from North America. George also joined with Pitt in keenly backing an expedition to capture Belle Isle, an island off the Breton coast, although it was not mounted until 1761. This was instructive as amphibious attacks on the French coast were very much associated with 'blue water' advocates and George was more usually linked to the focusing of British efforts on the Continent in the shape of a permanent wartime commitment of strength.

Robert Henley (later Earl of Northington), Keeper of the Great Seal from 1757 to 1761, indeed later told Augustus, 3rd Duke of Grafton, 'as a fact which he well knew, that had the king lived, he would have placed the full power, as his minister, into the hands of Mr. Pitt.'[84] Supporting evidence is lacking, although the tensions in the relationship between Pitt and the young Court that would have been produced by such a development would have pleased the King.

The Pitt-Newcastle ministry represented a return to the situation under Walpole, with George less prominent than he had been in the intervening years, not least because he was elderly and diminished in energy. However his continued and active presence ensured that an arbiter for the serious differences between the ministers remained. Such a position was, later, to give George III considerable margin for manoeuvre. Thus it would be a mistake to argue that the combination of two experienced and determined ministerial principals, with George's age, growing ill-health and a degree of passivity, similarly meant that the King was weak.

In June 1758, despite having a fever and problems with his sight, George had to read nine dispatch boxes on one day, which the doctors thought unhelpful for his sight.[85] Newcastle's papers make it quite clear that the now elderly King was still accustomed to receive masses of information, and able to offer a coherent understanding of the complexity of government business. A list of memoranda for the King drawn up in April 1759 included:

The news last night from Prince Ferdinand. Three battalions taken. The number of ships at Brest. Mor. Bothmar's Memorial with several new conditions sent to Lord Hardwicke. Mr. Norton.

Mr. Luttrell. Election at Wigan. The Minister of the Parish. Some Preferment. Lord Mansfield. My going to Claremont. Mr. Fairfax. D. Dorset. The Whig Cause in Kent . . . The Governor and Directors of the Bank. Their low condition. Lord Temple's behaviour is looked upon as a forerunner of a breach. Mr. Pitt's health. The season of admonition was not the end of the session. Their design is to fling everything upon the Treasury.[86]

Thus, George was provided with detailed material as well as that of more general significance. The list included not only war news and the state of public finances, but also indications of tension within the ministry, with the King exposed to the full flow of Newcastle's self-righteous concern about Pitt and the politics of shifting the buck. Detailed patronage issues also played a role. Wigan, which was a very difficult constituency to manage, had had a contested election for mayor the previous autumn and this had led to a lengthy legal case in which the ministry was involved since the mayoralty was seen as crucial to the Whig–Tory struggle in the constituency.

The King was also kept fully informed of the diplomatic correspondence, not only British but also Hanoverian. Five days after the above list was drawn up, Newcastle wrote to Joseph Yorke, Hardwicke's third son and the envoy at The Hague, with reference to a dispatch from the latter:

I have read almost all of it this day to the King. His Majesty was much pleased with the clearness of the account and the truth of it appears too plainly . . . the King allows me to give you such informations as may enable you to disabuse those who are not determined against us . . . The King has had letters from Copenhagen, that the Court of Denmark are horribly piqued at the dementi which France has given to their overture, made by the express order of the French court, to the King for peace; But His Majesty knows that Monseiur Bernstorff [the Danish minister] says that as long as it remains in the Cabinet only, they are not obliged to take notice of it; but that, if it should become public, and become the discourse, and observation of the world, their honour would then oblige them to take public notice; and this is now your business to bring about . . . I had a most cordial pretty letter from the honest Greffier [Dutch minister] which I read the greatest part of to the King.[87]

The sheer amount of time taken by senior ministers in dealing with the King emerges clearly, as does George's ability to keep his ministers up to the mark. This was seen when Hardwicke wrote to Newcastle on 3 April 1757:

the reception today at the Levée was as well, and as gracious as I could expect. The countenance was very well, and the questions were relative to my going out of town, and how long I stayed, and the business in the House of Lords. When I answered that I proposed to stay about a fortnight, the King said 'The Militia Bill is to come on in the House of Lords immediately after the recess' and said it in such a way as I thought looked like an intimation that I should attend it.[88]

An emphasis on George II's continued importance at this stage underlines the need for a careful analysis of George III's policies. On the one hand, it undermines claims about the novelty of George III's expectations about royal influence, but, on the other, it helps explain why ministers were so keen to persuade the new King to co-operate with them. George II's continued role in patronage issues shortly before his death, as well as his determination to retain control, was demonstrated in August 1760 when Newcastle wrote to Hugh, 3rd Earl of Marchmont after the death of Hugh's brother, Alexander Hume Campbell, who had been Lord Clerk Register in Scotland, about the latter's post:

The resolution which His Majesty took with regard to the manner of disposing of it was entirely the King's own and without any view to any particular person whatever. I did not indeed oppose it because I think it a very reasonable one. I can assure your Lordship that you were not out of my thoughts when the melancholy cause of the vacancy happened. I did imagine the King would never dispose of it more in the same manner, knowing the King's aversion to places for life, the making or continuing precedents of them and also to augmentations of salaries . . . the King was disposed to give it to my Lord Moreton and even declared his intention to do it upon his early application.[89]

George was too old to serve in the field, and indeed the considerably younger Louis XV did not take the field in the Seven Years' War. However, just as George had prevented Frederick, Prince of Wales from serving, so he also blocked his heir, the future George III, from doing so. This was despite the Prince's firmly pressed request to do so in 1759.[90] This refusal made the Prince angry and, more seriously, ensured that he continued to lack a role, and lessened the chance of winning him over to back the war. The King, however, was not interested in helping the Prince gain honour. In part, it was always hard for any ruler to give glory to the next monarch, but, in part, there was the issue of professionalism. The inexperienced Prince could not be given a responsible position, and there might be problems if he was left subordinate to a socially inferior commander. The dispatch of the Prince to Germany would also have made matters difficult for Prince Ferdinand of Brunswick, the commander of the Allied forces. Prince George's brother, Edward, Duke of York, however, was allowed to begin a military apprenticeship.

Although the King was generally fit and healthy, there were periods of illness, including in late 1753, September 1755, the spring of 1756, the late summer of 1757 and on three occasions in 1758. Foreign commentators, such as Frederick the Great, whose comments were frequently spiteful, wondered whether he would last much longer. In questioning the value of Britain as an ally, Count Wenzel Kaunitz, the Austrian Chancellor, pointed out in June 1755 that George might die soon.[91] Frederick also noted signs of deterioration in George's health. In 1754, he repeated reports from Hanover that George was nearly blind[92] and discussed the likely consequences if George died.[93] In contrast, in 1755, Joseph Yorke noted, in September, that the King ate heartily, while, the following month, Theophilus Lindsey wrote to his patron, Francis, 10th Earl of Huntingdon, that George 'never looked better or in better spirits than when he first came home [from Hanover], though his visage has been somewhat ruffled since by brawls and contentions amongst his servants'. However, a French memorandum advised that George's advanced age and the prospect of a new King were factors that could affect British policy.[94]

Indeed, the small-change of diplomatic opinion included the view that, because George was very old, his British ministers would want peace,[95] an inaccurate perception. George, however, was the oldest King of England since Edward the Confessor, who died in 1066, and George both lived and ruled for longer than Edward. In 1756, growing problems with his sight led George to press for the use of black ink in documents that he had to read, while, in February 1759, a serious bout of ill-health led George to give Yarmouth some bank bills.[96] This was at once a preparation for his death, and an important sign of his support for her. Increasing the sense of mortality, his (younger) sister, Sophia Dorothea, and his eldest granddaughter, Frederick, Prince of Wales's eldest daughter, Elizabeth, died in 1757, two of Sophia Dorothea's children, Wilhelmina and August Wilhelm, died the following year, and two of George's daughters, Anne and Caroline in 1759.

Nevertheless, the ability of George still to make key public gestures was shown in July 1759 when he reviewed two battalions of Norfolk militia in Hyde Park. This was an important move in the shadow of a threatened French invasion, not least because George was associating himself with the citizen soldiers of the militia whose role was pushed hard by Pitt. Unlike at the time of the Jacobite rising in 1745–6, there was no political crisis to overshadow this demonstration of the royal role. According to the hostile Horace Walpole, the officers of the militia 'were chiefly Tory gentlemen',[97] which suggested further unity in the face of invasion. Such unity, and George's role as a symbol of national determination, indeed a supportive counterpoint to Pitt in the public mind, was important because of the extent to which the war affected society. Far from being seen as a distant affair, the war had multiple consequences, not least in terms of purchase of supplies, concerns about invasion, and militia preparations.[98] War indeed was central to the developing character of national identity.[99]

George died on 25 October 1760 at Kensington Palace, the first of the Hanoverian monarchs to die in Britain. Having risen early, as was his fashion and drunk his chocolate, he retired to relieve himself on his close-stool, where, alone, he died from a heart-attack at 7.30 am. His valet, Schröder, heard a noise and found George dead on the floor. Time would tell whether the ongoing war abroad, and the new political confidence and co-operation that it had helped create at home, would bring further benefits to the regime of the new King.

The funeral took place in Westminster Abbey on 11 November 1760, a night-time ceremony that was particularly spectacular. George was buried in the Chapel of Henry VII, the last monarch to be buried there. As George had stated that his remains were to mingle with those of Caroline, his coffin was buried next to hers, and their adjacent sides were removed. Under his will, George left £50,000 to be divided among his surviving children, Cumberland, Amelia and Mary of Hesse. A substantial bequest of £9,000 in bank bills and 1,100 gold sovereigns was left to Yarmouth. The remains of his private fortune was, in accordance with a deed of 1743, given to Cumberland. This included his jewels, which were sold to George III for £54,000 and mortgages in Germany worth about £180,000.

The private tributes paid to George II when he died are striking, especially as it might not have been thought that the cantankerous monarch would have inspired such respect and affection. Characteristically emotional, Newcastle felt he had 'lost the best King, the best master, and the best friend that ever subject had. God knows what consequences it may have.' Angry and confused at the direction that policy was to take under George III, Newcastle was to resign in 1762. Granville (Carteret) wrote to his daughter that he had 'lost in common with the public an excellent King but also I can say with great truth a most gracious and good friend in particular'. For both men, this was the end of an era, and in the King's death they probably saw their own: Newcastle was to die in 1768 and Granville in 1763.

Others were appreciative from a distance. The radical Thomas Hollis noted in his diary that during the reign he had 'passed the principal part and flower of my life in peace and full security and happiness'. The 'blue-stocking' Elizabeth Montagu offered a very thoughtful assessment:

> With him our laws and liberties were safe, he possessed in a great degree the confidence of his people and the respect of foreign governments; and a certain steadiness of character made him of great consequence in these unsettled times. During his long reign we never were subject to the insolence and rapaciousness of favourites, a grievance of all others most intolerable . . . His character would not afford subject for epic poetry, but will look well in the sober page of history. Conscious perhaps of this he was too little regardful of sciences and the fine arts; he considered common sense as the best panegyric.

Most, however, turned with relief to the bright promise of a new, young and vigorous King, leaving Sarah Stanley to note on 7 December 1760: 'I can't help regretting our late Sovereign. If he had some defects, he had certainly many virtues, and he had experience, which nothing but time can give; he seems already to be almost forgotten.'[100]

10

George II's Reputation

The neglect of George II is longstanding. Without reliable access to Court news, ready to see George as manipulated, not least because that justified opposition, and keen to focus on partisan politics, most of the King's contemporaries were apt to concentrate on ministers, not the Crown, especially in the last years, which were dominated by Pitt. This stance was given added force during the long reign of George III (1760–1820) by the vigour of the Whig myth about the new King that began very early in his reign. This myth presented him as an innovator who overthrew the stable world of 'Old Corps' Whigs politics and the constitutional monarchy established after the Glorious Revolution of 1688–9. The account condemned George III's policies by a portrayal of the policies and policy-makers of the reign of George II that left scant role for the views and actions of the King, and, indeed, presented him not so much as happily co-operative, but as ductile, indeed as a 'king in toils'. The perception of George II as a cipher led by Pitt and Newcastle was indeed of great importance in the early 1760s. This view, however, was already strong in George II's reign, being used by critics of ministers, such as Robert Walpole, to argue that they had seized too much power, and were therefore misleading both monarch and people.

Such an image remained influential during the nineteenth century, and was encouraged by waspish remarks made about George II, and the minimizing of his influence, particularly by Horace Walpole and John, Lord Hervey. Walpole's account was published as *Memoires of the last ten years of the reign of George the Second* in 1822 and Hervey's *Some Materials towards Memoirs of the Reign of King George II* followed in 1848. These were to be the most influential of contemporary comments, the

Walpole being published in new editions in 1846, 1847 (a very slightly revised reprinting), and 1985; the Hervey in 1884 and 1931. Hervey, for example, was cited by William Makepeace Thackeray in his *The Four Georges* (1860), a work that described George as 'one who had neither dignity, learning, morals nor wit—he tainted a great society by bad example; who in youth, manhood, old age was gross, low and sensual'.

Horace Walpole made disparaging remarks throughout his *Memoirs*, but his summary of the King's character was not without some praise, although the overall impression was critical. This was particularly so if quotations from Walpole were taken out of the context of a writer who was generally waspish, if not hostile, in his judgments of most people:

> The King had fewer sensations of revenge, or at least knew how to hoard them better than any man who ever sat upon a throne. The insults he experienced from his own, and those obliged servants, never provoked him enough to make him venture the repose of his people, or his own. If any object of his hate fell in his way, he did not pique himself upon heroic forgiveness; but would indulge it at the expense of his integrity, though not of his safety. He was reckoned strictly honest; but the burning his father's will must be an indelible blot upon his memory; as a much later instance of his refusing to pardon a young man who had been condemned at Oxford for a most trifling forgery, contrary to all example when recommended to mercy by the judge, merely because Willes, who was attached to the Prince of Wales, had tried him, and assured him his pardon; will stamp his name with cruelty; though in general his disposition was merciful, if the offence was not murder. His avarice was much less equivocal than his courage . . . His understanding was not near so deficient, as it was imagined . . . His other passions were Germany, the army, and women . . . there were few arts by which he was not governed at some time or other of his life . . . He had the haughtiness of Henry the Eighth without his spirit; the avarice of Henry the Seventh without his exactions; the indignities of Charles the First without his bigotry for his prerogative; the vexations of King William [III] with as little skill in the management of parties; and the gross gallantry of his father without his good nature or his honesty—he might perhaps have been honest, if he had never hated his father, or had ever loved his son.[1]

Anger with George III, however, led Walpole to temper his criticism, and, in his memoirs of the first ten years of that reign, he wrote that George II 'terminated his career with glory both to himself and his people. He died crowned with years and honours, and respected from success, which with the multitude is the same as being beloved.'[2]

However influential, the oft-repeated gripes of Hervey and Horace Walpole need to be treated more as evidence of the criticism that was inseparable from royal Courts and British politics and indeed as resting with issues in the writers' own psyche, than as the basis for a modern objective judgment. Indeed, Horace Walpole did not go to Court during the period covered by his memoirs.[3] The early historiographical legacy is fraught with excessive condemnation, and only now can it be redressed systematically.

The reality is less lurid and more impressive than the caricature. George was a politically calculating man of ability, who cannot be dismissed as stupid. Furthermore, there were indications in the early legacy that were less critical. A memorandum in the Prime Minister's papers in 1821 noted diligence and duty in discussing George's visits to Hanover, 'His Majesty never quitted this country except during the recess of Parliament, even in the memorable year in which he went to join the army and gained the battle of Dettingen.'[4]

The focus on ministers, not monarch, nevertheless continued in the twentieth century. It was in his biography of Walpole (1906), that John Morley, a prominent liberal politician and active biographer, offered his account of George's character, one that presented the King as very much influenced by his wife. George was praised for physical courage, integrity (on the whole) and for being sober and temperate in most of his appetites, but also firmly criticized:

> In ordinary intercourse he was stiff, formal, and uneasy, as men are apt to be who privately doubt their own fitness for a post, but hope that their secret is not found out . . . He was avaricious and mean . . . His temper was passionate and splenetic, and he was an incessant railer. Though not exactly bad-hearted or malevolent, he was thoroughly unfeeling . . . the dapper martinet.[5]

Unlike his grandson, George did not make it into W.C. Sellar and R.J. Yeatman's *1066 and All That* (1930), the instructive pastiche of received opinion, although Walpole and Charles Edward Stuart did. Biographies appeared, but they were based on secondary or printed primary material, with some, but few, additions from manuscript sources. Reginald Lucas's *George II and his Ministers* (1910) was followed by John Davis's *George II. A King in Toils* (1938), and then by Charles Chevenix Trench's *George II* (1973). The last presented the King as personally vicious—'abominable temper, parsimony amounting to avarice, vanity and a somewhat unseemly sexual promiscuity', but a good judge of men who was the first who 'really understood the limitations on a constitutional monarch'.[6]

Neither did George do well at the collective level of the dynasty. In *The Four Georges* (1935; 2nd edn 1946), Sir Charles Petrie left him in Walpole's shadow. Petrie also displayed a Jacobite bias hostile to George, one that was typical of the Catholic historical tradition. No Stuart sympathizer or Catholic, J.H. Plumb, nevertheless, also left the King in Walpole's shadow, not only in his incomplete but influential biography of Walpole, but also in his unsatisfactory and critical portrayal of George in *The First Four Georges* (1956), a work that enjoyed considerable sales. When the latter was re-published in 2000, no effort was made to update it to take note of subsequent work. Plumb's work was the most widely read of all the books covering the King in its day, but it lacked any real engagement with the problems of the evidence, did not consider foreign policy adequately, and preferred aphorisms to scholarly rigour. In an important assessment of governance during the Seven Years' War that emphasized the role of George, Stephen Baxter was to argue that Plumb wrote 'history with the king left out'.[7]

At the scholarly level, the major advance after World War Two was by J.B. Owen who, in an important essay published in 1973, suggested that George was far from being an ineffectual monarch, a marked revision of the position taken in 1951 by Richard Pares who referred to his 'insignificance' and his very bad defence of his central position in the constitution.[8] Owen, in contrast, concluded, 'Within the context of eighteenth-century conventions George II managed to get his own way more often than has generally been recognized. Frequently, and often with impunity, he ignored or overrode the advice of his ministers; his was the dominant voice in the conduct of war and diplomacy.'[9] This approach, based essentially on Owen's work on the rise of the Pelhams in the 1740s,[10] did not, however, lead Owen to a more major study.

For a quarter-century after Owen's essay appeared, the situation was not very encouraging, and this despite the favourable response enjoyed by Ragnhild Hatton's impressive biography of George I, published in

1978, a work that had particular impact because she looked at George as Elector and King, as a part of both Continental politics and Hanoverian dynastic strategy. The decline of Whig historiography opened the way for reassessment of monarchical power, but George II did not benefit. In part, the problem can be reduced to the role of publishing initiative and individual scholarship. Historiographical discussion should not ignore this dimension, as it is generally apt to do, with its focus on the broad sweep and climates of opinion. This unfortunately neglects the extent to which the decisions of a small number of individuals in fact play a key role in what appears. Publishers, their advisers and potential authors comprise the individuals in question. For example, when, in the early 1990s, Cambridge University Press commissioned a 'British Lives' series, under the general editorship of Maurice Cowling and John Vincent, they sought volumes for the eighteenth century on Marlborough, Walpole, Pitt the Elder, and George III, but not on George II. Such decisions can be seen very much as those of individuals, and the emphasis can be on their views and connections, although it can be argued that the decision also reflects a sense of commercial opportunity, and thus a perception of the wider market. As a paperback series, 'British Lives', which in the event was a failure, was designed with high sales in mind, which raises the question of how far publishers choose to respond cautiously to a perceived market, a course that would deter them from approaching George II, and how far they seek to create an interest.

To turn to a decision to tackle George II, Methuen's prestigious 'British Monarchs' series, in which the books were sufficiently lengthy to permit detailed study, focused initially on medieval and Tudor monarchs, with distinguished studies of some rulers from Edward the Confessor to James I apearing. George II was eventually allocated in this series to Aubrey Newman, and knowledge of this discouraged other scholars from writing, and other publishers from commissioning studies. Newman's 1987 inaugural lecture, published as *The World Turned Inside Out. New Views on George II* (1988), indicated that he had carried out valuable archival work on the subject, but it did not represent a major advance on Owen, and Newman did not subsequently publish the long-awaited biography, nor any series of related scholarly publications. Reports that Stephen Baxter, who had offered a positive assessment of the King's role during the Seven Years' War in his (ed.), *England's Rise to Greatness 1660–1763* (1983), might produce a biography also proved fruitless. After the 'British Monarchs' series was taken over by Yale

University Press, and new titles were commissioned, there was talk of a co-publication by Newman and Paul Hyland, but it led nowhere.

In the meantime, relatively little appeared, although, in an article on Church patronage published in 1992, Stephen Taylor showed that George was no cipher in episcopal appointments.[11] Furthermore, the publication of an edition of *The Memoirs and Speeches of James, Second Earl Waldegrave, 1742–1763* (1988) by Jonathan Clark offered a valuable guide to Court attitudes, not least because it appeared with a lengthy introduction. Waldegrave, a Lord of the Bedchamber from 1743 to 1752, was a royal 'favourite' whom George thought of as a key figure for government in 1757. Clark's earlier *The Dynamics of Change. The Crisis of the 1750s and English Party Systems* (1982) threw much light on George's role in the ministerial politics of 1754–7, while the close of the reign was illuminated by Peter Brown and Karl Schweizer's edition of the diary of William, 4th Duke of Devonshire (1982).

More significant was the publication of work in German that threw considerable light on George as Elector and, at least tangentially, added to knowledge of him as King. Uriel Dann's *Hannover und England 1740–1760* (1986), a major work on foreign policy, was translated and slightly revised as *Hanover and Great Britain 1740–1760* (1991), but other work was not translated, particularly Uta Richter-Uhlig's *Hof und Politik unter den Bedingungen der Personalunion zwischen Hannover und England. Die Aufenthalte Georgs II in Hannover zwischen 1729 und 1741* (1992). Although brief, some useful perspectives were provided by Philip König's *The Hanoverian Kings and their Homeland* (1993).

The situation has very much improved since 1999. Indeed, a new biography of George has appeared, Mijndert Bertram's *George II. König und Kurfürst* (2003). Although brief and entirely based on published material, this offers a valuable German view. Queen Caroline features in two helpful collection edited by Clarissa Campbell Orr, *Queenship in Britain, 1660–1837: Royal Patronage, Court Culture and Dynastic Politics* (2002) and *Queenship in Europe, 1660–1815. The Role of the Consort* (2004). Studies of Court culture, an increasingly important subject with the subject being treated in an arresting inter-disciplinary fashion, made an important contribution, with David Flaten's 'King George II and the Politicians: The Struggle for Political Power' (PhD. Fordham, 1999), followed by Hannah Smith's 'Georgian Monarchical Culture in England, 1714–60' (PhD. Cambridge, 2001), an expanded version of which was published in 2006. Matthew Kilburn's 'Royalty and Public in Britain,

1714–1789' (D.Phil. Oxford, 1997) is also valuable. Lastly, the Newman slot in the 'British Monarchs' series has now been taken by Andrew Thompson, who is particularly strong on the German dimension, and has already published *Britain, Hanover and the Protestant Interest, 1688–1756* (2006). That subject has also been discussed in Mitchell Allen's 'The Anglo-Hanoverian connection: 1727–1760' (PhD. Boston, 2000) and *The Hanoverian Dimension in British History, 1714–1837* edited by Brendan Simms and Torsten Riotte (Cambridge, 2007). Nicholas Harding has considered 'Dynastic Union in British and Hanoverian Ideology, 1701–1803' (PhD. Columbia, 2003).

As an instance, however, of the persistence of traditional views, a critical view was offered in the 2006 script in the relevant episode for the third series of the 'Monarchy' programmes splendidly presented for Channel Four by David Starkey. For example:

> If it had been left to the Hanoverians themselves, who were the least able and attractive house to sit on the British throne, it is un-likely there would have been much [of the empire] to lose in the first place.
>
> But in fact Britain in the eighteenth century witnessed an extra-ordinary and unprecedented political development: the rise of a second, parallel monarchy in Britain—the premiership. It was monarchs of this new kind who created the first British Empire, and the old monarchy which eventually destroyed it.[12]

Leaving aside the difficulty of comparing dynasties across time (were the Hanoverians really less able and attractive than the Yorkists?), this approach reflects a disinclination to take on board the nuances of parliamentary monarchy and the qualities revealed by work on the Hanoverians. Starkey also argued that Caroline and Walpole together 'governed the king'.[13] Five years earlier, the eighth edition of a major American text for students, William B. Willcox and Walter L. Arnstein's *The Age of Aristocracy 1688–1830* (Boston, 2001) wrote of:

> . . . the odd little man who now took the throne. George II had led a difficult life, hated and bullied by his father and detesting him in return. He hid his loss of self-confidence behind a violent temper, a restlessness that kept him always moving and continually talking, and an almost neurotic preoccupation with the minutiae of his

daily routine . . . His weakness made him profoundly dependent, and he became that great rarity among his fellow monarchs, one who depended on his wife . . . her head was good enough to do her husband's thinking for him.[14]

The standard presentation was also seen in Kenneth Baker's popular-style *The Kings and Queens. An Irreverent Cartoon History of the British Monarchy* (1996): 'Caroline governed her husband by a combination of bullying and sensual gratification,'[15] and in Edward Pearce's *The Great Man. Sir Robert Walpole* (2007): 'George, fulminating in all directions . . . had no more real resolution. Caroline . . . issued few commands, doing it all through her guile and his infatuation'.[16] Such accounts indicate the persistence of traditional views and underline the need for a revision in assessment, one that, while alive to George's limitations, nevertheless understands his important abilities and significant achievements.

11

Conclusions

The figure of the monarch resonates because his importance within the political linkages and culture of the period is clear. The symbolic roles of monarchy and monarch were readily apparent. Thus, in a key development, George, who never visited Scotland, still became a major player in its reconciliation within a non-Stuart Britain. This was a matter of patronage, rather than legislation. The '45 indeed led to a major legislative programme that extended royal powers in Scotland. In 1746, an Act regulating Nonjuring meeting houses specified that the priests should pray for the King by name, thus making it clear that the Stuart Pretender was not intended. Thomas Sherlock, the influential Bishop of Salisbury, urged, that May, that 'the main thing to be provided for is we secure an execution of the *King's* laws in the country; which is at present under the absolute *will* of the lairds.'[1] Indeed, in 1747, the principal hereditable jurisdictions were abolished: the jurisdictions of regalities were assumed by the royal Courts, while heritable sheriffdoms were similarly abrogated and their powers transferred to the Crown. These, however, were measures pushed by the ministry, not the Crown, and George was somewhat disengaged, leaving Scottish patronage to the Argyll interest. In 1747, Chesterfield 'told the King his Majesty had got a pretty bill from Scotland . . . the King had said he had expected it, and he added Sir, I foretold you it would be so. The King said it was their business. Afterwards, the Duke of Argyll went in and he supposedly told a thousand lies'.[2]

George, nevertheless, took his part by ensuring that the relationship between Crown and Scottish élite was strengthened. The army, in particular, played a key role in the willing co-option of powerful Scots

263

through patronage. Sir Charles Hanbury Williams, a loyal Whig, was shocked to hear in 1753 that six English regiments had been placed under Scottish colonels, but George, who controlled army patronage, felt this a safe course of action. If Alexander Murray of Elibank took a central role in the Jacobite 'Elibank Plot' of 1751–3, his brother James played a key part in the battle outside Québec that led to the city's fall in 1759, while Lord John Murray, half-brother of Lord George Murray, the Jacobite commander in 1745–6, was an aide-de-camp to George, and eventually the senior general in the army. George's concern for the army does not only link into the development and strengthening of the empire in Scotland. In particular, but not only, via the Duke of Cumberland, it is also important to note the role of military appointees in the empire, which offers a very different model to that of the mercantile-based expansionism usually considered.[3]

George, however, was less successful as far as Hanover was concerned. In 1744, Marchmont recorded in his diary that George had told a Prussian diplomat 'that the people here were angry at his going to Hanover, when they went all out of town to their country-seats; but it was unjust, for Hanover was his country-seat, and he had no other.'[4] George's commitment to the Electorate was of course far greater. It affected contemporary British views of the King, as well as those of the future George III, and thus conditioned the subsequent assessment of both George II and the dynasty. British commentators who saw George as trying to lead Britain against its wishes were matched by foreign commentators, such as the hostile Frederick the Great in 1749.[5] Foreign governments also expected that Hanoverian interest would lead George to take particular initiatives, such as acceding to specific treaties.[6]

More generally, although George devoted much of his attention to foreign policy and war, he found it difficult to win lasting glory that way. John, 3rd Earl of Hyndford might refer to George in 1748 as 'the primum mobile' of 'the good cause',[7] but Hyndford was a royal agent and this was a view only episodically held in Britain. Furthermore, George's ambitions for the Electorate were not realized. He failed to acquire East Friesland, Hildesheim and Osnabrück. No opportunities came up akin to those offered his father, by the collapse of the Swedish empire, nor his grandson, in the Vienna negotiations in 1814–15, by the earlier demise of the German prince-bishoprics. In 1759, George was still pressing for gains as part of the peace settlement,[8] only to meet with firm opposition from Pitt, who was concerned about the likely response within Britain.[9] In July 1761, Haslang noted that whatever happened in the Empire would have little effect on British policy, adding 'Ce n'est plus le temps de George II.'[10] It is ironic that George III, who never visited Hanover, became its first King, and indeed acquired East Friesland, Hildesheim and Osnabrück, while George II, who made such major efforts, did not realize his goals.

Looked at in one light, George II's efforts on behalf of the dynasty, which included keeping Britain and Hanover together, reached fruition in the 1814–15 settlement. Considered differently, the occupations of Hanover by both Prussia and France during the Napoleonic Wars were an aspect of the failure that arose from this dynastic politics. Hanover was a tempting target that was unable, as a consequence of the British connection, to follow its own line. Leaving aside the failure of the 1800s, the Hanoverian neutralities of 1741 and 1757 were major blows to George and indicated the crippling vulnerability of the Electorate. The French conquest in 1757 proved particularly devastating and this influenced Hanoverian views of the union with Britain.[11]

Within Britain, George by his own actions did little to win popularity either for the new order created after the Glorious Revolution or for political stability, and certainly far less than his grandson, George III, was to do, eventually, for the latter. However, far more crucially, the extent to which George II's attitudes or policies actively sapped consent was limited. This was important when there was a rival dynasty in the shape of the Stuarts. George's place in British politics was not of his choosing, but a consequence of the limitations in royal authority and power that stemmed from the seventeenth-century struggles over Stuart policies, as well as changes following the Glorious Revolution. George was shrewd enough to adapt and survive. Despite his temper, he was a pragmatist, or rather the temper was the froth on his pragmatism. At the same time, the powers of the Crown remained a continual issue. Thus, in 1739, when war broke out with Spain, George wished to see new regiments raised at once, but the ministers were more concerned about due processes. Newcastle noted:

> His Majesty argued quite on the other side of the question, chiefly insisting in a strong manner, that the raising of the troops should arise originally from the Crown, which I did admit, but that it should be done in a regular way, by speech from the throne, and estimate. This did not convince, and I by no means made my court.[12]

Lacking the decisiveness, charisma and wiliness of Louis XIV of France, Peter the Great of Russia, or Frederick the Great of Prussia, George did not have an impact, nor win a reputation, comparable to them, but their ambitions were out of keeping with his position. Furthermore, in his early years as King, George did not suffer in comparison with his royal counterparts. The young Louis XV was no Louis XIV, while in Russia and Sweden the rulers (Peter II, Anna, Frederick I) were pale echoes of recent greatness (Peter the Great, Charles XII), and Philip V of Spain was widely regarded as eccentric to the point of madness, as well as dominated by his wife. His eldest son, Ferdinand VI, had poor mental health. Adolf Frederick of Sweden provided an example of an amiable, but weak, husband with a strong wife (Louisa Ulrica) in a parliamentary kind of state.

It was not until Frederick the Great became King of Prussia in 1740 that George came to seem less impressive in this comparative context. It was one that hit home because Frederick was a younger relative, and his prestige was won in war. Furthermore, Frederick's success left Hanover definitely a second-rank power in north Germany. This was not the legacy George sought, and it meant more to him than British imperial gains. A couplet in a newspaper toward the close of the reign ended 'The Prussian hero was great George's friend!', as if the only glory George could then enjoy was reflected from Frederick. The comparison was more marked because, until mid-century, the Prussian royal family appeared in almanacks as part of the British royal family. If before 1737, when Frederick Prince of Wales had his first child, the Hanoverians had suffered a dynastic lack of fertility similar to that suffered by the Stuarts, then the British Crown could conceivably have passed to the Prussians, who had been briefly lined up by some in Scotland to inherit an independent Scottish Crown before the Act of Union. Although George would have concentrated on the German dimension, the proximity of a Prussian succession to Britain would not have been far from his mind either.

With the exception of Frederick, however, George again did not suffer in comparison in his later years. Louis XV certainly did not improve greatly with the years. Indeed, writing to Cumberland from Paris in 1749, Joseph Yorke reported:

> I confess nothing since my coming into this country has surprised
> me more than to find the French King spoke of with so little

regard, which is so contrary to the notion one generally has conceived, of their outward at least affection for their monarch; but it
is certainly much otherwise at present.[13]

Austria and Russia were then under female rulers (Maria Theresa and
Elizabeth) with whom comparisons were difficult, and Ferdinand VI of
Spain, while lacking his father's eccentricities, was presented as a weak
man run by his wife.[14]

The life of George II invites comparison with that of George
III. This is both instructive in itself and also offers the possibility of
considering the development of British monarchy. George III died in
1820 over a century after George II became Prince of Wales in 1714.
By then the Revolution Settlement was established, but the position had
been very different when the future George II was born in 1683. In
many respects, indeed, Britain in 1683 was still similar to the situation
that had existed over the previous century and a half. Charles II was
then ruling without Parliament and it was by no means clear whether
the latter had an assured part in the political system. Charles's father had
been beheaded in 1649, but the sweeping political revolution that had
focused on this execution had failed and had then been reversed with
Charles's restoration in 1660. By 1683, Charles had overcome vigorous
political opposition, which had culminated in the Exclusion Crisis of
1678–81. His opponents were scattered, and the succession seemed
secure for his Catholic and authoritarian brother, James, Duke of York.
James II (and VII of Scotland) indeed came to the throne in 1685 and
easily overcame rebellions in both England and Scotland, led by the
Dukes of Monmouth and Argyll respectively. Furthermore, having
fallen out with Parliament, he dispensed with it. There were no sessions
in 1686 and 1687 and, in the meanwhile, James pressed on with the
creation of a substantial army that was designed to allow him to pursue
his own domestic political agenda.

In contrast, the situation in the early nineteenth century was very
different to that under James II and VII. The idea of the monarch
deploying force to achieve his own goals at the expense of the
assumptions and aspirations focused on Parliament would have seemed
bizarre. Radical critics made hostile comparisons, but it was the King-
in-Parliament, not the King alone, that was the centre of such criticism,
as had also been the case for the American Patriots. This was especially
the case from the 1790s, as first ministers, initially Pitt the Younger,

were seen as governing, with George III very much remaining in the background. Much of the importance of George II's reign rested on the degree to which it had prepared the way for this situation. Indeed, the influence of Newcastle and Pitt at the close of George's reign in many respects prefigured the situation in the 1790s and 1800s before George III became incapacitated from kingship.

The wider significance of both situation and shift can be assessed by considering the changes in British society and the pressures on its government. This provides a dynamic context for the consideration of monarchy, and one that registers the problems it, and government in general, grappled with at the time, problems that also affected the prospects for individual monarchs. If contrasts between 1683 and 1820 did not only focus on royal plans, that was not simply a matter of the monarchs sensibly learning lessons about the nature of politics. There was also an important transformation in the nature of British government and society, albeit one that was smaller than that over the preceding or subsequent 137 years. By 1957, Britain was a largely urban country, had a universal adult male and female franchise, and was a welfare state in which the government had a direct role in the livelihood and health of the population. Between 1546 and 1683, on the other hand, there were far less sweeping socio-economic changes than those in the period 1820–1957, but the changes in Church and state were crucial, although the abolition of monarchy in 1649 was reversed, as was the restoration of Catholicism under Mary (r. 1553–8). From 1683 to 1820, in contrast, government had primarily to respond to the problems posed by repeated wars (for national survival, in each of which there were threats of invasion. These wars were far more frequent than the major ones that occurred between 1820 and 1957). Government also had to respond to the major growth of urban life, and thus participatory politics, and to the difficulties of running what became the world's largest empire; although, by modern standards, the demands of economic and social management were limited.

In many respects, there was an apparent stability in the processes of government in this period, the long eighteenth century. This is particularly so if the start date is taken to be 1707 rather than 1683, as, by 1707, the key questions of the previous century and a half had been settled: the role of Parliament had been regularized; a financial settlement had left monarch and government dependent on Parliament and a publicly guaranteed national debt; a religious settlement had been enacted that was to last until, in the late 1820s, civil disabilities on Catholics and Nonconformists were ended; and political, governmental and economic relations between England and Scotland had been settled. Thus, it is possible to see 1708–1820 in terms of the working out of the 1688–1707 settlement, an essentially stable conception, or, instead, to put the emphasis on change, not least new challenges, which included rapid economic development as well as the problems of empire. The Hanoverian dynasty had a particularly important role if a stable conception of the period is adopted, as it represented and stabilized the political and religious settlements enacted in 1689–1707. Indeed, in 1732, Francis Squire, a parson in rural Somerset who favoured the conciliation of Dissent and the agricultural interest, in his tract *The West Country Farmer Number 2*, presented George as the safeguard of Britons against the Catholic threat,[15] in short the focus of true Patriotism. He was also a stabilizer and a dutiful, executive monarch.

Whichever the interpretation, the role of the monarch was as part of a system that was at once political and governmental. Within that system there was a major change in the long eighteenth century. Where best to date it is controversial, but George's reign was certainly important to both the establishment and the development of constitutional and political conventions. Constitutional history is an unduly neglected subject at present, surprisingly so given the extent of constitutional flux, in particular as far as relations with the European Union, Scotland, Wales and Northern Ireland are concerned. The major relevant work for the period of this book, E.N. Williams' *The Eighteenth-Century Constitution 1688–1815* (1960), discerned 'a slow and irregular process, the elimination of the Crown, and the establishment of the cabinet as the central organ of government' that was 'naturally accompanied by the growth of the office of Prime Minister'. Walpole and Pelham are presented as Prime Ministers but, after 1754, no clear one is seen 'till the younger Pitt; though it was becoming recognised that such an officer was a necessity to unify the government, though not, at this stage, to dominate the King.'[16]

Williams cited a meeting between George and Hardwicke in 1755 that reveals the King's frustration. It is an instructive account from the confidential correspondence between Hardwicke and Newcastle, although it is fair to note that the events of the subsequent two years scarcely suggested that government was as fixed, or Newcastle as dominant, as the passage might imply. Hardwicke reported George as growing 'warm' and saying:

> 'The Duke of Newcastle meddles in things he has nothing to do with. He would dispose of my Bedchamber, which is a personal service about myself, and I wont suffer anybody to meddle in.' His Majesty then talked of his Father's having been in the right in resolving to have no Groom of the Stole, and of Sunderland's having forced him to make him etc; that the Treasury was the Duke of Newcastle's department, and that was business enough etc; that your Grace had begun at the wrong end, and proposed Lords of the Bedchamber to him before there was any vacancy there. To this I said that the head of his Treasury was indeed an employment of great business, very extensive, which always went beyond the bare management of the revenue; that it extended through both Houses of Parliament, the members of which were naturally to look thither; that there must be some principal person to receive applications, to hear the wants and the wishes and the requests of mankind, with the reasons of them, in order to lay them before His Majesty for his determination; that it was impossible for the King to be troubled with all this himself. This he in part admitted, but there were some things nobody should meddle in etc. I said it was only a method of laying things before him, and the absolute final decision was in *him*; that it had been always the usage in this country, and I supposed was so in others; that without it no administration could be enabled to serve him, that ministers bore all the blame and resentment of disappointed persons, and they could never carry on his affairs without having some weight in the disposition of favours. The King said, he had seen too much of that in this country already, and it was time to change it to some degree'.[17]

At the same time, alongside royal complaints, it is necessary to note those of ministers. Four years earlier, Newcastle had complained that George only spoke to Henry Pelham about 'everything at home . . . I am with regard to the King as much a stranger as if I was not in the ministry.'[18]

One way to view the situation is to see George as the fixed figure and his ministers as serial characters: at times and in episodes, key people come and go from the scene, they play their part, and are gone.

In the end, in contrast, George remained, longevity helping ensure that, as Benjamin Kennicott, a Whig Oxford scholar, put it in 1756, he was 'so eminently the Father of his People'.[19] However implausible the description there was a political as well as a symbolic truth in this statement. His longevity ensured that, by 1756, he was the only King many adults could remember, in a society with a life expectancy lower than that of today. Moreover, George was politically knowledgeable, kept his options open, and rewarded duty and those who got the job done. He sought the best advice he could, and to see this as weakness is misleading. George was a King of duty, one who pursued his own goals, not due to any autocratic tendencies but because he thought them appropriate. He sought chiefly to undertake business efficiently. His view was that ministers and politics got in the way, hence the 'Ministers are the Kings in this country' exchange with Hardwicke (see p. 000).

George's frustration with having to bow to circumstances can, in the words of critics, make George appear ridiculous, but it is difficult not to feel sympathetic towards the King. Pitt was a megalomaniac and Newcastle not the most impressive of politicians. George gave the necessary support to Walpole and to Henry Pelham. William Hay MP observed of George and Walpole in 1742,

> His Majesty in regard to him, showed his constancy and goodness in supporting an old servant, of confessed abilities, and against whom nothing particular had been charged, as long as he could consistently with the constitution; afterwards dismissing him with honour. And as he showed his goodness in not dismissing him on popular clamour only; so he showed his prudence in dismissing him on the tacit advice of Parliament, before things came to extremity. And rather to suffer the advice of Parliament than the prerogative to prevent such advice.[20]

If pleasing the King could mean indulging the Elector, George tried to handle the Anglo-Hanoverian relationship without causing excessive problems for either. This was far from easy, but, in the end, there was a working out of the relationship when Pitt supported the dispatch of troops to help Hanover in 1758. This was a fitting legacy to the often complex politics of the reign, and one that enabled George to close it in a far more acceptable fashion than had seemed possible as recently as 1757. Compromise had prevailed alongside duty.

This had also been seen at the crisis of the reign, during the '45, when royal family played a key role, but George had to accept serious rebuff in ministerial politics. Earlier, Arthur Onslow, the Speaker of the House of Commons, responded to the news of the Jacobite victory at Prestonpans by going to Court. He recorded:

> When the King came into the Drawing Room . . . he looked as became him on the occasion, with a composedness that showed attention to what had happened, but void of the least appearance of fear or dejection, and just with cheerfulness enough to give spirit to others. I never saw him I think show so much of true greatness as he then did.

George asked Onslow if there would be a large attendance of MPs when Parliament met, adding:

> that he hoped for and chiefly depended upon the vigour of his Parliament on this occasion, that they must be his true support . . . he did not only now rely upon Parliament, but had always done so, for the support and security of his government; and however he might sometimes have disapproved of some particular men's behaviour there, yet in general he always liked and loved and trusted to Parliaments . . . afterwards with some little emotion, looking steadfastly at me, France, says he, has been the occasion of all this . . . and till her power is checked, or she is subdued (I cannot say which of the expressions) this nation will never be quiet.[21]

Notes

1. The Role of Monarchy in Eighteenth-Century Britain

1. N. Rogers, *Whigs and Cities: Popular Politics in the Age of Walpole and Pitt* (Oxford, 1989).
2. N. Henshall, The Myth of Absolutism. Change and Continuity in Early Modern European Monarchy (London, 1992); J. Black, Kings, Nobles and Commoners. States and Societies in Early Modern Europe. A Revisionist History (London, 2004).
3. J.A. Gierowski, The Polish-Lithuanian Commonwealth in the Eighteenth Century (Cracow, 1996).
4. T. Harris, *Restoration: Charles II and his Kingdoms, 1660–1685* (London, 2005).
5. H. Nenner, *The Right to be King. The Succession to the Crown of England, 1603–1714* (London, 1995).
6. B. Harris, *Politics and the Nation. Britain in the Mid-Eighteenth Century* (Oxford, 2002), p. 28.
7. A.W. Ward, *The Electress Sophia and the Hanoverian Succession* (London, 1909).
8. T. Harris, *Revolution: The Great Crisis of the British Monarchy, 1685–1720* (London, 2006).
9. T. Harris, *Politics under the Later Stuarts: Party Conflict in a Divided Society, 1660–1715* (London, 1993).
10. Lloyd, *Essay*, p. 199.
11. E. Gregg, *Queen Anne* (London, 1984); R.O. Bucholz, *The Augustan Court: Queen Anne and the Decline of Court Culture* (Stanford, 1993).
12. J. Brewer, *The Sinews of Power. War, Money and the English State, 1688–1783* (London, 1989).
13. The literature can be approached through B.W. Hill, *The Growth of Parliamentary Parties 1689–1742* (London, 1976) and F. O'Gorman, *The Emergence of the British Two-Party System, 1760–1832* (London, 1982).

14. See e.g. N. Rogers, *Whigs and Cities: Popular Politics in the Age of Walpole and Pitt* (Oxford, 1989) and E.P. Thompson, *Customs in Common* (London, 1991).

15. H. Smith, *Georgian Monarchy. Politics and Culture, 1714–1760* (Cambridge, 2006).

16. P.D. Brown and K.W. Schweizer (eds), *The Devonshire Diary. William Cavendish, Fourth Duke of Devonshire. Memoranda on State of Affairs, 1759–1762* (London, 1982), p. 50.

17. R. Browning, *The Duke of Newcastle* (New Haven, 1975).

18. H. Watanabe-O'Kelly, *Court Culture in Dresden. From Renaissance to Baroque* (Basingstoke, 2002); J. Duindam, *The Courts of Europe's Dynastic Rivals, 1550–1780* (Cambridge, 2003); C.C. Orr (ed.), *Queenship in Europe 1660–1815* (Cambridge, 2004).

19. L.J. Colley, *Britons. Forging the Nation, 1707–1837* (New Haven, 1992).

20. J.W. Merrick, *The Desacralization of the French Monarchy in the Eighteenth Century* (Baton Rouge, 1990).

21. E. Cruickshanks and J. Black (eds), *The Jacobite Challenge* (Edinburgh, 1988).

22. BL. Add. 33045 fol. 45.

23. BL. Add. 32859 fols 219–20.

24. NA. PRO. 30/29/1/14.

25. Horatio Walpole to Trevor, 22 Mar. (os) 1737, Aylesbury, Buckinghamshire CRO, Trevor papers, vol. 7.

26. Chamberlayne, *Magnae Britanniae Notitia* (1726), pp. 39–40.

27. NA. SP. 84/467, 6 Dec. 1754.

28. AE. CP. Ang. 437 fol. 422.

29. RA. CP. 33/24.

30. NAS. GD. 150/3476/41.

31. B. Harris, *Politics and the Nation*, p. 194.

32. RA. CP. 33/25.

33. HMC., *Polwarth V*, p. 330

34. Lascaris, 6 July 1752, AST. LM. Ing. 57.

35. Hervey, *Memoirs*, p. 670.

36. T.C.W. Blanning, *The Culture of Power and the Power of Culture, Old Regime Europe 1660–1789* (Oxford, 2002).

37. J. Black, *Natural and Necessary Enemies. Anglo-French Relations in the Eighteenth Century* (London, 1986).

38. Richard Blacow to Thomas Bray, 28 Jan. 1755, Exeter College Oxford, Bray papers; HMC., *10th Report, Part VI*, pp. 257–8.

39. E. Gregg, *Queen Anne* (London, 1984); R. Hatton, *George I* (2nd edn, New Haven, 2001).

40. Horatio Walpole to Robert Trevor, 30 Jan. (os) 1736, Aylesbury CRO. Trevor papers; A. Newman, 'Two Countries, One Monarch. The Union England/Hanover as the ruler's personal problem', in R. Recheuser (ed.), *Die Personalunionen von Sachsen-Polen 1697–1763 und Hannover-England 1714–1837. Ein Vergleich* (Wiesbaden, 2005), p. 357.

41. D'Aix, 22 Dec. 1727, Ossorio, 17 Jan. 1747, Perron, 15 Jan. 1750, AST. LM. Ing. 35, 53, 56.
42. AE. CP. Ang. 428 fol. 243.
43. J.A. Sweet, 'Bearing Feathers of the Eagle: Tomochichi's Trip to England', *Georgia Historical Quarterly*, 86 (2002), pp. 339–71 and *Negotiating for Georgia. British-Creek Relations in the Trustee Era 1733–1752* (Athens, Georgia, 2005), pp. 48–50.
44. Robinson to Lord Harrington, 20 June 1733, NA. SP. 80/93.
45. RA. CP. 32/220.

2. A New Dynasty and a Quarrelsome Prince of Wales, 1683–1727

1. There are two copies in the British Library, 10805aa52 and 900 C23(1); NA. SP. 84/319 fol. 119; Dayrolle to Tilson, 16 Aug., Waldegrave to Delafaye, 31 Aug., Waldegrave to Delafaye, 31 Aug., 3 Sept. 1732, NA. SP. 84/319, 78/201.
2. A. Hanham, 'Caroline of Brandenburg-Ansbach and the "Anglicisation" of the House of Hanover', in C.C. Orr (ed.), *Queenship in Europe 1660–1815: The Role of the Consort* (Cambridge, 2004), pp. 276–99.
3. Gansinot to Törring, 16 Ap. 1734, Munich, Kasten Schwarz 17326; HMC. *14th Report, Appendix 9. Onslow papers* (1895), p. 524.
4. J.C.D. Clark, *English Society 1660–1832. Religion, Ideology and Politics during the Ancien Regime* (2nd edn, Cambridge, 2000), pp. 94–5.
5. AE. CP. Ang. 259 fol. 39.
6. J. Toland, *An Account of the Courts of Prussia and Hanover* (London, 1705), p. 73.
7. Hatton, *George I*, p. 262.
8. Liselotte, *Letters from Liselotte*, translated and edited by M. Kroll (London, 1970), p. 171.
9. D. Szechi, *1715: The Great Jacobite Rebellion* (New Haven, 2006).
10. Hervey, *Memoirs*, p. 918.
11. J.F. Chance, *George I and the Northern War. A Study of British-Hanoverian Policy in the North of Europe in the Years 1709 to 1721* (London, 1909); J.J. Murray, *George I, the Baltic and the Whig Split* (London, 1969).
12. Darmstadt F23 fol. 125.
13. Darmstadt F23 fol. 128.
14. BL. Add. 61492 fols 201–2; NA. SP. 35/10 fol. 144; KAO U 1590 O 1590.
15. HHStA. GK. 42 fol. 29.
16. Bonet to Frederick William I of Prussia, 15 Mar. 1718, Berlin, Geheimes Staatsarchiv, Preussischer Kulturbesitz, Rep. 11 vol. 41; J.M. Beattie, *The English Court in the Reign of George I* (Cambridge, 1967).
17. BL. Add. 47028 fol. 223.

18. Darmstadt F23 fols 114–15, 170; James Craggs, Secretary of State, to Stair, 21 July (os) 1718, NAS. GD. 135/41/13B.
19. Darmstadt F23 fol. 155.
20. Darmstadt F23 fols 141–3; HL. LO. 7958; BL. Add. 17677 ZZZ fols 15–20, 61492 fols 203–6.
21. Robethon, member of the Hanoverian Chancery in London, to Stair, 30 Dec. 1717, NAS. GD. 135/141/12; Darmstadt F23 fol. 149; BL. Add. 47028 fols. 221–6; BL. Stowe Mss 246 fol. 78.
22. R. Hatton, *George I* (2nd edn, New Haven, 2001), pp. 214, 355.
23. Bonet to Frederick William, 25 Jan. 1718, in response to his of 11 Jan., Berlin, Rep. 11 vol. 41.
24. Darmstadt F23 fol. 146.
25. J. Black, *The Hanoverians* (London, 2004), p. 240 fn. 3.
26. D'Aix, 9, 26 June 1727, AST. LM. Ing. 35.
27. HMC., *Polwarth V*, p. 5.
28. M. Raeff, *The Well-Ordered Police State: Social and Institutional Change through the Law in the Germanies and Russia, 1600–1800* (New Haven, 1983).

3. The King's Realm

1. J. Black, *Trade, Empire and British Foreign Policy, 1689–1815. The Politics of a Commercial State* (London, 2007).
2. J. Black, *The Slave Trade* (London, 2007).
3. Hervey, *Memoirs*, p. 656.
4. Hervey, *Memoirs*, p. 499.
5. Devonshire to Fox, 4 Oct. 1755, HP., Chatsworth papers.
6. BL. Add. 64929 fols 85–6.
7. Southwell to –, 15 Feb. 1742, Bristol, City Library, Southwell papers vol. 7.
8. Hervey, *Memoirs*, p. 486.
9. BL. Add. 47069 fol. 6; HMC. *Hastings Mss*, p. 37.
10. HL.Mo. 3079.
11. Hervey, *Memoirs*, p. 915; *HW*, III, 121 no. 6.
12. Northumberland CRO. ZRI 27/5.
13. Bristol Record Office, Common Council Proceedings, 1722–38, fol. 135.

4. The New King, 1727–1731

1. G.S. Rousseau, "'This Grand and Sacred Solemnity . . . ": of coronations, republics, and poetry', *British Journal of Eighteenth-Century Studies*, 5 (1982), pp. 8–9.
2. Madame van Muyden (ed.), *A Foreign View of England in the Reigns of George I and George II: The Letters of Monsieur César de Saussure to his Family* (London, 1902), p. 265.

3. G.A. Tresidder, 'Coronation day celebrations in English towns, 1685–1821: élite hegemony and local relations on a ceremonial occasion', *British Journal for Eighteenth-Century Studies*, 15 (1992), pp. 2–9.

4. RA., Stuart Papers 108/79.

5. RA, Stuart Papers 108/79, 107/41.

6. P. King, *Life of John Locke* (2 vols, London, 1830), II, pp. 49–50,

7. E. Cruickshanks, *Political Untouchables. The Tories and the '45* (London, 1979).

8. Newcastle to Townshend, 15 June (os) 1727, BL. Add. 32687.

9. HMC, *14th Report, Appendix 9, Onslow* (1895), pp. 516–17, cf. D'Aix, 30 June 1727, AST. LM. Ing. 35.

10. King, *Locke*, II, p. 49–50.

11. Harriet Pitt, BL. Add. 69285, 27 June (os) 1727.

12. I owe this point to Andrew Thompson.

13. Horatio Walpole to Trevor, 25 Nov. (os) 1740, Aylesbury, Buckinghamshire CRO., Trevor papers, vol. 24.

14. Le Coq, 22 July 1727, Dresden 2676.

15. Fleury to George II, 2, 11 July 1727, NA. SP. 100/7.

16. Coxe, *Walpole* I, 286–7, II, 519–20.

17. Newcastle to Lord Blandford, 24 July (os) 1727, BL. Add. 32993.

18. Ipswich, CRO. HA 403/1/10; D'Aix, 11 Aug. 1727, AST. LM. Ing. 35, cf. 15 Dec. 1727.

19. D'Aix, 11 Aug. 1727, AST. LM. Ing. 35.

20. R. Drögereit, 'Das Testament Georgs I und die Frage der Personalunion zwischen England und Hannover', *Niedersächsisches Jahrbuch für Landesgeschichte*, 14 (1937), pp. 94–199; R. Hatton, *The Anglo-Hanoverian Connection 1714–1760* (London, 1982), p. 17.

21. Ipswich, CRO. HA 403/1/10; Le Coq, 22 July, 12, 26 Aug., 23 Sept. 1727, Dresden 2676.

22. NA. SP. 63/389.

23. HMC., *Polwarth V*, p. 7.

24. 16 Dec. 1727, Osnabrück 299.

25. AE. CP. Ang. 364 fols 397–8.

26. D'Aix, 29 Sept. 1727, AST. LM. Ing. 35; Le Coq, 23 Sept. 1727, Dresden, 2676.

27. King, *John Locke*, II, 47–8.

28. D'Aix, 22 Dec. 1727, AST. LM. Ing. 35.

29. *Mémoires . . . Villars* V, 96; Le Coq, 22 July 1727, Dresden, 2676.

30. D'Aix, 9 May 1728, AST. LM. Ing. 35.

31. Townshend to Waldegrave, 2 July (os) 1727, NA. SP. 80/62.

32. D'Aix, 9 May 1728, AST. LM. Ing. 35.

33. Du Bourgay to Townshend, 9 Aug. 1727, NA. SP. 90/22; Le Coq to Augustus, 25 July 1727, Dresden 2676.

34. D'Aix, 21 Ap. 1728, AST. LM. Ing. 35.

35. Delafaye, 8 Aug. (os) 1727, NA. SP. 78/187.

36. Hanoverian Council to George II, 5 Aug. 1727, Hanover, Cal. Brief 11 EI 274 M.
37. NA. SP. 78/187 fols 1–7.
38. BL. Add. 38507 fol. 231.
39. BL. Add. 38507 fol. 232.
40. BL. Add. 38507 fol. 233.
41. Townshend to Horatio Walpole, 31 July (os) 1728, Bradfer Lawrence.
42. BL. Add. 38507 fol. 227.
43. BL. Add. 38507 fol. 229.
44. Townshend to Finch, 12 Dec. (os) 1727, NA. SP. 84/294.
45. BL. Add. 38507 fol. 242.
46. D'Aix, 12 July 1728, AST. LM. Ing. 35.
47. D'Aix, 23 Aug. 1728, AST. LM. Ing. 35.
48. BL. Add. 38507 fol. 244.
49. D'Aix, 17 May 1728, AST. LM. Ing. 35.
50. BL. Add. 38507 fol. 247.
51. M. Richter-Uhlig, *Hof und Politik unter den Bedingungen der Personalunion zwischen Hannover und England. Die Aufenthalte Georgs II in Hannover zwischen 1729 und 1741* (Hanover, 1992).
52. Diemar, Hesse-Cassel envoy, to Landgrave Karl, 8, 13 Aug. 1729, Marburg, England 197.
53. Townshend to Newcastle, 6 Sept. 1729, NA. SP. 43/80.
54. Du Bourgay, 27 Aug. 1729, Dickens, 21 June 1738, NA. SP. 90/25, 44.
55. Trevor to Poyntz, 21 Dec. (os) 1729, BL. Althorp E3.
56. W. Coxe (ed.), *Memoirs of the Life and Administration of Sir Robert Walpole* (3 vols, London, 1798), II, 534–5.
57. Grumbkow to Reichenbach, 25 Mar. 1730, Hull, DDHo 3/3.
58. Tilson to Poyntz, 20 Jan. (os) 1730, BL. Althorp, E4.
59. Townshend to Hotham, 16 Ap. (os) 1730, NA. SP. 90/27.
60. J. Black, *The Collapse of the Anglo-French Alliance, 1727–1731* (Gloucester, 1987), p. 181.
61. J. Dureng, *Mission de Théodore Chevignard de Chavigny en Allemagne* (Paris, 1912).
62. BL. Add. 38507 fols 230, 240.
63. BL. Add. 38507 fol. 245.
64. Coxe, *Walpole*, I, 335.
65. Beinecke, Osborn Files, Sydney.
66. Coxe, *Walpole*, II, 667.
67. Reichenbach, 24, 28 Mar. 1730, Hull, DDHo 3/3.
68. J. Black, 'Fresh Light on the Fall of Townshend', *Historical Journal*, 29 (1986), pp. 41–64, and 'Additional Light on the Fall of Townshend', *Yale University Library Gazette* 63 (1989), pp. 132–6.
69. Townshend to Poyntz, 26 June (os) 1732, BL. Althorp E5.
70. Zamboni to Count Manteuffel, 1, 18 Aug. 1730, Bod., Rawlinson Letters, vol. 120.

5. Character and Concerns

1. BL. Add. 35416 fol. 100.
2. S. O'Connell, *London 1753* (London, 2003), p. 203.
3. W.A. Speck, *The Butcher. The Duke of Cumberland and the Suppression of the '45* (Oxford, 1981), p. 191.
4. J. Niemeyer, *Die Revue bei Bemerode, 1735. Eine kulturgeschichtliche und heereskundliche Betrachtung zu einem Gemälde von J.F. Lüders* (Beckum, 1985).
5. Zamboni to Landgrave of Hesse-Darmstadt, 19 Jan. 1748, Darmstadt, Staatsarchiv, E1 M10/6.
6. A. Guy, *Oeconomy and Discipline. Officership and Administration in the British Army 1714–63* (Manchester, 1985).
7. BL. Add. 35406 fol. 136, 35407 fol. 17.
8. HMC, *Polwarth V*, p. 30
9. Horatio Walpole to Trevor, 29 Ap. (os) 1740, Aylesbury CRO. Trevor papers vol. 21.
10. *Gentleman's Magazine*, XXVI, 408.
11. *HW*, II, 219.
12. *HW*, II, 223.
13. BL. Add. 32865 fols 251–2; William to Charles Hotham, 26 Oct. 1755, Hull UL., Hotham papers DDHo 4/6.
14. Aylesbury, CRO. Trevor papers 4, no. 20.
15. D'Aix, 23 Aug. 1728, AST. LM. Ing. 35.
16. P. Woodfine, *Britannia's Glories. The Walpole Ministry and the 1739 War with Spain* (Woodbridge, 1998), pp. 100–7.
17. Haslang, Bavarian envoy, 12, 16, 19 Jan. 1748, Munich, London, 220.
18. Robinson to Newcastle, 5 Ap. 1753, BL. Add. 32854 fol. 55.
19. BL. Eg. 3446 fols. 67, 105.
20. AE. CP. Ang. 425 fol. 325.
21. Chavigny to Chauvelin, 4 Sept. 1729, AE. CP. Br. –Han. 47; Eugene to Count Philip Kinsky, Austrian envoy in London, 2 May 1729, HHStA. GK. 94b.
22. N.A.M. Rodger, *The Insatiable Earl. A Life of John Montagu, 4th Earl of Sandwich 1718–1792* (London, 1993), p. 34.
23. Ryder diary, 2 Dec. 1753, Sandon; BL. Add. 35411 fol. 189.
24. Hervey, *Memoirs*, pp. 485–6.
25. Ossorio, before the end of April 1735, AST. LM. Ing. 42.
26. BL. Add. 32811 fol. 239.
27. BL. Add. 32816 fol. 148.
28. HMC, *Polwarth V*, p. 272.
29. *Egmont* I, p. 228.
30. Mahon, *History of England*, II, xxxii.
31. Beinecke, Osborn Shelves, Stair Letters, no. 22.
32. Horatio Walpole to Edward Weston, 3 July 1739, Farmington, Lewis Walpole Library, Weston papers, vol. 12.

33. Hanover, Des 91, G.A. Münchhausen I Nr. 36 fol. 7; BL. Add. 35410 fols 8, 91.

34. Hervey, *Memoirs*, p. 652; BL. Add. 32811 fol. 239.

35. *HW*, I, 135; R.R. Sedgwick (ed.), *The House of Commons* (2 vols, London, 1970) I, 60.

36. Harrington to Newcastle, 7 Aug. 1735, NA. SP. 43/87. Cf. re postwar moves in 1748, BL. Add. 35410 fol. 30.

37. BL. Add. 32995 fols 114, 203.

38. BL. Add. 32870 fol. 337, 35410 fols 74–5.

39. Newcastle to Dr Younge, 29 Mar. 1757, BL. Add. 32870 fol. 346.

40. *HW*, I, 45.

41. *HW*, I, 47.

42. CUL.C(H) corresp. 2440.

43. Ossorio, 21 May 1731, AST. LM. Ing. 38.

44. BL. Add. 38507.

45. Perron, 19 Sept. 1754, AST. LM. Ing. 58.

46. Hervey, *Memoirs*, p. 499.

47. R. Hatton, 'England and Hanover 1714–1837', in A.M. Birke and K. Kluxen (eds), *England und Hannover* (Munich, 1986), p. 27.

48. AE. CP. Ang. 265 fols 18, 24.

49. BL. Add. 20101 fol. 28.

50. M. Wilson, *William Kent. Architect, Designer, Decorator and Gardener 1688–1748* (London, 1984).

51. J. Cartwright (ed.), *Wentworth Papers*, p. 531.

52. C.C. Orr, 'Lost Hanoverian Royal Libraries and Hanoverian Court Culture', in J. Raven (ed.), *Lost Libraries: The Destruction of Great Book Collections since Antiquity* (Aldershot, 2004), p. 163–80.

53. Hervey, *Memoirs*, p. 261.

54. BL. Stowe Mss. 308 fol. 5.

55. U. Richter-Uhlig, 'London-Hannover-Göttingen: Die Reisen Georgs II nach Hannover und sein Verhältnis zu Göttingen', in E. Mitler (ed.), *'Eine Welt allein ist nicht genug'. Grossbritannien, Hannover und Göttingen 1714–1837* (Göttingen, 2005), pp. 147–59.

56. T. Biskup, 'The university of Göttingen and the Personal Union, 1737–1837', in B. Simms and T. Riotte (eds), *The Hanoverian Dimension in British History, 1714–1837* (Cambridge, 2007), p. 134.

57. BL. Add. 35410 fol. 1.

58. R. Hatton, *The Anglo-Hanoverian Connection 1714–1760* (London, 1982), p. 14.

59. BL. Add. 38507.

60. NA. SP. 84/343 fol. 168.

61. Ossorio, 7 Oct. 1732, AST. LM. Ing. 39.

62. Hervey, *Memoirs*, p. xxiv.

63. P. Toynbee (ed.), *Reminiscences Written by Mr. Horace Walpole* (Oxford, 1924), p. 110.

64. *HW*, I, 152.
65. Hervey, *Memoirs*, pp. 909–10.
66. Hervey, *Memoirs*, p. 814; C.C. Orr, 'Dynastic perspectives', in Simms and Riotte (eds), *Hanoverian Dimension*, pp. 213–28.
67. *Polit. Corresp.* VI, 362, 372.
68. V. Baker-Smith, 'The daughters of George II: marriage and dynastic politics', in C.C. Orr (ed.), *Queenship in Britain: Royal Patronage, Court Culture, and Dynastic Politics* (Manchester, 2002), pp. 193–206.
69. BL. Eg. 3446 fol. 116.
70. Holdernesse to Joseph Yorke, 1 Nov. 1754, and reply, 5 Nov., NA.SP. 84/467; AE. CP. Ang. 437 fol. 390; *Polit. Corr.* XI, 79, 355–6.
71. NA. SP. 90/65, 14 May 1756.
72. Stephen Poyntz, Cumberland's former Governor, to Trevor, 9 Jan. (os), 19 Mar. (os) 1745, Aylesbury, Trevor papers, vols 45–6.
73. Paris, Bibliothèque Nationale, naf. 10716 fol. 12.
74. Haslang, 16 Sept. 1754, Munich, London 229.
75. G. Wagner, *Thomas Coram, Gent, 1666–1751* (Woodbridge, 2004).
76. Ossorio, 15 Mar. 1748, AST. LM. Ing. 54.
77. *HW*, II, 191.
78. W. Coxe, *Pelham Administration* (2 vols, London, 1829) I, 103.
79. E. Harcourt (ed.), *The Harcourt Papers* (7 vols, Oxford, no date), III, 74.
80. BL. Add. 32693 fol. 326.
81. BL. Add. 35406 fol. 272.
82. Ossorio, 23 Feb. 1748, AST. LM. Ing. 54.

6. George and Walpole: Double Act or King in the Shadows? 1731–1741

1. 17 Jan. 1733, NA. SP. 107/8.
2. Newcastle to Waldegrave, 26 Mar. (os) 1731, BL. Add. 32772.
3. P. Langford, *The Excise Crisis* (Oxford, 1975); J. Price, 'The Excise Affair revisited', in S. Baxter (ed.), *England's Rise to Greatness* (Berkeley, 1983), pp. 257–321.
4. BL. Add. 64929 fol. 77.
5. BL. Add. 64929 fol. 77, 64939 fol. 81.
6. NAS. GD. 150/3474/21.
7. Beinecke, Stair Letters, no. 51.
8. BL. Add. 47033 fol. 62.
9. BL. Add. 74005 fol. 21.
10. BL. Add. 51437 fol. 14.
11. Broglie, 2 July 1730, AE. CP. Ang. 370.
12. J. Black, 'British Neutrality in the War of the Polish Succession, 1733–1735', *International History Review*, 8 (1986), pp. 345–66.

13. BL. Add. 23790 fol. 401.
14. J. Black, 'When "Natural Allies" Fall Out: Anglo-Austrian Relations, 1725–1740', *Mitteilungen des Österreichischen Staatsarchivs*, 36 (1983).
15. NA. SP. 84/311 fol. 109.
16. D'Aix, 9 May 1728, AST. LM. Ing. 35.
17. J. Black, *The Collapse of the Anglo-French Alliance, 1727–31* (Gloucester, 1987).
18. Ossorio, 29 Oct. 1731, AST. LM. Ing. 38.
19. B. Kappelhoff, *Absolutistsisches Regiment oder Ständeherrschaft? Landesherr und Landstände in Ostfriesland im ersten Drittel des* 18. *Jahrhunderts* (Hildesheim, 1982).
20. M. Hughes, *Law and Politics in Eighteenth Century Germany: The Imperial Aulic Council in the Reign of Charles VI* (Woodbridge, 1988).
21. Horatio Walpole to Robert Trevor, 26 Ap. (os) 1737, Aylesbury CRO. Trevor papers, vol. 8.
22. HHStA. GK. 85a.
23. Ossorio, 28 Sept. 1738, AST. LM. Ing. 45.
24. Robinson to Harrington, 28 Oct. 1733, NA. SP. 80/100.
25. Horatio to Robert Walpole, 10 July 1734, CUL. C(H) corresp. 2259.
26. NA. SP. 43/86.
27. De Löss report, 16 Aug., 2 Sept. 1736, Dresden, 638 IV 6. fols 130, 180–3.
28. Horatio Walpole to Trevor, 30 Jan. (os) 1736, Aylesbury, Trevor papers, Ossorio, 11 Feb., 4 Mar. 1737, AST. LM. Ing. 44.
29. AE. CP. Ang. 397 fols 252–3.
30. *HW*, I, 93.
31. Ossorio, 23 May 1740, AST. LM. Ing. 46.
32. W. Coxe, *Memoirs of . . . Walpole* (1798), III, 535–7.
33. BL. Add. 32689 fol. 212.
34. Beinecke, Stair Letters, no. 22.
35. BL. Add. 63749 fol. 253.
36. P. Yorke, *Walpoliana* (London, 1781), p. 6.
37. Ossorio, 19 Mar. 1736, AST. LM. Ing. 43.
38. Ossorio, 3 May 1736, AST. LM. Ing. 43.
39. Horatio Walpole to Trevor, 21 Oct. 1736, Aylesbury, Trevor papers, vol. 5; BL. Add. 4806 fol. 178.
40. RA. Stuart papers 207/133.
41. Ossorio, 10 May 1736, AST. LM. Ing. 43.
42. Hervey, *Memoirs*, p. 652.
43. Ossorio, 17 June 1737, AST. LM. Ing. 44.
44. BL. Add. 33045 fol. 27.
45. BL. Add. 33045 fol. 29.
46. S. Taylor and C. Jones (eds), *Tory and Whig. The Parliamentary Papers of Edward Harley and William Hay* (Woodbridge, 1998), pp. 24–6.
47. Weston to Titley, 25 Feb. 1737, BL. Eg. 2684.
48. BL. Add. 20815 p. 5.

49. BL. Add. 20815, pp. 17–19.
50. BL. Add. 33045 fol. 31.
51. Francis Hare, Bishop of Chichester, to his son, Francis Naylor, 18 Dec. (os) 1737, 26 Jan. (os) 1738 HMC., *14th Report, Appendix I* (1895), pp. 237–8.
52. Hervey, *Memoirs*, p. 919.
53. Ossorio, 5 May 1738, AST. LM. Ing. 45.
54. BL. Add. 32870 fols 58–62.
55. Haslang, 19 Jan. 1748, Munich, Bayr. Ges. London 220.
56. BL. Add. 35335 fol. 26.
57. Beinecke, Stair Letters, no. 18.
58. Couraud to Waldegrave, 31 Jan. (os) 1737, Chewton; Ossorio, 11, 25 Feb. 1737, AST. LM. Ing. 44.
59. HMC. *Carlisle*, p. 176.
60. BL. Add. 32692 fol. 164.
61. HMC. *Carlisle*, p. 172.
62. BL. Add. 9176 fols 32, 34; Horatio Walpole to Trevor, 10 Aug. (os) 1740, Aylesbury. CRO. Trevor papers, vol. 22.
63. Lowther to Spedding, 18 Nov. 1740, Carlisle, Cumbria CRO. D/Lons./W.
64. Ryder papers, Sandon Hall.
65. Cobbett, XI, 732.
66. Horatio Walpole to Trevor, 3 Jan. (os) 1738, Aylesbury CRO., Trevor papers, vol. 10.
67. Robert to Horatio, 21 Aug. 1739, BL. Add. 63749A fol. 320; Horatio to Trevor, 13 May (os), 21 June (os), 5 Dec. (os) 1740, Aylesbury CRO., Trevor papers, vols 21, 22, 24.
68. Horatio Walpole to Malton, 10 Oct. (os) 1738, NWM 3.
69. Chewton Mendip, Chewton House, Waldegrave papers.
70. CUL. C(H) corresp. 2716; BL. Add. 9132 fol. 96; Ossorio, 6 Jan. 1738, AST. LM. Ing. 45..
71. BL. Add. 35586 fols 47–8.

7. Turmoil and Crisis, 1741–1746

1. Ossorio, 10 July 1739, AST. LM. Ing. 46.
2. Ossorio, 21, 22 Nov. 1740, AST. LM. Ing. 46.
3. R. Browning, *The War of Austrian Succession* (Stroud, 1994); M.S. Anderson, *The War of Austrian Succession, 1740–1748* (London, 1995).
4. Ütterodt, 10 Jan. 1741, Dresden, 2677 III; Ossorio, 2 Jan. 1741, AST. LM. Ing. 47.
5. Walpole to Trevor, 19 Dec. (os) 1740, Aylesbury, Buckinghamshire CRO., Trevor Mss vol. 24; W. Mediger, 'Great Britain, Hanover and the Rise of Prussia', in R. Hatton and M.S. Anderson (eds), *Studies in Diplomatic History* (1970), p. 203; 26 Dec. (os) 1740, NA. SP. 84/388.

6. Ossorio, 24 Mar. 1741, AST. LM. Ing. 47.

7. Ossorio, 31 July 1741, AST. LM. Ing. 47.

8. BL. Add. 35407 fol. 43.

9. Harrington to Newcastle, 2 Aug. 1741, NA. SP. 43/101; BL. Add. 32697 fol. 240.

10. Harrington to Newcastle, 2 Aug. 1741, NA. SP. 43/101.

11. AE. CP. Brunswick-Hanovre 49, fols 99–100, 144–6, 149–50, 161–4; AE. MD. Brunswick-Hanovre 9 fols 164–250.

12. AE. CP. Brunswick-Hanovre 49 fols 162–214.

13. AE. CP. Espagne 470 fol. 95.

14. 3 Dec. (os) 1741, NA. SP. 92/44; Ossorio, 13 Dec. 1741, AST. LM. Ing. 47.

15. K. Wilson, 'Empire, trade and popular politics in mid-Hanoverian Britain: the case of Admiral Vernon', *Past and Present*, 121 (1988), pp. 74–109.

16. R.H. Harding, *Amphibious Warfare in the Eighteenth Century. The British Expedition to the West Indies, 1740–1742* (Woodbridge, 1991).

17. Horatio Walpole to Trevor, 17 Ap. (os) 1739, Aylesbury CRO. Trevor papers, vol. 17.

18. Amelot to Bussy, 5 Jan., Valory to Bussy, 13 Jan. 1742, NA. SP. 107/52. Hardenberg's reports are in Hanover, Calenberg Brief Archiv 24.

19. Trevor to Henry Pelham, 15 May 1744, Aylesbury, Trevor papers, vol. 39.

20. Zamboni to Haslang, 5 Jan. 1742, Munich, London 370.

21. BL. Add. 35587 fols 2–5.

22. HMC. *Egmont*, III, 239.

23. J.B. Owen, *The Rise of the Pelhams* (London, 1957), pp. 1–40.

24. *The Lives of Dr. Edward Pocock, Dr. Zachary Pearce, Dr. Thomas Newton and the Rev. Philip Shelton* (2 vols, London, 1816) II, 49, 69–70.

25. W.S. Lewis (ed.) *Horace Walpole's Correspondence* XVII, 318–19, 502.

26. BL. Add. 37934 fol. 32; Ossorio, 2 Ap. 1742, AST. LM. Ing. 48.

27. HL. STG. Box 191 (12).

28. BL. Add. 63749A fol. 339.

29. Sandon Mss. 21 R. 144.

30. Ossorio, 13 Ap. 1742, AST. LM. Ing. 48.

31. Taunton, Somerset CRO. Trollop-Bellew papers DD/TB 16 FT18; M. Orr, *Dettingen 1743* (London, 1972).

32. Aylesbury, Buckinghamshire CRO. D/X 1069/2/115.

33. Leonard to Molly Robinson, 18 June 1743, Warwick, The Queen's Own Hussars Museum.

34. BL. Add. 35396 fols 111–12, 32701 fols 37–8.

35. *Westminster Journal*, 17 Sept. (os), 13, 19 Nov. (os), 24 Dec. (os) 1743; Ossorio, 18 Feb. 1737, AST. LM. Ing. 44.

36. BL. Add. 32702 fol. 7.

37. S. Küster, *Vier Monarchien—Vier Öffentlichkeiten: Kommunikation um die Schlacht bei Dettingen* (Münster, 2004).

38. P. Mackesy, *The Coward of Minden* (London, 1979).

39. W. Coxe, *Pelham Administration* (2 vols, London, 1829), I, 103.
40. B. Simms, 'Pitt and Hanover', in Simms and T. Riotte (eds), *The Hanoverian Dimension in British History, 1714–1837* (Cambridge, 2007), p. 34.
41. Taunton, CRO. DD/SAS/FA 41/C; Warwick CRO. 136 B 2530/2.
42. *HW*, I, 71–2.
43. Northumberland CRO. ZAL 98 13/2; Bod. Ms. Don. C. 107 fols 117–18.
44. P. Yorke (ed.), *Life and Correspondence of Philip Yorke, Earl of Hardwicke* (3 vols, Cambridge, 1913) I, 383.
45. AE. CP. Bavière 110 fol. 71.
46. R. Lodge, 'The Hanau controversy in 1744 and the fall of Carteret', *English Historical Review*, 38 (1923), pp. 509–31.
47. *Bedford Corresp.* I, xxxvii–xxxviii.
48. RA. CP. 4/201–4; NA. SP. 43/115.
49. C. Duffy, *The '45* (London, 2003).
50. F. McLynn, *Charles Edward Stuart* (London, 1988), p. 144.
51. Bedford, CRO. HW 87/125.
52. Stanhope to George Stanhope, 11 Feb. 1746, Maidstone, Kent Archive Office, U1590C 708/1; *Hardwicke*, I, 499.
53. Goodwood, MS 104 fol. 297.
54. Bod. MS Don. c. 107 fols 226–7.
55. Coxe, *Pelham Administration*, I, 290.
56. G.H. Rose (ed.), *A Selection of the Papers of the Earls of Marchmont* (3 vols, London, 1831), I, 181, 187.

8. The Rule of the Pelhams? 1746–1754

1. U. Dann, *Hanover and Great Britain 1740–1760* (Leicester, 1991).
2. *Polit. Corresp.*, IV, 324.
3. Rose (ed.), *Marchmont*, I, 176; J. Black, *Pitt the Elder* (Stroud, 1999), pp. 65–6.
4. Ilchester (ed.), *Letters to Henry Fox*, pp. 12–13, 53.
5. BL. Add. 32810 fol. 391.
6. RA. CP. 32/303.
7. HMC. *Polwarth V*, pp. 258–9.
8. NLS. MS 16630 fol. 124.
9. BL. Add. 32707 fol. 492.
10. RA. CP. 32/121.
11. BL. Add. 15870 fol. 42.
12. 11 Ap. 1755, Newport, Public Library, Hanbury Williams papers.
13. R.R. Sedgwick (ed.), *The House of Commons* (2 vols, London, 1970) I, 57.
14. HMC. *Polwarth V*, p. 272.
15. RA. CP. 32/113–14.
16. Haslang, 2 Jan. 1748, Munich, Bayr. Ges. London 220; Ossorio, 2 Jan. 1748, AST. LM. Ing. 54.

17. BL. Add. 9147 fol. 14; Leeds, Archive Office, Newby Hall mss 2833 no. 71.
18. HMC. *Polwarth V*, p. 255.
19. Farmington, 67 fol. 155.
20. *Polit. Corresp.* X, 478.
21. Fox to Hanbury Williams, 10 May (os) 1750, Farmington, 52; Newcastle to Pelham, 13 Sept. 1750, BL. Add. 35411.
22. *Polit. Corresp.* X, 149–50.
23. BL. Add. 32816 fol. 142.
24. BL. Add. 21816 fol. 188.
25. BL. Add. 15873 fols 86, 84.
26. R.N. Middleton, 'French Policy and Prussia after the Peace of Aix-la-Chapelle, 1749–1753' (PhD. Columbia, 1968), pp. 170, 174; AE. CP. Prusse 171 fols 239–41.
27. *Polit. Corresp.* VIII, 538.
28. BL. Add. 32722 fol. 24, 32723 fols 134–5.
29. Perron, 6 Mar. 1755, AST. LM. Ing. 59.
30. Newcastle to Hanbury Williams, 5 Feb. (os) 1751, NA. SP. 88/71.
31. NA. SP. 84/454 fol. 61.
32. *HW*, I, 42.
33. BL. Add. 32810 fol. 411.
34. AE. CP. Ang. 428 fol. 7.
35. *HW*, I, 43.
36. Farmington, 54 fol. 11.
37. A.N. Newman (ed.), 'Leicester House Politics, 1750–60, from the papers of John, Second Earl of Egmont', *Camden Miscellany* (London, 1969), p. 208.
38. *HW*, I, 133.
39. W. Coxe, *Pelham Administration* (1829), II, 385.
40. BL. Add. 15873 fol. 82; *Gentleman's Magazine* 21 (1751), p. 522.
41. *HW*, I, 142.
42. NA. SP. 36/111 fol. 115.
43. HMC. *Polwarth V*, pp. 183–4.
44. *Hardwicke*, II, 43; J. Bullion, '"To play what game she pleased without observation": Princess Augusta and the political drama of succession, 1736–56', in Orr (ed.), *Queenship in Britain*, pp. 223–5.
45. *HW*, I, 79.
46. *HW*, I, 82.
47. *HW*, I, 103.
48. *HW*, I, 103.
49. G. Plank, *Rebellion and Savagery. The Jacobite Rising of 1745 and the British Empire* (Philadelphia, 2006).
50. *Polit. Corresp.* X, 118; Bedford CRO. Lucas papers 30/9/3/31; NA. SP. 36/118 fol. 343.
51. AE. MD. Ang. 51 fols 154–61; BL. Add. 35412 fol. 3.
52. BL. Add. 35412 fol. 132.

53. NA. SP. 36/118 fol. 299.
54. NA. SP. 36/119 fol. 143.
55. 2 Feb. 1753, NA. SP. 80/191.
56. BL. Add. 35412 fols 209, 184, 250.
57. *HW*, I, 236–7.
58. *HW*, I, 15.
59. Fox to Devonshire, 11 Dec. 1755, HP.
60. BL. Add. 32870 fol. 299.
61. BL. Add. 32731 fol. 260.

9. Last Years, 1754–1760

1. AE. MD. Ang. 1 fols 30, 39–40, 100–1.
2. B. Stone, *The French Parlements and the Crisis of the Old Regime* (Chapel Hill, 1986); J. Swann, *Politics and the Parlement of Paris under Louis XV, 1754–1774* (Cambridge, 1995).
3. P.C. Yorke (ed.), *The Life of Lord Chancellor Hardwicke* (3 vols, Cambridge, 1913), II, 214.
4. 24 July 1755, Newport, Hanbury Williams papers.
5. Ilchester (ed.), *Letters to Henry Fox*, p. 100.
6. Perron, 21 Nov., 5, 19 Dec. 1754, AST. LM. Ing. 58.
7. Leeds, Vyner papers no. 11863.
8. Alt, 17 Dec. 1754, Marburg 257.
9. BL. Add. 32856 fol. 380.
10. BL. Add. 32996 fols 81–2.
11. *Hardwicke*, II, 235.
12. AE. CP. Ang. 439 fol. 273; Viry, 25 Aug. 1755, AST. LM. Ing. 59.
13. BL. Add. 32856 fol. 380.
14. 11 Ap. 1755, Newport, Hanbury Williams papers; BL. Add. 32996 fol. 79.
15. *Polit. Corresp.* X, 386.
16. AE. CP. Ang. 439 fols 278–9, 287, 371–2, 438, fol. 349.
17. BL. Add. 35364 fol. 43.
18. AE. CP. Ang. 438 fol. 15.
19. AE. CP. Ang. 438 fol. 305, 439 fol. 169.
20. AE. CP. Ang. 438 fol. 50.
21. AE. CP. Ang. 438 fol. 50.
22. NA. SP. 84/468, 28 Jan.
23. *HW*, II, 48; Perron, 20 Mar. 1755, AST. LM. Ing. 59 cf. 17 Ap.
24. Viry, 8 Sept. 1755, AST. LM. Ing. 59; Potenger to Hanbury Williams, 17 June 1755, Newport, Hanbury Williams papers.
25. NA. SP. 80/196 fols. 37, 44.
26. BL. Add. 32857 fol. 54.
27. BL. Add. 32857 fols 4, 43.

28. BL. Add. 63750 fol. 42.
29. Benjamin Kennicott to Thomas Bray, no date, Exeter College, Oxford, Bray papers.
30. AE. CP. Ang. 438 fol. 311; Perron, 20 Mar. 1755, AST. LM. Ing. 59; *Harcourt Papers*, III, 69; Blacow to Bray, no date, and 7 Mar. 1755, Exeter College, Oxford, Bray Papers.
31. *Polit. Corresp.* XI, 193.
32. AE. CP. Ang. 438 fol. 443.
33. AE. CP. Ang. 438 fol. 418, fols 170, 226.
34. BL. Add. 32996 fols 150–1, 161.
35. AE. CP. Autriche 254 fol. 225.
36. AE. CP. Ang. 438 fol. 350.
37. AE. CP. Brunswick-Hanovre 52 fols 16–19.
38. BL. Add. 35415 fol. 3.
39. BL. Add. 32857 fols 44, 53.
40. *Harcourt Papers*, III, 72.
41. Bedford Corresp, II, 200–1; *HW*, II, 179.
42. BL. Add. 51387 fol. 49.
43. BL. Add. 33045 fol. 55.
44. BL. Add. 33045 fol. 56.
45. BL. Add. 33045 fols 80, 90.
46. BL. Add. 32870 fols 399, 423.
47. *HW*, II, 186; Fox to Egremont, 2 Nov. 1756, BL. Add. 51436 fol. 21.
48. *HW*, II, 187.
49. NA. SP. 90/67.
50. BL. Add. 32870 fol. 237.
51. BL. Add. 32870 fols 250, 264.
52. BL. Add. 32870 fols 287–90.
53. BL. Add. 32870 fol. 299.
54. BL. Add. 32870 fols 343–4.
55. BL. Add. 32870 fol. 395.
56. BL. Add. 32870 fol. 358.
57. BL. Add. 32870 fols 421, 423.
58. Clark, *Dynamics of Change*, p. 374.
59. NA. SP. 80/196 fol. 8.
60. BL. Add. 32870 fol. 73.
61. Clark, *Waldegrave*, p. 206.
62. BL. Add. 32870 fol. 378.
63. NeC 3158; Northampton CRO. F(M) G 808.
64. AE. CP. Autriche 254 fol. 135.
65. NA. SP. 80/196 fols 56–7.
66. W. Mediger, 'Hastenbeck and Zeven. Der Eintritt Hannovers in den Siebenjährigen Krieg', *Niedersächsisches Jahrbuch für Landesgeschichte*, 56 (1984), pp. 137–66.

67. K.W. Schweizer, *England, Prussia and the Seven Years' War* (Lewiston, 1989).
68. BL. Add. 35417 fol. 92.
69. H. Wellenreuther, 'Die Bedeutung des Siebenjährigen Krieges für die englisch-hannoveranischen Beziehungen', in A.M. Birke and K. Kluxen (eds), *England und Hannover* (Munich, 1986), pp. 170–2.
70. BL. Add. 35418 fol. 188.
71. BL. Add. 32899 fols 6–7.
72. AE. CP. Ang. 438 fol. 305, 439 fol. 169.
73. BL. Add. 35418 fol. 45.
74. BL. Add. 32897 fol. 87.
75. Newcastle to Rockingham, 1757, misdated 1751, Sheffield Archives, Wentworth Woodhouse papers, R1–5.
76. Haslang to Count Preysing, 7 Jan. 1757, Munich, London vol. 233.
77. HMC, *Polwarth V*, p. 272.
78. R.M. Hatton, *The Anglo-Hanoverian Connection 1714–1760* (London, 1982), p. 15.
79. NeC 3154; HP. transcripts of papers of James Harris, 13 May 1767.
80. W.J. Smith (ed.), *The Grenville Papers* (4 vols, London, 1852–3), I, 331–2, 337–8.
81. Holdernesse to Cumberland, 6 May 1757, BL. Eg. 3442; BL. Add. 35417 fol. 171.
82. BL. Add. 32870 fol. 220.
83. BL. Add. 35417 fols 187–8.
84. W.R. Anson (ed.), *Autobiography and Political Correspondence of Augustus Henry, 3rd Duke of Grafton* (London, 1898), pp. 12–13.
85. BL. Add. 32880 fol. 309.
86. BL. Add. 32890 fol. 35.
87. BL. Add. 32890 fols 106–8.
88. BL. Add. 32870 fol. 358.
89. HMC, *Polwarth V*, p. 351.
90. BL. Add. 32893 fols 154–5.
91. J.C. Batzel, 'Austria and the First Three Treaties of Versailles, 1755–1758' (PhD Brown Univ., 1974), p. 66.
92. *Polit. Corresp.* X, p. 422.
93. *Polit. Corresp.* X, p. 385.
94. HMC. *Hastings Mss*, pp. 104–6; AE. MD. Ang. 41 fol. 12.
95. Munich, Bayr. Ges. Paris 13, 28 Ap. 1755.
96. Fox to Devonshire, 5 Feb. 1756, HP. RA. 52980.
97. *HW*, III, 59.
98. S. Conway, *War, State and Society in Mid-Eighteenth-Century Britain and Ireland* (Oxford, 2006).
99. B. Harris, *Politics and the Nation: Britain in the Mid-Eighteenth Century* (Oxford, 2002).
100. BL. Add. 32913 fol. 399; Bod. MS. Lyell, empt. 35; F. Blackburne (ed.),

Memoirs of Thomas Hollis, Esq. (2 vols, London, 1780) I, 98; HL. Mo. 1404, 5084.

10. George II's Reputation

1. *HW*, I, 116–20.
2. *HW*, I, 6.
3. *HW*, I, xxx fn. 6.
4. BL. Add. 38575 fol. 3.
5. J. Morley, *Walpole* (London, 1906), pp. 91, 95.
6. C.C. Trench, *George II* (London, 1973), pp. 299–300.
7. S. Baxter (ed.), *England's Rise to Greatness 1660–1763* (Berkeley, 1983), p. 326.
8. R. Pares, *The Historian's Business and Other Essays* (Oxford, 1961), p. 109.
9. J.B. Owen, 'George II Reconsidered', in A. Whiteman, J.S. Bromley and P.G.M. Dickson (eds), *Statesmen, Scholars and Merchants. Essays in Eighteenth Century History presented to Dame Lucy Sutherland* (Oxford, 1973), pp. 113–34, at p. 129.
10. Owen, *The Rise of the Pelhams* (London, 1957).
11. See also J. Black, 'George II Reconsidered: A Consideration of George's Influence in the Conduct of Foreign Policy in the First Years of his reign', *Mitteilungen des Österreichischen Staatsarchivs*, 35 (1982), pp. 35–56.
12. See also, D. Starkey, *Monarchy. From the Middle Ages to Modernity* (2006), pp. 230–1.
13. *Ibid.*, p. 240.
14. Willcox and Arnstein, p. 96.
15. K. Baker, *Kings and Queens*, p. 34.
16. Pearce, *The Great Man*, p. 220.

11. Conclusions

1. Farmington, Weston papers, vol. 3.
2. HMC, *Polwarth V*, p. 253.
3. G. Plank, *Rebellion and Savagery: The Jacobite Rising of 1745 and the British Empire* (Philadelphia, 2006).
4. Rose (ed.), *Marchmont*, I, 54.
5. *Polit. Corresp.* VI, 362.
6. BL. Add. 32816 fol. 177, Russian memorial of 1749.
7. *Sbornik Imperatorskago Russkago Istoricheskago Obshchestva* (148 vols, St Petersburg, 1867–1916), CIII, p. 500.
8. Yorke, *Hardwicke*, III, 91.
9. BL. Add. 32897 fols 90, 500; Yorke, *Hardwicke*, III, 241–2.
10. 28 July 1761, Munich, London, 238.
11. N. Harding, 'Hanoverian Rulership and Dynastic Union with Britain, 1700–

1760', in R. Rexheuser (ed.), *Die Personalunionen von Sachsen-Polen 1697–1763 und Hannover-England 1714–1837. Ein Vergleich* (Wiesbaden, 2005), pp. 401–3, 412; T. Biskup, 'The university of Göttingen and the Personal Union, 1737–1837', in B. Simms and T. Riotte (eds), *The Hanoverian Dimension in British History, 1714–1837* (Cambridge, 2007), p. 136.

12. BL. Add. 35406 fol. 153.

13. RA. CP. 43/122.

14. NA. SP. 94/135 fol. 57.

15. W. Gibson, *Religion and the Enlightenment 1600–1800. Conflict and the Rise of Civic Humanism in Taunton* (Bern, 2007), pp. 303, 306.

16. Williams, p. 73.

17. Williams, pp. 130–1.

18. Sedgwick, *History of Parliament*, II, 331.

19. B. Kennicott, *A Word to the Hutchinsonians* (London, 1756), cited in J.C.D. Clark, *English Society 1660–1832. Religion, Ideology and Politics during the Ancien Regime* (Cambridge, 2000), p. 261.

20. Taylor and Jones (eds), *Tory and Whig*, p. 177.

21. MHC., *14th Report. Appendix 9*, pp. 523–4.

Selected Further Reading

All works published in London unless otherwise stated.

Arkell, R.L., *Caroline of Ansbach. George the Second's Queen* (1939)

Beattie, J.W., *The English Court in the Reign of George I* (Cambridge, 1967)

Bertram, M., *Georg II: König und Kurfürst* (Göttingen, 2003)

Bertram, M., *Das Königreich Hannover: Kleine Geschichte eines vergangenen deutschen States* (Hanover, 2003)

Birke, A.M. and Kluxen, K. (eds), *England und Hannover* (Munich, 1986)

Brooke, J. (ed.), *Memoirs of the Reign of George II by Horace Walpole* (3 vols, New Haven, 1985)

Brown, P.D. and Schweizer, K.W. (eds), *The Devonshire Diary, William Cavendish, Fourth Duke of Devonshire, Memoranda on State of Affairs* (1982)

Carlton, C., *Royal Warriors: A Military History of the British Monarchy* (Harlow, 2003)

Clark, J.C.D. (ed.), *The Memoirs and Speeches of James, 2nd Earl Waldegrave, 1742–1763* (Cambridge, 1968)

Clark, J.C.D., *English Society, 1688–1832* (Cambridge, 1985)

Colvin, H.M. et al., *The History of the King's Works, V, 1660–1782* (1976)

Cowper, M., *Diary of Mary Countess Cowper, Lady of the Bedchamber to the Princess of Wales, 1714–1720* (1864)

Dann, U., *Hanover and Great Britain, 1740–1760* (Leicester, 1991)

Davies, J.D.G., *A King in Toils* (1938)

De-la-Noy, M., *The King Who Never Was: The Story of Frederick, Prince of Wales* (1996)

Edwards, A., *Frederick Louis, Prince of Wales* (1947)

Hatton, R.M., *George I, Elector and King* (1978)

Hatton, R.M., *The Anglo-Hanoverian Connection, 1714–1760* (1982)

Konig, P., *The Hanoverian Kings and their Homeland* (1993)

McKelvey, J.L., *George III and Bute: The Leicester House Years* (Durham, North Carolina, 1973)

Oberschelp, R., *Politische Geschichte Niedersachsens, 1714–1803* (Hildesheim, 1983)

Orr, C.C. (ed.), *Queenship in Britain, 1660–1837: Royal Patronage, Court Culture and Dynastic Politics* (Manchester, 2002)

Plumb, J.H., *The First Four Georges* (1956)

Portzek, H., *Friedrich der Grosse und Hannover in ihrem gegenseitigen Urteil* (Hildesheim, 1958)

Richter-Uhlig, U., *Hof und Politik unter den Bedingungen der Personalunion zwischen Hannover und England: Die Aufenthalte Georgs II in Hannover zwischen 1729 und 1741* (Hanover, 1992)

Sedgwick, R.R. (ed.), *Memoirs of the Reign of George II, by John, Lord Hervey* (3 vols, 1931)

Simms, B. and Riotte, T. (eds), *The Hanoverian Dimension in British History, 1714–1837* (Cambridge, 2007)

Wilkins, W.H., *Caroline the Illustrious: Queen Consort of George II* (1901)

Yorke, P.C., *The Life and Correspondence of Philip Yorke, Earl of Hardwicke* (3 vols, Cambridge, 1913)

Index